GREENBOOK®
GUIDE TO
DEPARTMENT 56®
VILLAGES

EIGHTH EDITION
1998/1999

Including

THE ORIGINAL SNOW VILLAGE®
THE ORIGINAL SNOW VILLAGE® ACCESSORIES

MEADOWLAND

THE HERITAGE VILLAGE COLLECTION®
Dickens' Village Series®
New England Village®
Alpine Village Series™
Christmas In The City®
Little Town Of Bethlehem™
North Pole Series™
Disney Parks Village™
THE HERITAGE VILLAGE COLLECTION® ACCESSORIES

BACHMAN'S®

PROFILES™

ADDITIONAL VILLAGE ACCESSORIES

ORNAMENTS

The Most Respected Guides To Popular Collectibles
& Their After Market Values

P.O. Box 645
Pacific Grove, CA   93950
831.656.9000
FAX 831.656.9004
www.greenbooks.com

Printed in Canada

ISBN 0-923628-62-2

The GREENBOOK would like to thank –

Department 56, Inc.

Jeanne George.

The **collectors, retailers, secondary market dealers** and **newsletter publishers** across the country who take their valuable time to supply us with information including secondary market status and price.

Acknowledgments

We tallied up the pages and I couldn't figure out how we got to 352 of them. Then I remembered. The GREENBOOK History Lists.

Do you miss the *old* Department 56, Inc. History Lists? If you've been involved with the Villages for any number of years, like me, you probably grew up with them. The History Lists gave me my bearings. They provided definitive answers to questions such as the "Year Issued" for each piece because I always found the *"*Year of introduction indicates the year in which the piece was designed, sculpted, and copyrighted. It is possible these pieces may not be available to the collector until the following calendar year."* explanation baffling–especially when it came to midyear releases. With the History Lists, I didn't have to understand it. I could just look it up. I thought they were so illuminating, from the very beginning, we presented the Guide in History List order. I even incorporated similar charts in some of the other titles we publish.

Peter George, publisher of *the Village Chronicle* magazine and GREENBOOK's Department 56 Historian, and I had some of our best discussions debating whether or not to stray from the History Lists when things simply didn't make sense. My favorite was the *Village Potted Topiary Pair* being in the Original Snow Village® Accessories section. In the end, though we both felt very strongly these were an *Additional Village Accessories–Trees* item, conformity with the History List won out. (Don't you wish you could discuss a topic like that and call it work!)

This is a long way of telling you we miss them so much we decided to do our own. You'll find them as an introduction to each of the Village sections.

Incidentally, now that we're the author of our own History Lists, we've moved some stuff around. I checked all moves with Peter because, as GREENBOOK's best traveling emissary, he once jokingly told me, "You make a decision, and I live with it for a year."

We reviewed it last year, but I'd like to mention again this year that GREENBOOK TruMarket Values are from actual sales that have taken place in every region of the country. You can buy other "price guides" with values that are more fun. However, in a library, you'll find GREENBOOK in the Reference Section, not Fiction. Stop and think. Everything doesn't always go up. Some Secondary Market Dealers are willing accomplices with inflated price guides because they can charge you the real price and give you a bargain at the same time.

Enough said.

Thanks for buying the Guide.

Louise Patterson Langenfeld
Editor & Publisher

Note From The Publisher

Table Of Contents

Throughout this edition of GREENBOOK are a variety of articles by Peter George, GREENBOOK's Department 56® Historian, that *the* **Village Chronicle.** were previously printed in *the Village Chronicle* magazine. Though some of them appeared recently in the magazine and others are from issues dating back a year or more, the subject of each article is as valid now as when it was first published. These articles cover topics including particular buildings and accessories and collecting Department 56® in general. We think you will enjoy reading these articles for their historical, informational and entertaining values.

Peter is the publisher of *the Village Chronicle* magazine which he founded in 1991. Along with his publishing responsibilities, he also writes some of the articles and features for the magazine. Considered a Department 56® authority, he is a frequent guest speaker at gatherings and other Department 56, Inc. related events throughout the United States. As you might expect, one of his favorite pastimes is collecting Department 56® Villages. This is Peter's fifth year as GREENBOOK's Department 56® Historian.

If you enjoy the articles from *the Village Chronicle* subscribe to it today and continue the fun. Each issue entertains and informs you with page after page of:

- accurate, timely information
- articles about each of the Villages
- varied points of view from nationally recognized authorities
- display advice & tips
- product highlights
- secondary market updates
- a calendar of Department 56® events
- classified ads so you can buy, sell, and trade
- and always much more

$25 for one year - 6 issues   *(International: $30 US funds)*
$45 for two years - 12 issues   *(International: $50 US funds)*
                                    R.I. residents add 7% sales tax.

Visa, MasterCard, Discover, American Express, Checks accepted

Subscribe by phone, fax, mail, internet, or visit our web site.

Phone: 401-467-9343
Fax: 401-467-9359
Internet: d56er@aol.com
Web Site: http://www.villagechronicle.com
mail: the Village Chronicle
            757 Park Ave.
            Cranston, RI 02910

WE'RE A LITTLE STRANGE ... *Not that there's anything wrong with that!*

You know you're sane, and I know you're sane, but have others ever wondered just a bit about your competence when it comes to little houses? Surely someone—your spouse, children, neighbors, UPS driver—has mentioned that you're a little crazed. *Not that there's anything wrong with that!*

Think about it from their point of view for a minute or two, and you'll probably agree. But, so what? What's wrong with being overly...shall we say...infatuated with this hobby. It's clean, it's fun, and it's only harmful to your pocketbook.

So how do you defend yourself when those non-collectors suggest that you're like one of the buildings you collect? (The light's on but no one's home.) Well, you might want to point out what collectors of other products do. It just might make those of us who collect villages look slightly more in charge of our capacities.

We, as village collectors, are generally concerned with little more than the condition of the piece. Sure, we want it to be in its box and sleeve if possible, but if it's not and the price is right, it's not unlikely for us to scoop it up. Does that little hang tag have to be with it? Not necessarily. Is it a requirement for the brochure to be there? Few probably give it a second thought. (Many I've spoken to actually see them as a nuisance.) *Not that there's anything wrong with that!*

Variations *do* make us stand up and take notice. When purchasing a piece that has known variations on the secondary market, we're most often going to be particular. But we're not usually fanatical about that either.

Do some collectors know what was printed on a box for an early delivery as opposed to latter ones? Sure. Do some know when in a production run a variation changed? Of course, but don't ever let the non-collector become aware of these facts.

Instead, tell them about other collectibles and those who collect them. Do you know anyone who collects Hallmark ornaments? Perhaps you do yourself. If so, you already know that that little perforated retail price tag on the side of the box must be intact. Many Hallmark ornament collectors insist that a tag must be there, or the value of the item inside drops by at least 10 to 15%. *Not that there's anything wrong with that!*

Beanie Babies, now here's a fairly recent craze, but it hasn't taken long for collectors to have their own preferences/requirements for their collectible. The most common of these has to do with that red, heart-shaped tag. That tag has become so important *(Not that there's anything wrong with that!)* that companies now produce enclosures to keep the tag in mint condition.

Probably the most demanding collectors I've learned about so far are Harbour Lights collectors. They are so in tune with their collectible that they know where in the total number of a numbered limited edition a change took place. Then, in an effort to purchase the variation they desire, they search to locate a piece within that number range. Furthermore, they are often intent on locating a particular piece from a particular factory in a particular type box. *Not that there's anything wrong with that!*

Keep in mind that the majority of any collector base is made up of casual collectors who are not aware nor concerned with such specifics. But when confronting those who think you're a little over the edge, you might want to leave that part out, though you will be bending the truth a bit. *Not that there's anything wrong with that...at least not in this case!*

the **Village Chronicle**.

GREENBOOK
WHAT WE DO & HOW WE DO IT

ARTCHARTS & LISTINGS

The GREENBOOK ARTCHARTS developed for the Department 56® Villages feature color photographs, factual information and TRUMARKET VALUES for each piece.

Factual information consists of:
- Name
- Item Number
- Year Of Introduction
- Market Status
- Description
- Variations
- Particulars

GREENBOOK TRUMARKET VALUE Listings include:

- Original Suggested Retail Price
- GREENBOOK TRUMARKET Secondary Market Value (**GBTru$**)
- The percentage up or down as compared to last year's 7th Ed. Guide (or "No Change" if the price is unchanged)
- The GBTru History Line–tracking the GREENBOOK Secondary Market Value for each piece over the years. If a piece is Current, the GBTru History Line tracks the suggested retail price.

GREENBOOK TRUMARKET VALUES

Secondary Market prices are reported to us by retailers and collectors. The data is compiled, checked for accuracy, and a price established as a benchmark as a result of this research. There are many factors which determine the price a collector will pay for a piece; most acquisitions are a matter of personal judgement. The price will fluctuate with the time of year, section of the country and type of sale. GREENBOOK takes all of these factors into consideration when determining TRUMARKET Values, and so **GREENBOOK TRUMARKET Values are never an absolute number**. Use them as a basis for comparison, as a point of information when considering an acquisition, and as a guide when insuring for replacement value.

The GREENBOOK does not trade on the Secondary Market. The GREENBOOK monitors and reports prices, in the same way as the Wall Street Journal reports trades on the stock markets in the United States and abroad.

HOW TO USE THIS GUIDE

This Guide is divided into three main sections: The Original Snow Village®, The Heritage Village Collection® and Additional Village Accessories. Within each section, GREENBOOK Listings are in chronological date of introduction order. It's important to remember "the year of introduction indicates the year in which the piece was designed, sculpted and copyrighted" and the piece is generally available to collectors the following calendar year.

Within each year, the Listings are in Department 56® Item Number order.

Use the GREENBOOK History List (chronological date of introduction order, within each year–Department 56® Item Number order) as your map through each Village.

How To Use This Guide

THE VILLAGES

NEW ENGLAND VILLAGE®

Little Town of Bethlehem™

NORTH POLE SERIES™

Bachman's®

Profiles™

Meadowland

Ornaments

THE ACCESSORIES

The Original Snow Village® Accessories	The Heritage Village Collection® Accessories	Additional Village Accessories

Finding Your Way

9

The Original Snow Village®

When Department 56, Inc. introduced The Original Snow Village® in 1976, no one could have imagined what would happen during the next twenty years. What began as a line of giftware grew to be one of the most successful collectibles available today.

In 1977, the first six buildings arrived on dealers' shelves. Though not very detailed—many collectors consider them crude when contrasting them to today's designs—these ceramic buildings captured the hearts of consumers. Each year more designs were introduced, and the number of dealers selling the Villages continued to grow. In 1979, the first buildings—ten in all—retired, setting the stage for collectible status.

Representing the 1930's and '40's, The Original Snow Village® brought back memories to many collectors. They saw in it places of their childhood, the church where they got married, or the stores where they shopped, perhaps stores like the *Grocery*. The 1950's and '60's were ushered in with buildings like *Dinah's Drive-In* that inspired images of dancing at hops and listening to Rock & Roll. Recently, the Village entered the '90's with the introduction of Starbuck's® Coffee, though designs that represent past decades are continually being introduced.

The Original Snow Village® has hosted two "series within a series." The first, Meadowland, was introduced in 1979 and almost immediately retired in 1980. A summer-based series, it consisted of a cottage, church, trees, and sheep. The other series—a continuing one—is the *American Architecture Series*. Beginning with the *Prairie House* and *Queen Anne Victorian* in 1990, it has grown to include nine designs.

An intriguing and important development took place in 1994 when the first building featuring a licensed brand name was introduced—*Coca-Cola® brand Bottling Plant*. Since then, Department 56, Inc. has expanded this concept to include the *Coca-Cola® brand Corner Drugstore, Ryman Auditorium®, Starbuck's® Coffee, Harley-Davidson® Motorcycle Shop, McDonald's®*, and *Hershey's™ Chocolate Shop,* the latest addition.

For over twenty years, The Original Snow Village® has prospered while each year's designs have become more elaborate and more detailed. Likewise, it has become the second home for more and more collectors. It's evident that the lights in the Village will continue to burn brightly for years to come.

THE BOTTOM LINE:

Cost of all pieces introduced through the 1998 midyear introductions, including accessories: (This includes variations and adopted pieces such as *John Deere Water Tower*.) **$13,525.00**

GREENBOOK TruMarket Value of all pieces through the 1998 midyear introductions including accessories: (This includes variations and adopted pieces such as *John Deere Water Tower*.) **$61,120.00**

The Original Snow Village®

Since We Last Met...

... NEW FOR SALE LISTINGS

CHRISTMAS BARN DANCE - 1997

Take a look in the doors of this barn and you'll see the villagers dancing the night away. A translucent material depicting people dancing is positioned just inside the doors.

ITALIANTE VILLA - 1997

The *American Architecture Series* has a new building. This stately green and yellow villa is one of the new homes in the Village.

FARM HOUSE - 1997

A translucent material depicting the home's furnishings is placed inside. Just look through the windows and you'll see.

HERSHEY'S™ CHOCOLATE SHOP - 1997

Candy bars, kisses and other various chocolate delights have been a favorite for decades. It's no doubt that this building is going to be a favorite, too.

MCDONALD'S® - 1997

McDonald's is our kind of place ... That's what the villagers will be singing. Though it hasn't been around as long as Coca-Cola®, McDonald's® is certainly a bit of Americana, and like Coca-Cola®, it's now represented in the Village.

GRACIE'S DRY GOODS & GENERAL STORE, SET OF 2 - 1997

What would a small town be without a general store? This one will fit in well near a fishing area because it offers tackle at the side door.

ROLLERAMA ROLLER RINK - 1997

Everybody loves to skate, and they can skate at this rink that utilizes a Quonset hut design that was popular in the 1950's.

LINDEN HILLS COUNTRY CLUB, SET OF 2 - 1997

It's tee time! Now that the snow is melting, the residents of the Village can relax and hit a round or two at the club.

THE BRANDON BUNGALOW - 1997

10056 is the street address of this classic bungalow with attached garage. The car is parked partially out of the garage, ready to go for a spin.

ROCK CREEK MILL - 1998

This mill is very detailed and features a large wheel that extends from the building, a first for the Village.

THE CARNIVAL CAROUSEL - 1998

Everyone loves a carousel, and you'll love this one. It's animated and plays 30 songs. Notice that there's no snow on it!

HAUNTED MANSION - 1998

This animated building is a departure from what collectors have come to expect. Not only is it a Halloween-related design, but it also has no snow on it.

SNOWY PINES INN EXCLUSIVE GIFT SET - 1998

A set of 9 pieces, this Gift Set features a country inn. It includes two children decorating a tree, snow, trees, a road, and is trimmed with real tinsel garland.

... NO LONGER ON THE MARKET

5070-9	All Saints Church
5404-6	Gothic Farmhouse
5438-0	Village Station
5443-7	Village Public Library
5446-1	Dairy Barn
5465-8	Federal House
5466-6	Carmel Cottage
5468-2	Glenhaven House
5469-0	Coca-Cola® brand Bottling Plant
5470-4	Marvel's Beauty Salon
5485-2	Peppermint Porch Day Care
54855	Ryman Auditorium®
54873	Boulder Springs House
54874	Reindeer Bus Depot

The Original Snow Village®

AMERICAN ARCHITECTURE SERIES

5156-0 Prairie House
5157-8 Queen Anne Victorian
5403-8 Southern Colonial
5404-6 Gothic Farmhouse
5437-2 Craftsman Cottage
5465-8 Federal House
54856 Dutch Colonial
54884 Shingle Victorian
54911 Italianate Villa

HOMES FOR THE HOLIDAYS

54623 Snow Village Starter Set, 1994
    • Shady Oak Church Building
    • Sunday School Serenade
      Accessory
54902 The Original Snow Village Start
      A Tradition Set, 1997
    • Kringles Toy Shop & The Hot
      Chocolate Stand Buildings
    • Saturday Morning Down-
      town Accessory
54934 Snowy Pines Inn
      Exclusive Gift Set, 1998
    • Snowy Pines Inn
    • Decorate The Tree Accessory

Quik Reference

RETIRED BUILDINGS

5000-8	1984	Town Hall
5001-3	1979	Mountain Lodge
5001-6	1985	Grocery
5002-1	1979	Gabled Cottage
5002-4	1984	Victorian Cottage
5003-2	1985	Governor's Mansion
5003-9	1979	The Inn
5004-0	1986	Turn Of The Century
5004-7	1979	Country Church
5005-4	1979	Steepled Church
5005-9	1986	Main Street House
5006-2	1979	Small Chalet
5006-7	1989	St. Anthony Hotel & Post Office
5007-0	1979	Victorian House
5007-5	1986	Stratford House
5008-3	1987	Haversham House
5008-8	1979	Mansion
5009-1	1985	Galena House
5009-6	1979	Stone Church
5010-5	1987	River Road House
5011-2	1984	Homestead
5012-0	1980	General Store
5012-1	1986	Delta House
5013-0	1989	Snow Village Factory
5013-8	1980	Cape Cod
5014-6	1986	Nantucket
5015-3	1979	Skating Rink/ Duck Pond Set
5015-6	1986	Bayport
5016-1	1989	Small Double Trees
5017-2	1984	Skating Pond
5019-9	1984	Street Car
5019-9	1990	Cathedral Church
5020-2	1984	Centennial House
5021-0	1984	Carriage House
5022-9	1984	Pioneer Church
5023-7	1984	Swiss Chalet
5024-5	1983	Bank
5024-5	1995	Cumberland House
5026-1	1984	Village Church
5027-0	1990	Springfield House
5028-8	1986	Gothic Church
5029-6	1985	Parsonage
5030-0	1988	Lighthouse
5031-8	1985	Wooden Church
5032-6	1984	Fire Station
5033-4	1985	English Tudor
5034-2	1985	Congregational Church
5035-0	1986	Trinity Church
5036-9	1985	Summit House
5037-7	1986	New School House
5039-3	1986	Parish Church
5041-5	1986	Waverly Place
5042-3	1986	Twin Peaks
5043-1	1986	2101 Maple
5044-0	1991	Village Market
5045-8	1986	Stucco Bungalow
5046-6	1988	Williamsburg House
5047-4	1987	Plantation House
5048-2	1988	Church Of The Open Door
5049-0	1987	Spruce Place
5050-4	1987	Duplex
5051-2	1988	Depot And Train With 2 Train Cars
5052-0	1987	Ridgewood
5054-2	1982	Victorian
5054-7	1990	Kenwood House
5055-9	1981	Knob Hill
5056-7	1981	Brownstone
5057-5	1981	Log Cabin
5058-3	1984	Countryside Church
5059-1	1980	Stone Church
5060-1	1988	Lincoln Park Duplex
5060-9	1982	School House
5061-7	1981	Tudor House
5062-5	1980	Mission Church
5062-8	1988	Sonoma House
5063-3	1980	Mobile Home
5063-6	1988	Highland Park House
5065-2	1988	Beacon Hill House
5065-8	1982	Giant Trees
5066-0	1988	Pacific Heights House
5066-6	1980	Adobe House
5067-4	1981	Cathedral Church
5067-9	1989	Ramsey Hill House
5068-2	1982	Stone Mill House
5068-7	1988	Saint James Church
5070-9	1982	Colonial Farm House
5070-9	1997	All Saints Church
5071-7	1982	Town Church
5071-7	1988	Carriage House
5072-5	1984	Wooden Clapboard
5073-3	1982	English Cottage

5073-3	1990	Toy Shop
5074-1	1984	Barn
5076-8	1983	Corner Store
5076-8	1990	Apothecary
5077-6	1983	Bakery
5077-6	1991	Bakery
5078-4	1982	English Church
5078-4	1987	Diner
5080-6	1989	Large Single Tree
5081-4	1983	Gabled House
5081-4	1992	Red Barn
5082-2	1983	Flower Shop
5082-2	1991	Jefferson School
5083-0	1984	New Stone Church
5084-9	1984	Chateau
5085-6	1985	Train Station With
		3 Train Cars
5089-0	1992	Farm House
5091-1	1989	Fire Station No. 2
5092-0	1989	Snow Village
		Resort Lodge
5097-0	1996	The Christmas Shop
5114-4	1991	Jingle Belle Houseboat
5119-5	1992	Colonial Church
5120-9	1992	North Creek Cottage
5121-7	1990	Maple Ridge Inn
5122-5	1992	Village Station And Train
5123-3	1992	Cobblestone
		Antique Shop
5124-1	1991	Corner Cafe
5125-0	1990	Single Car Garage
5126-8	1991	Home Sweet Home
		House & Windmill
5127-6	1992	Redeemer Church
5128-4	1991	Service Station
5140-3	1994	Stonehurst House
5141-1	1990	Palos Verdes
5142-0	1993	Paramount Theater
5143-8	1992	Doctor's House
5144-6	1993	Courthouse
5145-4	1992	Village Warming House
5149-7	1992	J. Young's Granary
5150-0	1995	Pinewood Log Cabin
5151-9	1992	56 Flavors Ice Cream
		Parlor
5152-7	1992	Morningside House
5153-5	1993	Mainstreet Hardware
		Store

5154-3	1993	Village Realty
5155-1	1992	Spanish Mission Church
5156-0	1993	Prairie House
5157-8	1996	Queen Anne Victorian
5400-3	1994	Oak Grove Tudor
5401-1	1993	The Honeymooner Motel
5402-0	1995	Village Greenhouse
5403-8	1994	Southern Colonial
5404-6	1997	Gothic Farmhouse
5405-4	1993	Finklea's Finery
		Costume Shop
5406-2	1994	Jack's Corner
		Barber Shop
5407-0	1994	Double Bungalow
5420-8	1996	Grandma's Cottage
5421-6	1994	St. Luke's Church
5422-4	1995	Village Post Office
5423-2	1995	Al's TV Shop
5424-0	1996	Good Shepherd Chapel &
		Church School
5425-9	1994	Print Shop &
		Village News
5426-7	1995	Hartford House
5427-5	1995	Village Vet And Pet Shop
5437-2	1995	Craftsman Cottage
5438-0	1997	Village Station
5439-9	1996	Airport
5442-9	1996	Mount Olivet Church
5443-7	1997	Village Public Library
5444-5	1996	Woodbury House
5445-3	1996	Hunting Lodge
5446-1	1997	Dairy Barn
5447-0	1996	Dinah's Drive In
5448-8	1996	Snowy Hills Hospital
5462-3	1996	Snow Village Starter Set
5462-3	1996	Shady Oak Church
5465-8	1997	Federal House
5466-6	1997	Carmel Cottage
5468-2	1997	Glenhaven House
5469-0	1997	Coca-Cola® brand
		Bottling Plant
5470-4	1997	Marvel's Beauty Salon
5485-2	1997	Peppermint Porch
		Day Care
54855	1997	Ryman Auditorium®
54856	1996	Dutch Colonial
54873	1997	Boulder Springs House
54874	1997	Reindeer Bus Depot

GREENBOOK HISTORY LIST

ITEM #	NAME	ISSUED	RETIRED	GBTRU$
5001-3	Mountain Lodge	1976	1979	390.00
5002-1	Gabled Cottage	1976	1979	380.00
5003-9	The Inn	1976	1979	450.00
5004-7	Country Church	1976	1979	355.00
5005-4	Steepled Church	1976	1979	580.00
5006-2	Small Chalet	1976	1979	425.00
5007-0	Victorian House	1977	1979	465.00
5008-8	Mansion	1977	1979	590.00
5009-6	Stone Church–Original, Ver. 1	1977	1979	645.00
5009-6	Stone Church–Original, Ver. 2	1977	1979	640.00
5011-2	Homestead	1978	1984	215.00
5012-0	General Store–White	1978	1980	490.00
5012-0	General Store–Tan	1978	1980	565.00
5012-0	General Store–Gold	1978	1980	505.00
5013-8	Cape Cod	1978	1980	360.00
5014-6	Nantucket	1978	1986	260.00
5015-3	Skating Rink/Duck Pond Set	1978	1979	1070.00
5016-1	Small Double Trees–Blue Birds	1978	1989	165.00
5016-1	Small Double Trees–Red Birds	1978	1989	50.00
5054-2	Victorian	1979	1982	385.00
5055-9	Knob Hill–Gray	1979	1981	330.00
5055-9	Knob Hill–Yellow	1979	1981	380.00
5056-7	Brownstone	1979	1981	600.00
5057-5	Log Cabin	1979	1981	465.00
5058-3	Countryside Church	1979	1984	260.00
5059-1	Stone Church	1979	1980	975.00
5060-9	School House	1979	1982	400.00
5061-7	Tudor House	1979	1981	320.00
5062-5	Mission Church	1979	1980	1310.00
5063-3	Mobile Home	1979	1980	1650.00
5065-8	Giant Trees	1979	1982	280.00
5066-6	Adobe House	1979	1980	2500.00
5067-4	Cathedral Church	1980	1981	2700.00
5068-2	Stone Mill House	1980	1982	565.00
5070-9	Colonial Farm House	1980	1982	285.00
5071-7	Town Church	1980	1982	350.00
5086-5	Train Station With 3 Train Cars	1980	1985	400.00
5072-5	Wooden Clapboard	1981	1984	255.00
5073-3	English Cottage	1981	1982	290.00
5074-1	Barn	1981	1984	425.00
5076-8	Corner Store	1981	1983	250.00
5077-6	Bakery	1981	1983	275.00
5078-4	English Church	1981	1982	370.00
5080-6	Large Single Tree	1981	1989	55.00
5085-6	Train Station With 3 Train Cars	1981	1985	385.00

The Original Snow Village®

ITEM #	NAME	ISSUED	RETIRED	GBTRU$
5017-2	Skating Pond	1982	1984	350.00
5019-9	Street Car	1982	1904	380.00
5020-2	Centennial House	1982	1984	315.00
5021-0	Carriage House	1982	1984	295.00
5022-9	Pioneer Church	1982	1984	320.00
5023-7	Swiss Chalet	1982	1984	440.00
5024-5	Bank	1982	1983	620.00
5081-4	Gabled House	1982	1983	370.00
5082-2	Flower Shop	1982	1983	465.00
5083-0	New Stone Church	1982	1984	375.00
5000-8	Town Hall	1983	1984	325.00
5001-6	Grocery	1983	1985	350.00
5002-4	Victorian Cottage	1983	1984	375.00
5003-2	Governor's Mansion	1983	1985	315.00
5004-0	Turn Of The Century	1983	1986	255.00
5025-3	Gingerbread House	1983	1984	345.00
5026-1	Village Church	1983	1984	420.00
5028-8	Gothic Church	1983	1986	245.00
5029-6	Parsonage	1983	1985	385.00
5031-8	Wooden Church	1983	1985	355.00
5032-6	Fire Station	1983	1984	575.00
5033-4	English Tudor	1983	1985	280.00
5084-9	Chateau	1983	1984	495.00
5005-9	Main Street House	1984	1986	250.00
5007-5	Stratford House	1984	1986	190.00
5008-3	Haversham House	1984	1987	280.00
5009-1	Galena House	1984	1985	355.00
5010-5	River Road House	1984	1987	205.00
5012-1	Delta House	1984	1986	315.00
5015-6	Bayport	1984	1986	225.00
5034-2	Congregational Church	1984	1985	595.00
5035-0	Trinity Church	1984	1986	275.00
5036-9	Summit House	1984	1985	345.00
5037-7	New School House	1984	1986	255.00
5039-3	Parish Church	1984	1986	335.00
5045-8	Stucco Bungalow	1985	1986	370.00
5046-6	Williamsburg House	1985	1988	165.00
5047-4	Plantation House	1985	1987	110.00
5048-2	Church Of The Open Door	1985	1988	135.00
5049-0	Spruce Place	1985	1987	270.00
5050-4	Duplex	1985	1987	150.00
5051-2	Depot And Train With 2 Train Cars	1985	1988	165.00
5052-0	Ridgewood	1985	1987	170.00

The Original Snow Village®

ITEM #	NAME	ISSUED	RETIRED	GBTRU$
5041-5	Waverly Place	1986	1986	315.00
5042-3	Twin Peaks	1986	1986	425.00
5043-1	2101 Maple	1986	1986	345.00
5060-1	Lincoln Park Duplex	1986	1988	140.00
5062-8	Sonoma House	1986	1988	145.00
5063-6	Highland Park House	1986	1988	170.00
5065-2	Beacon Hill House	1986	1988	180.00
5066-0	Pacific Heights House	1986	1988	105.00
5067-9	Ramsey Hill House	1986	1989	100.00
5068-7	Saint James Church	1986	1988	175.00
5070-9	All Saints Church	1986	1997	65.00
5071-7	Carriage House	1986	1988	130.00
5073-3	Toy Shop	1986	1990	100.00
5076-8	Apothecary	1986	1990	110.00
5077-6	Bakery	1986	1991	85.00
5078-4	Diner	1986	1987	650.00
5006-7	St. Anthony Hotel & Post Office	1987	1989	115.00
5013-0	Snow Village Factory	1987	1989	150.00
5019-9	Cathedral Church	1987	1990	115.00
5024-5	Cumberland House	1987	1995	70.00
5027-0	Springfield House	1987	1990	90.00
5030-0	Lighthouse	1987	1988	550.00
5081-4	Red Barn	1987	1992	105.00
5082-2	Jefferson School	1987	1991	160.00
5089-0	Farm House	1987	1992	75.00
5091-1	Fire Station No. 2	1987	1989	195.00
5092-0	Snow Village Resort Lodge	1987	1989	150.00
5044-0	Village Market	1988	1991	95.00
5054-7	Kenwood House	1988	1990	145.00
5121-7	Maple Ridge Inn	1988	1990	75.00
5122-5	Village Station And Train	1988	1992	120.00
5123-3	Cobblestone Antique Shop	1988	1992	65.00
5124-1	Corner Cafe	1988	1991	100.00
5125-0	Single Car Garage	1988	1990	60.00
5126-8	Home Sweet Home/House/Windmill	1988	1991	120.00
5127-6	Redeemer Church	1988	1992	75.00
5128-4	Service Station	1988	1991	260.00
5140-3	Stonehurst House	1988	1994	70.00
5141-1	Palos Verdes	1988	1990	90.00
5114-4	Jingle Belle Houseboat	1989	1991	165.00
5119-5	Colonial Church	1989	1992	75.00
5120-9	North Creek Cottage	1989	1992	75.00
5142-0	Paramount Theater	1989	1993	195.00
5143-8	Doctor's House	1989	1992	105.00
5144-6	Courthouse	1989	1993	195.00
5145-4	Village Warming House	1989	1992	75.00
5149-7	J. Young's Granary	1989	1992	85.00
5150-0	Pinewood Log Cabin	1989	1995	70.00

The Original Snow Village®

ITEM #	NAME	ISSUED	RETIRED	GBTRU$
5151-9	56 Flavors Ice Cream Parlor	1990	1992	175.00
5152-7	Morningside House	1990	1992	65.00
5153-5	Mainstreet Hardware Store	1990	1993	90.00
5154-3	Village Realty	1990	1993	75.00
5155-1	Spanish Mission Church	1990	1992	85.00
5156-0	Prairie House	1990	1993	70.00
5157-8	Queen Anne Victorian	1990	1996	75.00
5097-0	The Christmas Shop	1991	1996	65.00
5400-3	Oak Grove Tudor	1991	1994	70.00
5401-1	The Honeymooner Motel	1991	1993	85.00
5402-0	Village Greenhouse	1991	1995	70.00
5403-8	Southern Colonial	1991	1994	80.00
5404-6	Gothic Farmhouse	1991	1997	70.00
5405-4	Finklea's Finery Costume Shop	1991	1993	70.00
5406-2	Jack's Corner Barber Shop	1991	1994	75.00
5407-0	Double Bungalow	1991	1994	70.00
5420-8	Grandma's Cottage	1992	1996	70.00
5421-6	St. Luke's Church	1992	1994	75.00
5422-4	Village Post Office	1992	1995	80.00
5423-2	Al's TV Shop	1992	1995	65.00
5424-0	Good Shepherd Chapel & Church School	1992	1996	95.00
5425-9	Print Shop & Village News	1992	1994	75.00
5426-7	Hartford House	1992	1995	80.00
5427-5	Village Vet And Pet Shop	1992	1995	70.00
5437-2	Craftsman Cottage	1992	1995	75.00
5438-0	Village Station	1992	1997	80.00
5439-9	Airport	1992	1996	85.00
5441-0	Nantucket Renovation	1993	1993 Annual	70.00
5442-9	Mount Olivet Church	1993	1996	80.00
5443-7	Village Public Library	1993	1997	65.00
5444-5	Woodbury House	1993	1996	70.00
5445-3	Hunting Lodge	1993	1996	140.00
5446-1	Dairy Barn	1993	1997	75.00
5447-0	Dinah's Drive-In	1993	1996	95.00
5448-8	Snowy Hills Hospital	1993	1996	90.00
5460-7	Fisherman's Nook Resort	1994	Current	75.00
5461-5	FISHERMAN'S NOOK CABINS, Set/2	1994	Current	50.00
5461-5	Fisherman's Nook Bass Cabin	1994	Current	*
5461-5	Fisherman's Nook Trout Cabin	1994	Current	*
5462-3	Snow Village Starter Set	1994	1996	75.00
5464-0	Wedding Chapel	1994	Current	55.00
5465-8	Federal House	1994	1997	70.00
5466-6	Carmel Cottage	1994	1997	65.00
5467-4	Skate & Ski Shop	1994	Current	50.00
5468-2	Glenhaven House	1994	1997	60.00
5469-0	Coca–Cola® brand Bottling Plant	1994	1997	85.00
5470-4	Marvel's Beauty Salon	1994	1997	50.00

The Original Snow Village®

ITEM #	NAME	ISSUED	RETIRED	GBTRU$
5483-6	Christmas Cove Lighthouse	1995	Current	60.00
5484-4	Coca–Cola® brand			
	Corner Drugstore	1995	Current	55.00
54850	Snow Carnival Ice Palace	1995	Current	95.00
54851	Pisa Pizza	1995	Current	35.00
5485-2	Peppermint Porch Day Care	1995	1997	70.00
54853	Village Police Station	1995	Current	48.00
54854	Holly Brothers Garage	1995	Current	48.00
54855	Ryman Auditorium®	1995	1997	90.00
54856	Dutch Colonial	1995	1996	70.00
54857	Beacon Hill Victorian	1995	Current	60.00
54858	Bowling Alley	1995	Current	42.00
54859	Starbucks® Coffee	1995	Current	48.00
54871	Nick's Tree Farm	1996	Current	40.00
54872	Smokey Mountain Retreat	1996	Current	65.00
54873	Boulder Springs House	1996	1997	70.00
54874	Reindeer Bus Depot	1996	1997	60.00
54880	Rockabilly Records	1996	Current	45.00
54881	Christmas Lake High School	1996	Current	52.00
54882	Birch Run Ski Chalet	1996	Current	60.00
54883	Rosita's Cantina	1996	Current	50.00
54884	Shingle Victorian	1996	Current	55.00
54885	The Secret Garden Florist	1996	Current	50.00
54886	Harley-Davidson® Motorcycle Shop	1996	Current	65.00
8802	Bachman's® Flower Shop	1997	1997 Annual	75.00
8960	Ronald McDonald House®	1997	Special	465.00
54887	Mainstreet Gift Shop	1997	1997 Annual	90.00
54902	The Original Snow Village			
	Start A Tradition Set	1997	Current	100.00
54903	Old Chelsea Mansion	1997	Current	85.00
54904	New Hope Church	1997	Current	60.00
54910	Christmas Barn Dance	1997	Current	65.00
54911	Italianate Villa	1997	Current	55.00
54912	Farm House	1997	Current	50.00
54913	Hershey's™ Chocolate Shop	1997	Current	55.00
54914	McDonald's®	1997	Current	65.00
54915	Gracie's Dry Goods &			
	General Store	1997	Current	70.00
54916	Rollerama Roller Rink	1997	Current	56.00
54917	Linden Hills Country Club	1997	Current	60.00
54918	The Brandon Bungalow	1997	Current	55.00
2210	Ronald McDonald House®	1998	Ltd Ed 5,600	NE
2203	Bachman's® Greenhouse	1998	1998 Annual	60.00
54932	Rock Creek Mill House	1998	Current	64.00
54933	Carnival Carousel	1998	Current	150.00
54934	Snowy Pines Inn Exclusive Gift Set	1998	1998 Annual	65.00
54935	Haunted Mansion	1998	Current	110.00

The Original Snow Village®

MOUNTAIN LODGE

ITEM #	INTRO	RETIRED	OSRP	GBTRU	↑
5001-3	1976	1979	$20	**$390**	4%

Particulars: One of the "Original 6." Color on roof is different from piece to piece. Bright colored skis lean against two-story lodge, upper windows painted to appear as lead panes, sunburst on end of building, snow laden tree at side.

'91	'92	'93	'94	'95	'96	'97
$525	550	405	370	375	325	375

GABLED COTTAGE

ITEM #	INTRO	RETIRED	OSRP	GBTRU	↑
5002-1	1976	1979	$20	**$380**	4%

Particulars: One of the "Original 6." Four-peaked roof with two chimneys, curtained windows, welcome mat, Ivy climbs walls to roof and door, several windows have wreath design. Attached snow laden tree with bluebird.

'91	'92	'93	'94	'95	'96	'97
$450	475	395	385	350	350	365

THE INN

ITEM #	INTRO	RETIRED	OSRP	GBTRU	↑
5003-9	1976	1979	$20	**$450**	6%

Particulars: One of the "Original 6." Colors on roof are not consistent. Two large brick chimneys, full length covered porch, welcome mat at timbered front doors, attached snow laden tree on side, bright yellow door on opposite side.

'91	'92	'93	'94	'95	'96	'97
$525	500	475	490	450	365	425

COUNTRY CHURCH

ITEM #	INTRO	RETIRED	OSRP	GBTRU	↓
5004-7	1976	1979	$18	**$355**	1%

Particulars: One of the "Original 6." Also known as "Wayside Chapel." Vines and painted welcome on walls, short-spired, door ajar, circular upper window, painted side windows, snow laden tree shades one wall. Authentic Department 56® pieces have hand-lettered signs. If they appear "rubber-stamped," they are not Department 56.

'91	'92	'93	'94	'95	'96	'97
$325	435	375	375	385	345	360

The Original Snow Village®

STEEPLED CHURCH

Item #	Intro	Retired	OSRP	GBTru	↑
5005-4	1976	1979	$25	**$580**	5%

Particulars: One of the "Original 6." Colors on roof are not consistent. One spire, large circular window over double wood front doors flanked by leaded lattice design windows, side chapel, snow covered tree, bluebird on steeple.

'91	'92	'93	'94	'95	'96	'97
$775	675	675	640	625	515	550

SMALL CHALET

Item #	Intro	Retired	OSRP	GBTru	↓
5006-2	1976	1979	$15	**$425**	4%

Particulars: One of the "Original 6." Also known as "Gingerbread Chalet." Variation in number of flowers in box (4, 5 or 7) and in color—tan to dark brown. Two-story small gingerbread look home, flower box with snow covered plants, attached tree.

'91	'92	'93	'94	'95	'96	'97
$360	415	415	365	400	375	445

VICTORIAN HOUSE

Item #	Intro	Retired	OSRP	GBTru	↑
5007-0	1977	1979	$30	**$465**	8%

Particulars: Variations in color—rust/white, salmon/white, pink/white & orange/yellow. Variations in birds–none to some. Orange/yellow color combination has no attached tree. Textured to portray shingles and clapboard. Steps lead up to front door. Stained glass inserts above windows.

'91	'92	'93	'94	'95	'96	'97
$400	485	375	435	455	395	430

MANSION

Item #	Intro	Retired	OSRP	GBTru	↑
5008-8	1977	1979	$30	**$590**	15%

Particulars: Variation in roof color–either forest green or turquoise. Forest green is considered to be the first shipped and is much harder to find. Amount and placement of snow varies with the roof colors. Building is white brick with porch supported by pillars, windows are shuttered, two chimneys plus cupola on roof. Attached snow laden evergreen tree.

'91	'92	'93	'94	'95	'96	'97
$600	600	500	550	495	495	515

The Original Snow Village®

STONE CHURCH–"ORIGINAL, VERSION 1"

Item #	Intro	Retired	OSRP	GBTru	↑
5009-6	1977	1979	$35	**$645**	16%

Particulars: There are two Stone Churches: 1977, #5009-6 and 1979, #5059-1. There are two versions of #5009-6. Both versions of the original 1977 Church have 10 ½" steeples. The color on Version 1 is usually a pale mint green; the finish is very glossy. Version 1's top step on the tree side is flush with the edge of the bottom step. Both versions have a separate bell, attached by wire.

'91	'92	'93	'94	'95	'96	'97
$825	715	650	725	625	555	555

STONE CHURCH–"ORIGINAL, VERSION 2"

Item #	Intro	Retired	OSRP	GBTru	↑
5009-6	1977	1979	$35	**$640**	15%

Particulars: The color on Version 2 of the original Church is usually a deeper greenish yellow. Version 2's top step is indented from the bottom step on the right-hand side.

'91	'92	'93	'94	'95	'96	'97
$825	715	650	725	625	555	555

HOMESTEAD

Item #	Intro	Retired	OSRP	GBTru	↓
5011-2	1978	1984	$30	**$215**	12%

Particulars: Old fashioned farmhouse, front porch full length of house. Second floor bay windows. Triple window in front gable. Attached tree.

'91	'92	'93	'94	'95	'96	'97
$250	310	285	240	250	195	245

GENERAL STORE–"WHITE"

Item #	Intro	Retired	OSRP	GBTru	↑
5012-0	1978	1980	$25	**$490**	8%

Particulars: Variations in color–White, Tan & Gold–affect GBTru Price. This "White" General Store w/gray roof is considered to be the first shipped, however the "Tan" and "Gold" are much harder to find. The sign on the "White" General Store most often is, "General Store, Y & L Brothers." All three colors have Christmas trees on the porch roof. General Stores supply food, postal service and gas.

'91	'92	'93	'94	'95	'96	'97
$440	500	450	450	450	435	455

GENERAL STORE—"TAN"

	ITEM #	INTRO	RETIRED	OSRP	GBTRU	↓
	5012-0	1978	1980	$25	**$565**	6%

Particulars: This is the "Tan" General Store. The sign above the porch most often reads, "General Store, S & L Brothers."

'91	'92	'93	'94	'95	'96	'97
$440	500	605	605	585	535	600

GENERAL STORE—"GOLD"

	ITEM #	INTRO	RETIRED	OSRP	GBTRU	↓
	5012-0	1978	1980	$25	**$505**	4%

Particulars: This is the "Gold" General Store. The sign above the porch most often reads simply, "General Store."

'91	'92	'93	'94	'95	'96	'97
$440	500	560	560	550	545	525

CAPE COD

	ITEM #	INTRO	RETIRED	OSRP	GBTRU	↓
	5013-8	1978	1980	$20	**$360**	4%

Particulars: Steep gabled roof with chimney, small dormer and painted landscaping. Attached snow laden tree.

'91	'92	'93	'94	'95	'96	'97
$385	385	375	360	375	385	375

NANTUCKET

	ITEM #	INTRO	RETIRED	OSRP	GBTRU	↑
	5014-6	1978	1986	$25	**$260**	2%

Particulars: Yellow cottage with green roof. Small front porch, attached greenhouse. Attached tree. Some have garland above two front windows, some don't. Also see the *Nantucket Renovation,* 1993, #5441-0.

'91	'92	'93	'94	'95	'96	'97
$235	250	250	315	275	235	255

SKATING RINK/DUCK POND SET

ITEM #	INTRO	RETIRED	OSRP	GBTRU	↑
5015-3	1978	1979	$16	**$1070**	2%

Particulars: Lighted. Set of 2. (The *Skating Rink* is the piece with the snowman, the *Duck Pond* is the piece with the bench and blue birds.) One of the first non-house pieces. In this set the trees were attached directly to the pond bases where their size and weight caused frequent breakage, therefore they were retired in 1979. The revised *Skating Pond* in 1982, #5017-2, was also a set of 2 with one piece being the pond and the other piece double lighted trees. Because the *Skating Rink* and *Duck Pond* are frequently sold separately on the secondary market there is confusion between the *Skating Rink* and *Skating Pond*. The Rink has one single lighted tree attached to the base, the Pond has separate double trees.

	'91	'92	'93	'94	'95	'96	'97
	$1100	1200	950	1000	1000	970	1045

SMALL DOUBLE TREES— "BLUE BIRDS"

ITEM #	INTRO	RETIRED	OSRP	GBTRU	↓
5016-1	1978	1989	$13.50	**$165**	8%

Particulars: Lighted. One of the first non-house accessory pieces. Approximately 8 to 8 ½" tall. Variations in color of birds–blue or red–affect GBTru Price. Blue are considered to be the first ones shipped; the change to red was made in late 1979. There were mold changes and a variation in the amount of snow over the years as well.

	'91	'92	'93	'94	'95	'96	'97
	$150	150	225	175	175	175	180

SMALL DOUBLE TREES— "RED BIRDS"

ITEM #	INTRO	RETIRED	OSRP	GBTRU	↑
5016-1	1978	1989	$13.50	**$50**	11%

Particulars: This is the Small Double Trees—"Red Birds" and a photo illustrating changes in the mold and the variation in the amount of snow.

	'91	'92	'93	'94	'95	'96	'97
	$40	48	48	52	50	40	45

VICTORIAN

ITEM #	INTRO	RETIRED	OSRP	GBTRU	↑
5054-2	1979	1982	$30	**$385**	10%

Particulars: There are variations in color and in exterior finish. They are peach with smooth walls (1979), gold with smooth walls (1980) and gold clapboard (1981 on). The peach is the most difficult to find but the gold and gold clapboard look nicer and are preferred by collectors.

'91	'92	'93	'94	'95	'96	'97
$345	440	435	380	350	315	350

KNOB HILL—"GRAY"

ITEM #	INTRO	RETIRED	OSRP	GBTRU	↓
5055-9	1979	1981	$30	**$330**	6%

Particulars: Variations in color in this three story San Francisco-style Victorian row house—"Gray" or "Yellow"—affect GBTru Price. This is the "Gray" Knob Hill with a red roof and black trim. The "Gray" Knob Hill is considered to be the first shipped.

'91	'92	'93	'94	'95	'96	'97
$350	350	350	350	295	265	350

KNOB HILL—"YELLOW"

ITEM #	INTRO	RETIRED	OSRP	GBTRU	↑
5055-9	1979	1981	$30	**$380**	4%

Particulars: This is the "Yellow" Knob Hill with a red roof and gray trim.

'91	'92	'93	'94	'95	'96	'97
$350	350	350	350	375	345	365

BROWNSTONE

ITEM #	INTRO	RETIRED	OSRP	GBTRU	↑
5056-7	1979	1981	$36	**$600**	6%

Particulars: There are two roof colors—originally introduced with a gray roof, the following year the roof was red. Red is the most desired. Building is three stories with wreath trimmed bay windows on all floors, overall flat roof.

'91	'92	'93	'94	'95	'96	'97
$475	495	540	560	575	545	565

LOG CABIN

ITEM #	INTRO	RETIRED	OSRP	GBTRU	↑
5057-5	1979	1981	$22	$465	6%

Particulars: Rustic log house with stone chimney, roof extends to cover porch, log pile at side, skis by door.

'91	'92	'93	'94	'95	'96	'97
$450	475	475	475	475	400	440

COUNTRYSIDE CHURCH

ITEM #	INTRO	RETIRED	OSRP	GBTRU	↓
5058-3	1979	1984	$27.50	$260	5%

Particulars: White clapboard church with central bell steeple, attached tree has all lower branches pruned. For a no snow version, see 1979 MEADOWLAND *Countryside Church*, #5051-8.

'91	'92	'93	'94	'95	'96	'97
$275	295	295	295	295	260	275

STONE CHURCH

ITEM #	INTRO	RETIRED	OSRP	GBTRU	↑
5059-1	1979	1980	$32	$975	2%

Particulars: 8 1/2" steeple. The color is yellow. It has a Department 56® sticker dated 1980 on the bottom. Also see the original *Stone Church*, 1977, #5009-6.

'91	'92	'93	'94	'95	'96	'97
$750	850	910	1000	1000	915	955

SCHOOL HOUSE

ITEM #	INTRO	RETIRED	OSRP	GBTRU	↑
5060-9	1979	1982	$30	$400	11%

Particulars: Color varies from rust to dark brown. The first design to feature the American flag. It flies from a roof peak above the brick one-room school. The flag pole is metal and removable.

'91	'92	'93	'94	'95	'96	'97
$400	360	405	340	345	365	360

TUDOR HOUSE

ITEM #	INTRO	RETIRED	OSRP	GBTRU	↑
5061-7	1979	1981	$25	**$320**	8%

Particulars: Brick chimney and fireplace on simple L-shaped timber trimmed home, split-shingle roof.

'91	'92	'93	'94	'95	'96	'97
$415	385	330	330	325	285	295

MISSION CHURCH

ITEM #	INTRO	RETIRED	OSRP	GBTRU	↑
5062-5	1979	1980	$30	**$1310**	3%

Particulars: Sun dried clay with structural timbers visible at roof line. Small arched bell tower above entry. Ceramic bell is attached by wire.

'91	'92	'93	'94	'95	'96	'97
$785	950	950	1260	1250	1100	1275

MOBILE HOME

ITEM #	INTRO	RETIRED	OSRP	GBTRU	↓
5063-3	1979	1980	$18	**$1650**	4%

Particulars: Similar to aluminum skinned Airstream mobile home. To be towed by car or truck for travel.

'91	'92	'93	'94	'95	'96	'97
$1350	1625	1700	1700	1750	1865	1725

GIANT TREES

ITEM #	INTRO	RETIRED	OSRP	GBTRU	↓
5065-8	1979	1982	$20	**$280**	5%

Particulars: Lighted snow covered large evergreen trees. Approximately 11" tall. Birds perch on branches.

'91	'92	'93	'94	'95	'96	'97
$310	295	295	360	360	335	295

ADOBE HOUSE

ITEM #	INTRO	RETIRED	OSRP	GBTRU	↑
5066-6	1979	1980	$18	**$2500**	4%

Particulars: Small sun dried clay home. Outside oven on side, chili peppers hang from roof beams.

'91	'92	'93	'94	'95	'96	'97
$1000	2000	2400	2495	2500	2150	2400

CATHEDRAL CHURCH

ITEM #	INTRO	RETIRED	OSRP	GBTRU	↑
5067-4	1980	1981	$36	**$2700**	8%

Particulars: First of two Original Snow Village® Cathedral Churches. (See also 1987, #5019-9.) This church has a central dome with two shorter bell towers. The stained glass windows are acrylic. Production problems (fragile domes) forced retirement after one year. Inspired by St. Paul's Cathedral in St. Paul, MN.

'91	'92	'93	'94	'95	'96	'97
$725	825	2300	1895	2000	2100	2500

STONE MILL HOUSE

ITEM #	INTRO	RETIRED	OSRP	GBTRU	↑
5068-2	1980	1982	$30	**$565**	6%

Particulars: Water wheel on dark weathered stone block mill, separate bag of oats hung with wire from block and tackle, another bag propped by door. Many pieces available on the secondary market are missing the separate bag of oats. **The GBTru for a piece without the bag of oats is $450.**

'91	'92	'93	'94	'95	'96	'97
$635	635	575	545	495	425	535

COLONIAL FARM HOUSE

ITEM #	INTRO	RETIRED	OSRP	GBTRU	↓
5070-9	1980	1982	$30	**$285**	12%

Particulars: House with wide front porch, two front dormers in attic, symmetrical layout of windows. The same Item # was used for the 1986 *All Saints Church*.

'91	'92	'93	'94	'95	'96	'97
$425	425	400	365	375	315	325

The Original Snow Village®

TOWN CHURCH

ITEM #	INTRO	RETIRED	OSRP	GBTRU	NO
5071-7	1980	1982	$33	**$350**	CHANGE

Particulars: A short bell tower rises from central nave area, an attached tree tucks in close to the side chapel. The same Item # was used for the 1986 *Carriage House*.

'91	'92	'93	'94	'95	'96	'97
$410	385	385	355	375	355	350

TRAIN STATION WITH 3 TRAIN CARS

ITEM #	INTRO	RETIRED	OSRP	GBTRU	NO
5087-3	1980	1985	$100	**$400**	CHANGE
5086-5					

Particulars: Set of 4. First Original Snow Village® train and station design. *Train Station With 3 Train Cars* was sold until 1981 under the Item #s 5087-3 and 5086-5, respectively. Though boxed separately, they were sold together. This Station has 6 window panes, a round window in the door, and brick on the front only. The three lighted train cars–an engine, passenger car and baggage/mail caboose have "G & N RR" on the cars. All four pieces are lit and were made in Japan. After their introduction it was thought the train was too large for the station, so in 1981 a new larger station, now packaged with the train, #5085-6, was released.

'91	'92	'93	'94	'95	'96	'97
$350	375	375	375	395	425	400

WOODEN CLAPBOARD

ITEM #	INTRO	RETIRED	OSRP	GBTRU	↑
5072-5	1981	1984	$32	**$255**	11%

Particulars: White house with green roof and trim and wraparound porch. Red brick chimney.

'91	'92	'93	'94	'95	'96	'97
$300	320	300	260	260	210	$230

Does Anybody Really Know What Time It Is?

Department 56, Inc. has elected to place clocks on buildings throughout the years as well as produce accessories relating to the time devices. Clocks have been used on the buildings for a number of reasons. Within the designs they have been an integral part of the buildings' use—schools, train stations, etc. Municipal buildings have had them included in their designs to add an illusion of authority. Others have them to represent the business taking place inside.

Quick... What was the first building to have a clock on it? Hint: If your first reaction is to start thinking about The Original Snow Village®, you're on the right track. OK, I'll give you a second here before giving you the answer. Ready? If you guessed *Train Station With 3 Train Cars* from 1980, you're right. If you have the Station, take a look above the door. There it is...a clock...of sorts. It has the perimeter of a clock face but no hands. The face does have Roman numerals indicating 3, 6, 9 and 12.

After the introduction of the Station, there was a four year gap before we saw the second clock. This one was on the *New School House*. It informs the school children that it is 3:00—school is over for the day.

Another four years passed before the next clock showed its face in the Village. This time, however, it was in a different form. The clock found on *Cobblestone Antique Shop* is not on the actual building. It's on the window decal which gives it the illusion of being a clock hanging on the wall inside the shop.

In 1989, the stately *Courthouse* appeared with its clock telling the citizens of the Village that it's 11:00. By 1992, the clocks in The Original Snow Village® had come full circle. *Village Station* is the most recent building to have a clock on it. Strangely enough, its clock says that the time is 5 of 6, a time that will show up time and again.

You might expect there to be many clocks introduced into The Heritage Village Collection® over the years—with seven villages, it would seem obvious. But this is not the case. In 1987, Alpine Village Series™ debuted the first clock. This was on *Alpine Church*.

As the pendulum continued to swing in this Village, the *Bahnhof* was a natural candidate for a clock since trains are so dependent on time. Train stations are known for keeping the correct time, therefore, it would seem that the churchgoers were called to service early. The clock on the station appears to read 7:25 while the one on the church reads 8:00.

In the meantime, a timekeeper appeared in 1988 on the Christmas In The City® *City Hall*. Its time is 8 of 6. Could it be that this was supposed to be 5 of 6?

Dickens' Village Series® residents couldn't check the time on a building until 1989 when *Victoria Station* opened its doors just in time for a morning commute. It read 7:20.

In 1992, two buildings were introduced that housed businesses related to selling and repairing clocks. Alpine Village Series™ had the *Kukuck Uhren*, and Christmas In The City® had the *City Clockworks*. Though the *Kukuck Uhren* has a cuckoo clock on the front of the building, it has no hands telling the time. The City piece displays 5 of 6 on two clocks—one above the door (the only one to date that is an attachment) and one next to the door.

A year later, time was being kept in the land to the north. The *North Pole Chapel* lets the elves know that it's 5 past 5. A second clock was introduced to the elves in 1995

continued page 32

Does Anybody Really Know What Time It Is?

continued from page 31

when the *Weather & Time Observatory* arrived. You would expect that a time observatory would have the correct time, so you have to assume that once again those attending religious services were early. The *Observatory's* clocks read 3:40 making the *Chapel's* 1 hour and 25 minutes fast. The North Pole Series'™ latest clock can be found on the *Hall Of Records*. It reads 3:40.

Christmas In The City® also got another clock in 1995. This one came on the *Brighton School*. Like the *Clockworks*, it too read 5 of 6. Figuring that the *City Hall* clock is running three minutes slow, Christmas In The City® would be the only village to have all its clocks telling the same time if it wasn't for the village's newest clock, the one on the *Grand Central Railway Station* introduced in 1996. It reads 12:53.

Two clocks were introduced for the Dickens' Village Series® in 1996, one on *The Olde Camden Town Church* and one on *Quilly's Antiques.* The one on the church is set at 4:45, and the one on the shop (actually a clock stands outside the shop) reads 1:25.

In 1997, the Alpine Village Series™ got another timepiece. Sitting high on the *Spielzeug Laden's* tower, it happily announces the time which is 3:35.

The latest building to be directly related to keeping track of time was introduced into the Dickens' Village Series® in 1998. Reading 3:50, a clock hangs from the side of the *Thomas Mudge Timepieces* building.

Six accessories have included clocks—the *Town Clock, Four Calling Birds* from the Twelve Days of Dickens' Village Series, the *Chelsea Market Curiosity Monger & Cart, Cobbler & Clock Peddler*, the *Village Square Clock Tower* that actually works, and the North Pole Series'™ *End of the Line.*

Who ever thought that we would have a working clock one day? I didn't. But now, I have to wonder if there will ever be a working clock built into a building. I think it's a natural progression, and that we may see it in the future (Lefton's Colonial Village already has such a building). Only time will tell.

As for the different times within the same village, it would be understandable if all future clocks were positioned at 5 of 6 as this is a Department 56® logo. So why hasn't it been this way? Well, maybe Chicago answered it best in their hit song in the '70's when they answered the question "Does anybody really know what time it is?" Their answer..."Does anybody really care?"

the Village Chronicle.

ENGLISH COTTAGE

Item #	Intro	Retired	OSRP	GBTru	↓
5073-3	1981	1982	$25	**$290**	2%

Particulars: Cottage with thatched roof and timbered frame, two chimneys, 1 ½ stories. The roof comes down to meet the top of the first story. Available for only one year.

'91	'92	'93	'94	'95	'96	'97
$300	350	325	285	295	275	295

BARN

Item #	Intro	Retired	OSRP	GBTru	↓
5074-1	1981	1984	$32	**$425**	1%

Particulars: Red barn and silo. Gray roof, two vents on roof ridge, root cellar on side, hay loft over animals and equipment. Also known as the "Original Barn."

'91	'92	'93	'94	'95	'96	'97
$450	425	425	460	460	410	430

CORNER STORE

Item #	Intro	Retired	OSRP	GBTru	↑
5076-8	1981	1983	$30	**$250**	2%

Particulars: Red brick building with one large display window, entry door on corner, bay window in family living area, shutters on windows, shingled roof. The same Item # was used for the 1986 *Apothecary*.

'91	'92	'93	'94	'95	'96	'97
$260	260	260	260	245	205	245

BAKERY

Item #	Intro	Retired	OSRP	GBTru	↑
5077-6	1981	1983	$30	**$275**	4%

Particulars: This is the original *Bakery*. The same Item # was used for the 1986 *Bakery*–a new and different design. This building with a bakery store beneath the family living area and a half turret form giving a unique angle to the front and second story bay window is white with a green roof. The 1986 *Bakery* is brown. There is a wide difference in secondary market value between the two bakery designs. Check all your factual information prior to a purchase. The original *Bakery* is modeled after The Scofield Building in Northfield, MN.

'91	'92	'93	'94	'95	'96	'97
$275	275	275	275	250	255	265

The Original Snow Village®

ENGLISH CHURCH

ITEM #	INTRO	RETIRED	OSRP	GBTRU	↓
5078-4	1981	1982	$30	**$370**	1%

Particulars: Church with steep pitched roof, side chapel, a steeple topped by a gold cross, arched windows, and triangular window in gable above the entry double doors. The cross is separate and inserts into the steeple. The same Item # was used for the 1986 *Diner*. Only available for one year.

'91	'92	'93	'94	'95	'96	'97
$250	375	375	390	395	365	375

LARGE SINGLE TREE

ITEM #	INTRO	RETIRED	OSRP	GBTRU	↑
5080-6	1981	1989	$17	**$55**	22%

Particulars: One lighted snow covered evergreen tree approximately 9" tall with birds perched on the branches. There were mold changes and variations in the amount of snow over the years.

'91	'92	'93	'94	'95	'96	'97
$50	50	50	55	45	35	45

TRAIN STATION WITH 3 TRAIN CARS

ITEM #	INTRO	RETIRED	OSRP	GBTRU	↑
5085-6	1981	1985	$100	**$385**	7%

Particulars: Set of 4. Revised Original Snow Village® train and station design. (Original was 1980, #5087-3 and #5086-5.) All 4 pieces are lit. This larger station, w/8 window panes, 2 windows in the door, brick on the front & side wings & tudor style cross beams, is in better proportion to the train cars.

'91	'92	'93	'94	'95	'96	'97
$350	375	325	325	325	330	360

SKATING POND

ITEM #	INTRO	RETIRED	OSRP	GBTRU	↓
5017-2	1982	1984	$25	**$350**	1%

Particulars: Set of 2. A small snow covered skating pond with a snowman on the edge and tree trunks piled together to provide seating is one piece. The second piece is two lighted evergreen trees. This set replaced and is sometimes confused with the *Skating Rink/Duck Pond Set,* 1978, #5015-3. In this piece, the trees are separate from the pond.

'91	'92	'93	'94	'95	'96	'97
$350	350	350	390	380	360	355

STREET CAR

ITEM #	INTRO	RETIRED	OSRP	GBTru	↑
5019-9	1982	1984	$16	**$380**	1%

Particulars: Lighted bright yellow with green "Main Street" sign on side. #2 car, hook-up on top for pole to connect to electric power. Same Item # was used for the 1987 *Cathedral Church*.

'91	'92	'93	'94	'95	'96	'97
$375	350	325	368	395	325	375

CENTENNIAL HOUSE

ITEM #	INTRO	RETIRED	OSRP	GBTru	↓
5020-2	1982	1984	$32	**$315**	3%

Particulars: Two story clapboard house, square tower, carved and curved window frames, wooden balcony and porch

'91	'92	'93	'94	'95	'96	'97
$365	365	370	350	350	305	325

CARRIAGE HOUSE

ITEM #	INTRO	RETIRED	OSRP	GBTru	↓
5021-0	1982	1984	$28	**$295**	6%

Particulars: In this carriage house, bright lamps flank the entry to the storage area for the carriages. The driver has a small apartment above.

'91	'92	'93	'94	'95	'96	'97
$300	315	300	305	325	290	315

PIONEER CHURCH

ITEM #	INTRO	RETIRED	OSRP	GBTru	NO CHANGE
5022-9	1982	1984	$30	**$320**	

Particulars: Simple cedar shake shingle church with front notice board sending joy to all who pass. Building has a short steeple on the front of the roof ridge.

'91	'92	'93	'94	'95	'96	'97
$285	355	305	310	300	310	320

The Original Snow Village®

SWISS CHALET

ITEM #	INTRO	RETIRED	OSRP	GBTRU	↑
5023-7	1982	1984	$28	**$440**	2%

Particulars: Stone base walls support the timber upper stories of the chalet. The upper floor has a front balcony with a railing and is enclosed by a roof overhang. This building has a very unusual roof.

'91	'92	'93	'94	'95	'96	'97
$335	450	435	415	450	410	430

BANK

ITEM #	INTRO	RETIRED	OSRP	GBTRU	↑
5024-5	1982	1983	$32	**$620**	3%

Particulars: Building is a corner bank with entry by revolving door. Outside there's a covered stairway leading to a second story. The "BANK" sign is part of the corner design. The same Item # was used for the 1987 *Cumberland House.* The Bank was available for only one year.

'91	'92	'93	'94	'95	'96	'97
$415	635	715	600	600	585	600

GABLED HOUSE

ITEM #	INTRO	RETIRED	OSRP	GBTRU	↑
5081-4	1982	1983	$30	**$370**	4%

Particulars: Production pieces of this design are quite different from the house pictured on the Original Snow Village® poster. The house is white shingled with a very dark blue-green variegated four gabled roof. In addition, the building has two small covered porches. The same Item # was used for the 1987 *Red Barn.* Piece was an Early Release to Gift Creations Concepts (GCC).

'91	'92	'93	'94	'95	'96	'97
$350	400	425	360	390	320	355

FLOWER SHOP

ITEM #	INTRO	RETIRED	OSRP	GBTRU	↓
5082-2	1982	1983	$25	**$465**	3%

Particulars: Flower boxes rest outside by the large display window. Shop has rolled up awnings above the front windows. There is a variation in the color of the window frames–they are either green or brown. The same Item # was used the the 1987 *Jefferson School.*

'91	'92	'93	'94	'95	'96	'97
$420	450	475	425	450	450	480

NEW STONE CHURCH

ITEM #	INTRO	RETIRED	OSRP	GBTRU	↑
5083-0	1982	1984	$32	**$375**	1%

Particulars: Church of stone block construction with long nave with side chapel, steeple rises on side opposite chapel. Front has arched windows and two lamps. Early release to Gift Creations Concepts (GCC).

'91	'92	'93	'94	'95	'96	'97
$245	325	325	370	395	330	370

TOWN HALL

ITEM #	INTRO	RETIRED	OSRP	GBTRU	↓
5000-8	1983	1984	$32	**$325**	3%

Particulars: Brick & stone Town Hall with 2 corner covered side entries. Building has symmetrical design (window over window) and a steeple above the front main wall. There's a ceramic bell in the tower. A separate, stamped metal weathervane came in an envelope inside the box. It's rare to find a piece that still has it. No doubt many were unknowingly discarded. Available for only one year.

'91	'92	'93	'94	'95	'96	'97
$225	300	330	330	345	315	335

GROCERY

ITEM #	INTRO	RETIRED	OSRP	GBTRU	↓
5001-6	1983	1985	$35	**$350**	3%

Particulars: Red brick grocery with full painted display windows and decorative cornice trim above and below front windows. The outside staircase leads to family quarters.

'91	'92	'93	'94	'95	'96	'97
$250	325	325	300	325	325	360

VICTORIAN COTTAGE

ITEM #	INTRO	RETIRED	OSRP	GBTRU	↑
5002-4	1983	1984	$35	**$375**	4%

Particulars: Cottage has ornate carved woodwork on front and an ornamental arched entry. First floor French windows are separated by pillars.

'91	'92	'93	'94	'95	'96	'97
$340	375	350	360	365	305	360

The Original Snow Village®

GOVERNOR'S MANSION

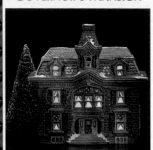

Item #	Intro	Retired	OSRP	GBTru	↑
5003-2	1983	1985	$32	**$315**	3%

Particulars: Brick mansion with metal ironwork featured on the roof cupola (missing from photo). Building has wide entry steps, a repetitive design above the door, a second story and central attic windows.

'91	'92	'93	'94	'95	'96	'97
$285	285	290	300	275	280	305

TURN OF THE CENTURY

Item #	Intro	Retired	OSRP	GBTru	↑
5004-0	1983	1986	$36	**$255**	2%

Particulars: Steps lead to the covered entry and a front triangular ornate design crown the front gable of this building. A squared turret rises from the left front corner and ends in the highest roof peak. The pictured piece is missing a chimney–the center peak should have a chimney. The bottom of the piece reads, "Turn The Time Of Century."

'91	'92	'93	'94	'95	'96	'97
$250	265	265	235	235	245	250

GINGERBREAD HOUSE

Item #	Intro	Retired	OSRP	GBTru	↑
5025-3	1983	1984	$24	**$345**	3%

Particulars: Two Versions: Lighted house and coin bank–not lighted. The coin bank version is extremely difficult to find. Designed like a Christmas edible treat. Cookies trim sides while candy canes and sugar hearts decorate the roof.

'91	'92	'93	'94	'95	'96	'97
$310	370	395	270	270	280	335

VILLAGE CHURCH

Item #	Intro	Retired	OSRP	GBTru	↑
5026-1	1983	1984	$30	**$420**	6%

Particulars: Stone steps of the church lead to double carved doors. The design over the door repeats on the roof trim. The steeple has long narrow openings and pointed arch windows are featured. Collectors often confuse this piece with the *Parish Church*, #5039-3. Early release to Gift Creations Concepts (GCC).

'91	'92	'93	'94	'95	'96	'97
$290	330	335	375	375	385	395

GOTHIC CHURCH

Item #	Intro	Retired	OSRP	GBTRU	↓
5028-8	1983	1986	$36	**$245**	4%

Particulars: Stone block church with the steeple rising straight from large double doors ending in a cross. The bell chamber has ornate grillwork. Smaller entry doors flank the central area repeating the design.

'91	'92	'93	'94	'95	'96	'97
$225	250	245	275	275	235	255

PARSONAGE

Item #	Intro	Retired	OSRP	GBTRU	↑
5029-6	1983	1985	$35	**$385**	3%

Particulars: A tower rises above the entry of the parsonage. The front gable has ornate coping topped by a cross. The coping details are repeated around the windows, doors and small balcony. There are community rooms on first floor and the family lives upstairs.

'91	'92	'93	'94	'95	'96	'97
$225	375	380	380	350	300	375

WOODEN CHURCH

Item #	Intro	Retired	OSRP	GBTRU	↑
5031-8	1983	1985	$30	**$355**	1%

Particulars: White clapboard church with crossed timber design that repeats over the door, roof peak and steeple. The side chapel has a separate entry door.

'91	'92	'93	'94	'95	'96	'97
$400	400	375	375	350	285	350

FIRE STATION

Item #	Intro	Retired	OSRP	GBTRU	NO CHANGE
5032-6	1983	1984	$32	**$575**	

Particulars: The central door of the fire station opens to reveal a red fire truck. Brick columns from the base to the roof add to the sturdy look. A Dalmatian sits by the entry, ready when necessary. Some pieces are without the dog.

'91	'92	'93	'94	'95	'96	'97
$675	675	650	650	625	550	575

ENGLISH TUDOR

Item #	Intro	Retired	OSRP	GBTru	↑
5033-4	1983	1985	$30	**$280**	2%

Particulars: Stucco finish building with brick chimneys. The three front roof peaks create the front gable design.

'91	'92	'93	'94	'95	'96	'97
$275	300	300	260	295	225	275

CHATEAU

Item #	Intro	Retired	OSRP	GBTru	↑
5084-9	1983	1984	$35	**$495**	4%

Particulars: First story large windows which include front and side bow windows are a feature of this building. There's a diamond design on the roof shingles, stone for walls and a cylindrical chimney with a domed flue cap. The front dormers and side peaks exhibit an ornate carved design. Early release to Gift Creations Concepts (GCC).

'91	'92	'93	'94	'95	'96	'97
$290	375	420	470	475	445	475

MAIN STREET HOUSE

Item #	Intro	Retired	OSRP	GBTru	↑
5005-9	1984	1986	$27	**$250**	4%

Particulars: White and green 1 ½-story house with clapboard lower story and timbered upper story. There are two lamps on either side of the front door. Early release to Gift Creations Concepts (GCC).

'91	'92	'93	'94	'95	'96	'97
$165	250	250	250	275	225	240

STRATFORD HOUSE

Item #	Intro	Retired	OSRP	GBTru	↑
5007-5	1984	1986	$28	**$190**	9%

Particulars: English Tudor style house featuring vertical ornamental timbers. All gables rise to the same height.

'91	'92	'93	'94	'95	'96	'97
$110	225	225	215	195	165	175

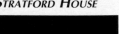

The Original Snow Village®

HAVERSHAM HOUSE

ITEM #	INTRO	RETIRED	OSRP	GBTRU	NO
5008-3	1984	1987	$37	**$280**	CHANGE

Particulars: All gables, balconies and porch are decorated with ornately carved woodwork. Early release to Gift Creations Concepts (GCC). Early release pieces are larger than subsequent ones.

'91	'92	'93	'94	'95	'96	'97
$200	240	295	310	300	240	280

GALENA HOUSE

ITEM #	INTRO	RETIRED	OSRP	GBTRU	↑
5009-1	1984	1985	$32	**$355**	11%

Particulars: Steps lead to double entry doors of this brick home. A bay window fills one side. The second floor is incorporated into the roof construction. Available for one year only.

'91	'92	'93	'94	'95	'96	'97
$285	330	330	330	345	285	320

RIVER ROAD HOUSE

ITEM #	INTRO	RETIRED	OSRP	GBTRU	↑
5010-5	1984	1987	$36	**$205**	3%

Particulars: A large and grand white house with many windows. There are 3 Versions. The First Version has cut out transoms above the two front windows, as is the middle arch above the front door. The Second Version repeats the cut out transoms with a solid middle arch. The Third Version has a cut out middle arch and solid transoms. Early release to Gift Creations Concepts (GCC).

'91	'92	'93	'94	'95	'96	'97
$150	150	220	220	215	185	200

DELTA HOUSE

ITEM #	INTRO	RETIRED	OSRP	GBTRU	↑
5012-1	1984	1986	$32	**$315**	5%

Particulars: A large brick house with a balcony above the wraparound porch which is separate from the entry. The decorative porch trim design is repeated where the roof and brick meet and on turret. The photograph is without the ornamental "iron works" atop the tower. Many collectors are unaware of the trim, in fact it's rare to find a piece that still has it. It came in an envelope inside the box.

'91	'92	'93	'94	'95	'96	'97
$350	325	335	345	310	260	300

BAYPORT

ITEM #	INTRO	RETIRED	OSRP	GBTru	↓
5015-6	1984	1986	$30	**$225**	4%

Particulars: Gray clapboard corner entry home with a turret addition positioned between the two main wings of the two-story house.

'91	'92	'93	'94	'95	'96	'97
$215	230	230	230	235	210	235

CONGREGATIONAL CHURCH

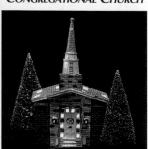

ITEM #	INTRO	RETIRED	OSRP	GBTru	↓
5034-2	1984	1985	$28	**$595**	8%

Particulars: Brick church with fieldstone front. The stone is repeated on the steeple. There are louver vents on the belfry. This is a difficult piece to locate on the secondary market due in part to the fact that it was available for only one year.

'91	'92	'93	'94	'95	'96	'97
$250	360	415	540	595	615	645

TRINITY CHURCH

ITEM #	INTRO	RETIRED	OSRP	GBTru	↓
5035-0	1984	1986	$32	**$275**	4%

Particulars: Church has steeples of different heights, clerestory windows to bring additional light to the nave and two large wreaths by the front doors.

'91	'92	'93	'94	'95	'96	'97
$220	265	305	305	305	245	285

SUMMIT HOUSE

ITEM #	INTRO	RETIRED	OSRP	GBTru	↑
5036-9	1984	1985	$28	**$345**	1%

Particulars: Pink corner house features a rounded turret and large entry door with side lights. Cornices appear to support the roof edge. Each second story window is capped by a molded projection. Available for one year only.

'91	'92	'93	'94	'95	'96	'97
$375	375	395	385	385	310	340

NEW SCHOOL HOUSE

ITEM #	INTRO	RETIRED	OSRP	GBTRU	↑
5037-7	1984	1986	$35	**$255**	9%

Particulars: Two-story schoolhouse with bell tower and clock. There is a separate cloth flag on a wooden pole that can be inserted into a hole in the base.

'91	'92	'93	'94	'95	'96	'97
$240	270	275	275	275	215	235

PARISH CHURCH

ITEM #	INTRO	RETIRED	OSRP	GBTRU	↑
5039-3	1984	1986	$32	**$335**	6%

Particulars: White country church with unique three level steeple has arched windows, a red door and a circular window over the entry. Collectors often confuse this piece with the *Village Church*, #5026-1.

'91	'92	'93	'94	'95	'96	'97
$310	345	370	370	370	285	315

STUCCO BUNGALOW

ITEM #	INTRO	RETIRED	OSRP	GBTRU	↑
5045-8	1985	1986	$30	**$370**	1%

Particulars: Two-story small house with one roof dormer as a mini tower has a second dormer featuring a timbered design. The entry door is built into the archway under a low roof peak. A wreath and garland decorate the door. This is a difficult piece to locate on the secondary market as it was available for only one year.

'91	'92	'93	'94	'95	'96	'97
$105	375	360	385	395	340	365

WILLIAMSBURG HOUSE

ITEM #	INTRO	RETIRED	OSRP	GBTRU	
5046-6	1985	1988	$37	**$165**	NO CHANGE

Particulars: A traditional two-story colonial with all windows shuttered, three dormers, two chimneys and a covered entry topped by a second floor balcony.

'91	'92	'93	'94	'95	'96	'97
$95	110	135	145	135	165	165

The Original Snow Village®

PLANTATION HOUSE

Item #	Intro	Retired	OSRP	GBTru	↓
5047-4	1985	1987	$37	**$110**	4%

Particulars: The house features an entry with two-story wood columns, three dormers, two chimneys and four first floor windows with canopies.

'91	'92	'93	'94	'95	'96	'97
$80	95	118	118	115	120	115

CHURCH OF THE OPEN DOOR

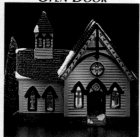

Item #	Intro	Retired	OSRP	GBTru	↓
5048-2	1985	1988	$34	**$135**	7%

Particulars: Church with a steeple on the side chapel has design over front entry above circular window that is repeated in motif on eaves.

'91	'92	'93	'94	'95	'96	'97
$110	105	135	135	125	130	145

SPRUCE PLACE

Item #	Intro	Retired	OSRP	GBTru	
5049-0	1985	1987	$33	**$270**	NO CHANGE

Particulars: Victorian house has a windowed turret rising above a covered porch. There's decorative molding above the porch, windows and dormer. A circular window over the porch is decorated with a wreath.

'91	'92	'93	'94	'95	'96	'97
$275	315	320	270	275	255	270

DUPLEX

Item #	Intro	Retired	OSRP	GBTru	↓
5050-4	1985	1987	$35	**$150**	9%

Particulars: The duplex is a two-family house with a shared entry. Each family has up and down rooms and a bay window. The building has a small second story balcony and roof dormers.

'91	'92	'93	'94	'95	'96	'97
$100	105	110	165	165	155	165

DEPOT AND TRAIN WITH 2 TRAIN CARS

ITEM #	INTRO	RETIRED	OSRP	GBTRU	↑
5051-2	1985	1988	$65	**$165**	3%

Particulars: Set of 4. Second Original Snow Village® train & station design. Train is non-lighting. Depot has 2 wings, each w/ chimney, connected by a central area. There are 3 Versions: 1st Version of the depot (pictured) was brown w/gray corner stones & yellow passenger car windows; 2nd Version was a variegated brick w/no corner stones & yellow passenger car windows; 3rd Version was the brick w/white passenger car windows.

'91	'92	'93	'94	'95	'96	'97
$110	125	135	135	145	150	160

RIDGEWOOD

ITEM #	INTRO	RETIRED	OSRP	GBTRU	↓
5052-0	1985	1987	$35	**$170**	6%

Particulars: Porches run the length of both the first and second story on this house. The first floor front windows are arched as are the window over the front door and in the attic.

'91	'92	'93	'94	'95	'96	'97
$125	130	150	165	170	180	180

WAVERLY PLACE

ITEM #	INTRO	RETIRED	OSRP	GBTRU	↑
5041-5	1986	1986	$35	**$315**	5%

Particulars: This ornate Victorian home has two different turret-like window designs. The second story features half moon window highlights and carved moldings. Designed after the Gingerbread Mansion in Ferndale, CA. Early release to Gift Creations Concepts (GCC), in the Fall of 1985.

'91	'92	'93	'94	'95	'96	'97
$265	300	300	300	325	290	300

TWIN PEAKS

ITEM #	INTRO	RETIRED	OSRP	GBTRU	↓
5042-3	1986	1986	$32	**$425**	3%

Particulars: Building has two matching three-story stone turrets with a multitude of windows on each story to soften the fortress look. Wide steps lead to the red entry doors. Early release to Gift Creations Concepts (GCC), Fall 1985.

'91	'92	'93	'94	'95	'96	'97
$275	285	325	510	525	445	440

2101 Maple

Item #	Intro	Retired	OSRP	GBTru	NO
5043-1	1986	1986	$32	**$345**	CHANGE

Particulars: Brick two-story home with the side of the front porch built out from a stone turret. The second story windows are capped by a half circle window. Early release to Gift Creations Concepts (GCC), Fall 1985.

'91	'92	'93	'94	'95	'96	'97
$195	330	330	360	375	325	345

Lincoln Park Duplex

Item #	Intro	Retired	OSRP	GBTru	↑
5060-1	1986	1988	$33	**$140**	4%

Particulars: Two-family attached home reminiscent of Chicago's Lincoln Park. Occupants share a front door. The floor plan's unique feature is the placement of chimneys–as if the floor plans are reversed–one is at the front, the other is at the rear.

'91	'92	'93	'94	'95	'96	'97
$90	115	100	125	125	135	135

Sonoma House

Item #	Intro	Retired	OSRP	GBTru	NO
5062-8	1986	1988	$33	**$145**	CHANGE

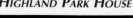

Particulars: Building exhibits the flavor of the Southwest with stucco walls and red roof. The decorative curved front rises 2 ½ stories. A square turret adjacent to the front door is capped by the same decorative design which also repeats on the chimney. Early release to Gift Creations Concepts (GCC), Fall 1985.

'91	'92	'93	'94	'95	'96	'97
$85	110	115	118	120	140	145

Highland Park House

Item #	Intro	Retired	OSRP	GBTru	↑
5063-6	1986	1988	$35	**$170**	6%

Particulars: Brick, timbered, and gabled house brings English Tudor design to cozy home. Rounded arch front door repeats theme in two windows in mid-roof gable. Brick chimney on side. Early release to Gift Creations Concepts (GCC), Fall 1986.

'91	'92	'93	'94	'95	'96	'97
$100	105	120	150	150	160	160

The Original Snow Village®

BEACON HILL HOUSE

ITEM #	INTRO	RETIRED	OSRP	GBTRU	↑
5065-2	1986	1988	$31	**$180**	3%

Particulars: A green with black roof row house, typical of urban Boston, MA neighborhoods. Home features bay windows on first and second story highlighted by paneled framing.

'91	'92	'93	'94	'95	'96	'97
$95	120	150	165	150	165	175

PACIFIC HEIGHTS HOUSE

ITEM #	INTRO	RETIRED	OSRP	GBTRU	↑
5066-0	1986	1988	$33	**$105**	5%

Particulars: A beige with tan roof West Coast row house that appears tall and narrow due to the vertical theme of the front porch balcony support columns.

'91	'92	'93	'94	'95	'96	'97
$115	90	95	100	100	105	100

RAMSEY HILL HOUSE

ITEM #	INTRO	RETIRED	OSRP	GBTRU	
5067-9	1986	1989	$36	**$100**	NO CHANGE

Particulars: Victorian home with double chimneys. There are steps to the front door and a porch adjacent to the entry. The side door also features a small porch. A low balustrade fronts the second story windows. Hand painting adds detailing to the design. Early release to Gift Creations Concepts (GCC), Fall 1986. The early release piece colors are more vibrant.

'91	'92	'93	'94	'95	'96	'97
$90	96	96	98	95	95	100

SAINT JAMES CHURCH

ITEM #	INTRO	RETIRED	OSRP	GBTRU	↑
5068-7	1986	1988	$37	**$175**	9%

Particulars: Church with long central nave flanked by lower roofed side sections fronted by two towers. The main center cross is reinforced by smaller crosses on each section of the tower roof. Smaller round side windows repeat the central window shape.

'91	'92	'93	'94	'95	'96	'97
$105	140	170	160	175	155	160

All Saints Church

Item #	Intro	Retired	OSRP	GBTru	↑
5070-9	1986	1997	$38	**$65**	44%

Particulars: A small country church with simple design of long nave and entry door in the base of the bell tower. The same Item # was used for the 1980 *Colonial Farm House.*

'91	'92	'93	'94	'95	'96	'97
$45	45	45	45	45	45	45

Carriage House

Item #	Intro	Retired	OSRP	GBTru	↑
5071-7	1986	1988	$29	**$130**	4%

Particulars: A small converted home from a building originally used to house carriages. A second story is achieved with many dormer windows. The fieldstone foundation allowed great weight when it was used for carriages. The same Item # was used for the 1980 *Town Church.*

'91	'92	'93	'94	'95	'96	'97
$95	110	110	110	110	115	125

Toy Shop

Item #	Intro	Retired	OSRP	GBTru	↑
5073-3	1986	1990	$36	**$100**	5%

Particulars: The shop's front windows display toys while the roof molding draws attention to the teddy bear under the pediment. This Main Street design is based on the Finch Building in Hastings, MN.

'91	'92	'93	'94	'95	'96	'97
$75	100	95	90	90	90	95

Apothecary

Item #	Intro	Retired	OSRP	GBTru	↑
5076-8	1986	1990	$34	**$110**	5%

Particulars: This Main Street design is based on the former City Hall in Hastings, MN. Two doors flank a central display bow window. A mortar and pestle, symbolizing the profession of the proprietor, is on the front panel above the second floor family quarters windows. Some sleeves read "Antique Shop." The same Item # was used for the 1981 *Corner Store.*

'91	'92	'93	'94	'95	'96	'97
$70	92	92	85	90	100	105

BAKERY

Item #	Intro	Retired	OSRP	GBTru	↓
5077-6	1986	1991	$35	**$85**	6%

Particulars: This Main Street design is based on the Scofield Building in Northfield, MN. The corner bakery has two large multi-paned display windows protected by a ribbed canopy. Greek key designs around the roof edging highlight the bas-relief cupcake topped by a cherry that is centrally placed over the entry. The same Item # was used for the first Original Snow Village® *Bakery* in 1981.

	'91	'92	'93	'94	'95	'96	'97
	$37.50	80	70	80	85	85	90

DINER

Item #	Intro	Retired	OSRP	GBTru	↓
5078-4	1986	1987	$22	**$650**	1%

Particulars: Also known as "Mickey's." Designed after Mickey's Diner in St. Paul, MN. Diners are an eating place based on the railroads' famous dining cars with a reputation for good, wholesome food. The glass block entry protects diners from the weather. Available for only one year. The same Item # was used for the 1981 *English Church.*

	'91	'92	'93	'94	'95	'96	'97
	$270	420	425	530	550	650	655

ST. ANTHONY HOTEL & POST OFFICE

Item #	Intro	Retired	OSRP	GBTru	↑
5006-7	1987	1989	$40	**$115**	10%

Particulars: This Main Street design three-story red brick building with green trim is dated "1886" and has an address of "56 Main Street." An American flag flies outside the ground floor of the Post Office. Metal flag is separate.

	'91	'92	'93	'94	'95	'96	'97
	$85	100	110	115	110	115	105

SNOW VILLAGE FACTORY

Item #	Intro	Retired	OSRP	GBTru	↑
5013-0	1987	1989	$45	**$150**	11%

Particulars: Set of 2. Smokestack is separate. The wood building rises on a stone block base with a tall smokestack at the rear. Factory products are sold in the small shop in the front.

	'91	'92	'93	'94	'95	'96	'97
	$90	105	110	110	120	130	135

The Original Snow Village®

CATHEDRAL CHURCH

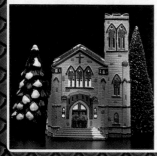

ITEM #	INTRO	RETIRED	OSRP	GBTRU	↑
5019-9	1987	1990	$50	**$115**	5%

Particulars: Second of two Original Snow Village® Cathedral Churches. (See also 1980, #5067-4.) Cathedral has mosaic "stained glass" decorating the Gothic windows on all sides as well as the large turret. Same Item # was used for the 1982 *Street Car*.

'91	'92	'93	'94	'95	'96	'97
$85	110	110	110	100	105	110

CUMBERLAND HOUSE

ITEM #	INTRO	RETIRED	OSRP	GBTRU	↓
5024-5	1987	1995	$42	**$70**	7%

Particulars: Large garland decorated house has multicolored roof supported by four columns, two chimneys and shuttered windows. The same Item # was used for the 1982 *Bank*.

'91	'92	'93	'94	'95	'96	'97
$44	44	45	45	45	65	75

SPRINGFIELD HOUSE

ITEM #	INTRO	RETIRED	OSRP	GBTRU	↑
5027-0	1987	1990	$40	**$90**	13%

Particulars: Williamsburg blue clapboard home's lower level has two multi-paned bay windows–one is bowed. The upper level windows are shuttered. Roof dormers are half-circle sunbursts. A stone chimney completes this house.

'91	'92	'93	'94	'95	'96	'97
$90	100	85	100	75	80	80

LIGHTHOUSE

ITEM #	INTRO	RETIRED	OSRP	GBTRU	↓
5030-0	1987	1988	$36	**$550**	8%

Particulars: A favorite with collectors. Five story lighthouse beacon rises from sturdy stone slab base and is connected to a caretaker's cottage. There are two versions of the piece. One has a white unglazed tower, the other has an off-white glazed tower.

'91	'92	'93	'94	'95	'96	'97
$255	340	340	650	595	605	595

The Original Snow Village®

RED BARN

Item #	Intro	Retired	OSRP	GBTru	↑
5081-4	1987	1992	$38	**$105**	24%

Particulars: Wooden barn has stone base, double cross-buck doors on the long side, and hayloft above the main doors. There are three ventilator cupolas on the roof ridge. A cat sleeps in the hayloft. The same Item # was used for the 1982 *Gabled House*. Early release to Gift Creations Concepts (GCC).

'91	'92	'93	'94	'95	'96	'97
$42	42	75	75	75	85	85

JEFFERSON SCHOOL

Item #	Intro	Retired	OSRP	GBTru	↓
5082-2	1987	1991	$36	**$160**	6%

Particulars: A two-room schoolhouse with large multi-paned windows with top transoms. There's a short bell tower incorporated into the roof. The same Item # was used for the 1982 *Flower Shop*. Early release to Gift Creations Concepts (GCC).

'91	'92	'93	'94	'95	'96	'97
$40	90	108	115	145	155	170

FARM HOUSE

Item #	Intro	Retired	OSRP	GBTru	NO CHANGE
5089-0	1987	1992	$40	**$75**	

Particulars: A 2 1/2-story wood frame home with front full-length porch. The roof interest is two low, one high peak with attic window in highest peak.

'91	'92	'93	'94	'95	'96	'97
$44	45	70	75	65	75	75

FIRE STATION NO. 2

Item #	Intro	Retired	OSRP	GBTru	↓
5091-1	1987	1989	$40	**$195**	3%

Particulars: Fire Station has two large double doors housing two engines, the side stair leads to living quarters. It's a brick building with a stone arch design at engine doors and front windows. Early release to Gift Creations Concepts (GCC).

'91	'92	'93	'94	'95	'96	'97
$70	120	140	140	185	220	200

SNOW VILLAGE RESORT LODGE

ITEM #	INTRO	RETIRED	OSRP	GBTRU	↑
5092-0	1987	1989	$55	**$150**	3%

Particulars: Bright yellow and green lodge with scalloped roof, covered porch and side entry. There are bay windows on the front house section. The back section rises to dormered 3 1/2 stories. Ventilator areas are directly under the roof cap.

'91	'92	'93	'94	'95	'96	'97
$100	120	120	120	140	145	145

VILLAGE MARKET

ITEM #	INTRO	RETIRED	OSRP	GBTRU	↑
5044-0	1988	1991	$39	**$95**	27%

Particulars: Silk-screened "glass" windows detail the merchandise available at the market. A red and white canopy protects shoppers using the in/out doors. There's a sign over the second story windows. The color varies from mint green to cream. Sisal tree on top is separate. Early release to Gift Creations Concepts (GCC).

'91	'92	'93	'94	'95	'96	'97
$40	85	74	75	65	75	75

KENWOOD HOUSE

ITEM #	INTRO	RETIRED	OSRP	GBTRU	↑
5054-7	1988	1990	$50	**$145**	12%

Particulars: Three-story home has an old-fashioned wraparound veranda with arched openings. The front facade features scalloped shingles on third story. Early release to Gift Creations Concepts (GCC).

'91	'92	'93	'94	'95	'96	'97
$100	105	105	100	125	130	130

MAPLE RIDGE INN

ITEM #	INTRO	RETIRED	OSRP	GBTRU	NO CHANGE
5121-7	1988	1990	$55	**$75**	

Particulars: Inn is a replica of a Victorian mansion. The ornamental roof piece concealed lightning rods. This piece is an interpretation of an American landmark in Cambridge, NY. 1991 Gift Creations Concepts (GCC) Catalog Exclusive at $75.00.

'91	'92	'93	'94	'95	'96	'97
$100	98	92	75	65	75	75

VILLAGE STATION AND TRAIN

ITEM #	INTRO	RETIRED	OSRP	GBTRU	↑
5122-5	1988	1992	$65	**$120**	9%

Particulars: Set of 4. The third Original Snow Village® train and station design. Station features an outside ticket window, soft drink vending machine and outside benches. The three train cars do not light.

'91	'92	'93	'94	'95	'96	'97
$70	70	105	105	100	115	110

COBBLESTONE ANTIQUE SHOP

ITEM #	INTRO	RETIRED	OSRP	GBTRU	↓
5123-3	1988	1992	$36	**$65**	13%

Particulars: The silk-screened front windows display antiques for sale and a bay window fills the second story width. A building date of "1881" is on the arched cornice.

'91	'92	'93	'94	'95	'96	'97
$37.50	37.50	65	70	65	70	75

CORNER CAFE

ITEM #	INTRO	RETIRED	OSRP	GBTRU	NO
5124-1	1988	1991	$37	**$100**	CHANGE

Particulars: There's "Pie" and "Coffee" silk-screened on the windows of this corner restaurant with red, white, and blue striped awnings. A building date of "1875" is inscribed on the turret.

'91	'92	'93	'94	'95	'96	'97
$37.50	75	75	80	90	90	100

SINGLE CAR GARAGE

ITEM #	INTRO	RETIRED	OSRP	GBTRU	↑
5125-0	1988	1990	$22	**$60**	9%

Particulars: Double doors open to house the car, there are two outside lights for safety and convenience. Designed to look like a house, the windows have shutters and the roof has dormers. The roof projects over a wood pile keeping it dry.

'91	'92	'93	'94	'95	'96	'97
$50	50	50	65	50	55	55

The Original Snow Village®

HOME SWEET HOME/ HOUSE & WINDMILL

ITEM #	INTRO	RETIRED	OSRP	GBTRU	NO
5126-8	1988	1991	$60	**$120**	CHANGE

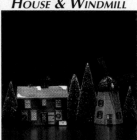

Particulars: Set of 2. Inspired by the East Hampton, NY landmark historic home of John Howard Payne, composer of "Home Sweet Home." The saltbox home has an asymmetrical arrangement of windows. Doors for root cellar are at the front corner and there's one central brick chimney. The four-bladed metal windmill is separate.

'91	'92	'93	'94	'95	'96	'97
$60	105	105	110	115	120	120

REDEEMER CHURCH

ITEM #	INTRO	RETIRED	OSRP	GBTRU	↑
5127-6	1988	1992	$42	**$75**	7%

Particulars: The stone corners add strength and support to this church and bell tower. Arched windows and heavy wooden double doors complete the design.

'91	'92	'93	'94	'95	'96	'97
$45	45	74	75	60	70	70

SERVICE STATION

ITEM #	INTRO	RETIRED	OSRP	GBTRU	↓
5128-4	1988	1991	$37.50	**$260**	2%

Particulars: More commonly known as "Bill's Service Station." Set of 2 includes building and gas pumps. Pumps do not light. There's a big difference in the secondary market value if the pumps are missing. Bill's has a candy machine, restroom, work area and office.

'91	'92	'93	'94	'95	'96	'97
$37.50	90	112	165	295	295	265

STONEHURST HOUSE

ITEM #	INTRO	RETIRED	OSRP	GBTRU	↑
5140-3	1988	1994	$37.50	**$70**	8%

Particulars: Home of red brick punctuated with black and white painted bricks. The half circle sunburst design second story dormers restate the arch shape of the first floor windows.

'91	'92	'93	'94	'95	'96	'97
$37.50	37.50	37.50	37.50	60	65	65

PALOS VERDES

ITEM #	INTRO	RETIRED	OSRP	GBTRU	↑
5141-1	1988	1990	$37.50	**$90**	6%

Particulars: Spanish style stucco home with green tiled roof, covered entry porch, and second floor shuttered windows. Coming forward from the main wing is a two-story round turret and ground floor window alcove. There's a separate potted miniature sisal tree on the porch.

'91	'92	'93	'94	'95	'96	'97
$60	85	75	75	80	85	85

JINGLE BELLE HOUSEBOAT

ITEM #	INTRO	RETIRED	OSRP	GBTRU	↑
5114-4	1989	1991	$42	**$165**	10%

Particulars: This floating house sports a Christmas tree on the wheelhouse roof and rear deck. The boat's name is stenciled on the bow and life preservers. The stamped metal bell that hangs on the side is separate and often lost.

'91	'92	'93	'94	'95	'96	'97
$42	90	80	80	100	115	150

COLONIAL CHURCH

ITEM #	INTRO	RETIRED	OSRP	GBTRU	↑
5119-5	1989	1992	$60	**$75**	7%

Particulars: Church has front entry with four floor-to-roof columns supporting the roof over the porch. The front facade repeats the design with four half columns set into the wall. A metal cross tops the three-tier steeple bell tower. Early release to Gift Creations Concepts (GCC).

'91	'92	'93	'94	'95	'96	'97
$60	60	85	75	75	80	70

NORTH CREEK COTTAGE

ITEM #	INTRO	RETIRED	OSRP	GBTRU	↑
5120-9	1989	1992	$45	**$75**	15%

Particulars: Cape cod style home with a colonial columned front porch. In addition, there's an attached garage with a deck on top, a front dormer and stone chimney. Early release to Gift Creations Concepts (GCC).

'91	'92	'93	'94	'95	'96	'97
$45	45	70	65	55	70	65

PARAMOUNT THEATER

ITEM #	INTRO	RETIRED	OSRP	GBTRU	↑
5142-0	1989	1993	$42	**$195**	22%

Particulars: The theater is a Spanish theme Art Deco building with double marques. A ticket booth in the center is flanked by two double doors. Corner billboards advertise "White Christmas" is *Now Showing* and "It's A Wonderful Life" is *Coming Soon*.

'91	'92	'93	'94	'95	'96	'97
$42	42	42	78	85	125	160

DOCTOR'S HOUSE

ITEM #	INTRO	RETIRED	OSRP	GBTRU	NO
5143-8	1989	1992	$56	**$105**	CHANGE

Particulars: The Doctor's home and office are within this house. A rounded turret completes the front. The three-story building has arched, porthole, and bay windows to add to its Victorian charm.

'91	'92	'93	'94	'95	'96	'97
$56	56	85	85	95	100	105

COURTHOUSE

ITEM #	INTRO	RETIRED	OSRP	GBTRU	↑
5144-6	1989	1993	$65	**$195**	8%

Particulars: Courthouse has four corner roof turrets with a central clock tower, windows with half circle sunbursts, decorative molding on the second story with two front windows being clear half-circles. The design is based on the Gibson County Courthouse in Princetown, IN.

'91	'92	'93	'94	'95	'96	'97
$65	65	65	110	125	150	180

VILLAGE WARMING HOUSE

ITEM #	INTRO	RETIRED	OSRP	GBTRU	↑
5145-4	1989	1992	$42	**$75**	15%

Particulars: Used by skaters to warm up from the chill, this small red house has a steep front roof. The bench at the side is available for a brief rest. Sisal trees detach.

'91	'92	'93	'94	'95	'96	'97
$42	42	70	60	60	70	65

J. YOUNG'S GRANARY

ITEM #	INTRO	RETIRED	OSRP	GBTRU	↑
5149-7	1989	1992	$45	**$85**	6%

Particulars: Granary has a central water wheel for grinding grain, a stone silo on one side and a small store and storage area on other side. Named for Julia Young, a Department 56® retailer in New Jersey.

'91	'92	'93	'94	'95	'96	'97
$45	45	65	75	65	75	80

PINEWOOD LOG CABIN

ITEM #	INTRO	RETIRED	OSRP	GBTRU	↑
5150-0	1989	1995	$37.50	**$70**	17%

Particulars: Cabin of log construction with two fireplaces for heating and cooking, tree trunk porch pillars, firewood stack and attached tree. The house name appears on the sign above the porch. Early release to Gift Creations Concepts (GCC), Fall 1990.

'91	'92	'93	'94	'95	'96	'97
$37.50	37.50	37.50	37.50	37.50	60	60

56 FLAVORS ICE CREAM PARLOR

ITEM #	INTRO	RETIRED	OSRP	GBTRU	↑
5151-9	1990	1992	$42	**$175**	21%

Particulars: Ice cream parlor is decorated like a sundae. Peppermint pillars flank the door, there's a sugar cone roof with a cherry on its peak and window boxes hold ice cream cones. Cherry and stem on top are extremely fragile. Early release to Gift Creations Concepts (GCC).

'91	'92	'93	'94	'95	'96	'97
$42	45	78	80	80	105	145

MORNINGSIDE HOUSE

ITEM #	INTRO	RETIRED	OSRP	GBTRU	↑
5152-7	1990	1992	$45	**$65**	8%

Particulars: Home is a pink split level house with one car garage. It has a fieldstone chimney, curved front steps and terraced landscaping with removable sisal trees.

'91	'92	'93	'94	'95	'96	'97
$45	45	55	50	50	65	60

MAINSTREET HARDWARE STORE

ITEM #	INTRO	RETIRED	OSRP	GBTRU	↑
5153-5	1990	1993	$42	**$90**	13%

Particulars: A three-story building with the store on the ground level. Access to the rental rooms on the second and third story is by the outside staircase. The store was originally photographed with blue awnings and window trim, however production pieces had green awnings and trim.

'91	'92	'93	'94	'95	'96	'97
$42	42	42	55	65	75	80

VILLAGE REALTY

ITEM #	INTRO	RETIRED	OSRP	GBTRU	↑
5154-3	1990	1993	$42	**$75**	7%

Particulars: The two story main building houses a real estate office. A front bay display window showcases available properties. "J. Saraceno" over the door is a tribute to Department 56, Inc.'s late National Sales Manager. The small adjacent building is an intimate Italian dining place with colorful striped awning.

'91	'92	'93	'94	'95	'96	'97
$42	42	42	60	70	75	70

SPANISH MISSION CHURCH

ITEM #	INTRO	RETIRED	OSRP	GBTRU	↑
5155-1	1990	1992	$42	**$85**	6%

Particulars: Sun-dried clay creates this adobe Spanish style church. The arcade along one side gives protected access. Designed after the Enga Memorial Chapel In Minneapolis, MN.

'91	'92	'93	'94	'95	'96	'97
$42	42	72	72	60	75	80

PRAIRIE HOUSE

ITEM #	INTRO	RETIRED	OSRP	GBTRU	NO CHANGE
5156-0	1990	1993	$42	**$70**	

Particulars: Two-story home with upper floor set in and back atop the first story. A large chimney rises up through the first story. Two large pillars support the covered entry with separate, removable sisal trees on either side. Part of the American Architecture Series.

'91	'92	'93	'94	'95	'96	'97
$42	42	44	50	60	70	70

The Original Snow Village®

QUEEN ANNE VICTORIAN

ITEM #	INTRO	RETIRED	OSRP	GBTru	↑
5157-8	1990	1996	$48	**$75**	15%

Particulars: Broad steps lead up to a pillared porch with a unique corner gazebo style sitting area. An ornate turret on the corner of the second story is decorated with scalloped shingles. Part of the American Architecture Series.

'91	'92	'93	'94	'95	'96	'97
$48	48	50	50	50	50	65

THE CHRISTMAS SHOP

ITEM #	INTRO	RETIRED	OSRP	GBTru	↑
5097-0	1991	1996	$37.50	**$65**	8%

Particulars: Pediment on the brick building advertises the holiday, the French "NOEL." There's a large teddy bear by the front window. Early release to Gift Creations Concepts (GCC) and Showcase Dealers.

'91	'92	'93	'94	'95	'96	'97
$37.50	37.50	37.50	37.50	37.50	37.50	60

OAK GROVE TUDOR

ITEM #	INTRO	RETIRED	OSRP	GBTru	↑
5400-3	1991	1994	$42	**$70**	8%

Particulars: Red brick base with stucco and timbered second-story home. There's a fireplace of brick and stone by the entry door. Rough stone frames the door and foundation. Early release to Showcase Dealers.

'91	'92	'93	'94	'95	'96	'97
$42	42	42	42	60	65	65

THE HONEYMOONER MOTEL

ITEM #	INTRO	RETIRED	OSRP	GBTru	↑
5401-1	1991	1993	$42	**$85**	6%

Particulars: A moon and stars sign above the office door is an advertisement for the motel. Motel is a white building with blue awnings and doors. There's a soda and ice machine by the office door. Middle class auto travelers were attracted to stay-over facilities that offered privacy and luxury offered by the Mom & Pop enterprises. By the 1940's there were motels coast to coast. Early release to Showcase Dealers.

'91	'92	'93	'94	'95	'96	'97
$42	42	44	75	70	70	80

VILLAGE GREENHOUSE

ITEM #	INTRO	RETIRED	OSRP	GBTRU	↑
5402-0	1991	1995	$35	**$70**	8%

Particulars: Plant growing area has bricked bottom and "glass" roof to allow sunlight in. Attached small store sells accessories. It has brick chimney, shingled roof and covered entry.

'91	'92	'93	'94	'95	'96	'97
$35	35	36	36	36	75	65

SOUTHERN COLONIAL

ITEM #	INTRO	RETIRED	OSRP	GBTRU	↑
5403-8	1991	1994	$48	**$80**	7%

Particulars: Four columns rise from the ground to the roof with a second-story veranda across the front. Double chimneys are surrounded by a balustrade. Shutters by each window both decorate and shut out the heat of the sun. Two urns flank steps of entryway. Part of the American Architecture Series.

'91	'92	'93	'94	'95	'96	'97
$48	48	50	50	65	75	75

GOTHIC FARMHOUSE

ITEM #	INTRO	RETIRED	OSRP	GBTRU	↑
5404-6	1991	1997	$48	**$70**	46%

Particulars: Clapboard home with diamond patterned roof shingles has columned front porch and entry. The first floor has a large bay window. The second story rises to a gable with carved molding which is repeated on the two dormer windows over the porch. Part of the American Architecture Series.

'91	'92	'93	'94	'95	'96	'97
$48	48	48	48	48	48	48

FINKLEA'S FINERY COSTUME SHOP

ITEM #	INTRO	RETIRED	OSRP	GBTRU	↑
5405-4	1991	1993	$45	**$70**	17%

Particulars: Dressed stone trims the facade of the three-story brick building. There are red awnings over the first floor display windows and a hood projects over the third floor piano teacher's windows. The attached side setback is two stories with a decorated rental return door and an awning on upper window.

'91	'92	'93	'94	'95	'96	'97
$45	45	45	70	55	60	60

JACK'S CORNER BARBER SHOP

	ITEM #	INTRO	RETIRED	OSRP	GBTru	↑
	5406-2	1991	1994	$42	**$75**	7%

Particulars: The barber shop also houses M. Schmitt Photography Studio and a second-floor tailor shop. A two-story turret separates two identical wings of the brick building. The fantail window design is repeated on the doors and on roof peaks. M. Schmitt is in honor of Department 56 photographer, Matthew Schmitt.

'91	'92	'93	'94	'95	'96	'97
$42	42	42	42	55	65	70

DOUBLE BUNGALOW

	ITEM #	INTRO	RETIRED	OSRP	GBTru	↑
	5407-0	1991	1994	$45	**$70**	8%

Particulars: An early two-family home—double entry doors, each side has bow window downstairs, a roof dormer, and own chimney. A brick facade dresses up the clapboard house.

'91	'92	'93	'94	'95	'96	'97
$45	45	45	45	55	65	65

GRANDMA'S COTTAGE

	ITEM #	INTRO	RETIRED	OSRP	GBTru	↑
	5420-8	1992	1996	$42	**$70**	8%

Particulars: A small porch is nestled between two identical house sections. Each section has a hooded double window, flanked by evergreens. Chimneys rise off the main roof. Early release to Gift Creations Concepts (GCC).

'92	'93	'94	'95	'96	'97
$42	45	45	45	45	65

ST. LUKE'S CHURCH

	ITEM #	INTRO	RETIRED	OSRP	GBTru	↑
	5421-6	1992	1994	$45	**$75**	15%

Particulars: Brick church features three square based steeples. The central steeple rises off the nave roof. The side steeples have doors at their base and are at the front corners of church. Trefoil designs on either side are repeated on the center main entry doors. Early release to Gift Creations Concepts (GCC).

'92	'93	'94	'95	'96	'97
$45	45	45	60	70	65

VILLAGE POST OFFICE

ITEM #	INTRO	RETIRED	OSRP	GBTRU	↑
5422-4	1992	1995	$35	**$80**	14%

Particulars: Doric columns support porch to the double entry doors. Building is a two-story brick with a two-story turret rising above the sign. A Greek key incised design separate the stories. Early release to Showcase Dealers.

'92	'93	'94	'95	'96	'97
$35	37.50	37.50	37.50	70	70

AL'S TV SHOP

ITEM #	INTRO	RETIRED	OSRP	GBTRU	NO
5423-2	1992	1995	$40	**$65**	CHANGE

Particulars: TV Shop has antenna on the roof. There are red awnings on the upper windows and a red canopy over the lower display window. The store entry is on the corner of the building.

'92	'93	'94	'95	'96	'97
$40	40	40	40	65	65

GOOD SHEPHERD CHAPEL & CHURCH SCHOOL

ITEM #	INTRO	RETIRED	OSRP	GBTRU	NO
5424-0	1992	1996	$72	**$95**	CHANGE

Particulars: Set of 2. The white chapel with a red roof rises on a stone base and has a steeple at the front entry. The church school has double doors, tall windows, a small bell tower, and a stone chimney on the side. The church side door meets the school side door.

'92	'93	'94	'95	'96	'97
$72	72	72	72	72	95

PRINT SHOP & VILLAGE NEWS

ITEM #	INTRO	RETIRED	OSRP	GBTRU	↑
5425-9	1992	1994	$37.50	**$75**	7%

Particulars: The stone in the front pediment notes a "1893" construction date. A symmetrical building design is emphasized by double chimneys, matching windows and columns. The brick building also houses a Muffin Shop.

'92	'93	'94	'95	'96	'97
$37.50	37.50	37.50	55	60	70

The Original Snow Village®

HARTFORD HOUSE

ITEM #	INTRO	RETIRED	OSRP	GBTRU	NO
5426-7	1992	1995	$55	**$80**	CHANGE

Particulars: Home has a steeply pitched roof with an ornate front covered entry pediment design which is repeated in the steep front gable. Molding surrounds windows and is on the side porch columns.

'92	'93	'94	'95	'96	'97
$55	55	55	55	80	80

VILLAGE VET AND PET SHOP

ITEM #	INTRO	RETIRED	OSRP	GBTRU	↑
5427-5	1992	1995	$32	**$70**	8%

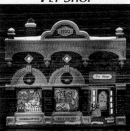

Particulars: Building has arched crescents over picture windows that are screened designs depicting dogs, kittens, fish and birds. An ornamental molding outlines the roof edge. A dog sits on the entry steps to the Vet's Office. In the first shipments hand lettered sign was misspelled "Vetrinary."

'92	'93	'94	'95	'96	'97
$32	32	32	32	65	65

CRAFTSMAN COTTAGE

ITEM #	INTRO	RETIRED	OSRP	GBTRU	NO
5437-2	1992	1995	$55	**$75**	CHANGE

Particulars: A stone based porch extends across the front of the house ending in a stone chimney. Large squared pillars are part of the support for the second story room above the entryway. There's a small dormer by chimney. Part of the American Architecture Series.

'92	'93	'94	'95	'96	'97
$55	55	55	55	75	75

VILLAGE STATION

ITEM #	INTRO	RETIRED	OSRP	GBTRU	↑
5438-0	1992	1997	$65	**$80**	23%

Particulars: A clock tower rises on one side of the two story red brick station. The platform sign behind a stack of luggage announces arrivals and departures. The many windowed waiting room for travelers extends the length of the station.

'92	'93	'94	'95	'96	'97
$65	65	65	65	65	65

AIRPORT

ITEM #	INTRO	RETIRED	OSRP	GBTRU	↑
5439-9	1992	1996	$60	**$85**	13%

Particulars: The airport's semicircular vaulted roof extends the length of the plane hangar with the control tower rising off the central rear of the building. A one-engine prop plane sits in the hangar entrance. There's a fuel tank pump at the corner, plus thermometer, and a crop dusting schedule. The door at the opposite front corner is for passengers and freight business.

'92	'93	'94	'95	'96	'97
$60	60	60	60	60	75

NANTUCKET RENOVATION

ITEM #	INTRO	RETIRED	OSRP	GBTRU	↓
5441-0	1993	1993 ANNUAL	$55	**$70**	7%

Particulars: Available for one year only through retailers who carried Original Snow Village® in 1986, Showcase Dealers and select buying groups. For the original *Nantucket* see 1978, Item #5014-6. Special box and hang tag. Blueprints of the renovation included.

'93	'94	'95	'96	'97
$55	105	70	75	75

MOUNT OLIVET CHURCH

ITEM #	INTRO	RETIRED	OSRP	GBTRU	NO
5442-9	1993	1996	$65	**$80**	CHANGE

Particulars: Handsome brick church with large circular stained glass window above double door entry. Square bell tower with steeple roof. Smaller stained glass window design repeated on side chapel entry.

'93	'94	'95	'96	'97
$65	65	65	65	80

VILLAGE PUBLIC LIBRARY

ITEM #	INTRO	RETIRED	OSRP	GBTRU	↑
5443-7	1993	1997	$55	**$65**	18%

Particulars: Sturdy brick and stone building with four Greek columns supporting the front portico. Entry is from the side steps through the double doors. A brick cupola rises from the center of the roof.

'93	'94	'95	'96	'97
$55	55	55	55	55

WOODBURY HOUSE

Item #	Intro	Retired	OSRP	GBTru	↑
5444-5	1993	1996	$45	**$70**	8%

Particulars: Turned spindle posts support the front porch of this clapboard home. It has a double gable design with the lower gable featuring two story bow windows. A brick chimney extends through the roof.

	'93	'94	'95	'96	'97
	$45	45	45	45	65

HUNTING LODGE

Item #	Intro	Retired	OSRP	GBTru	↑
5445-3	1993	1996	$50	**$140**	75%

Particulars: Lodge is a rustic log structure on a stone foundation with stone fireplace. Antlers decorate the front gable above the porch entry. Wreaths and garland add the final touch.

	'93	'94	'95	'96	'97
	$50	50	50	50	80

DAIRY BARN

Item #	Intro	Retired	OSRP	GBTru	↑
5446-1	1993	1997	$55	**$75**	36%

Particulars: Cow barn with attached silo, tin mansard roof and cow weather vane. Silo holds grain for winter feed. Wind-run ventilator fan keeps hay bales from collecting moisture.

	'93	'94	'95	'96	'97
	$55	55	55	55	55

DINAH'S DRIVE-IN

Item #	Intro	Retired	OSRP	GBTru	↑
5447-0	1993	1996	$45	**$95**	27%

Particulars: A burger in a bun and a bubbly soda top the circular fast food drive-in. As car travel increased, so did a need for informal eating places. A favorite stop for teenagers, children, and parents on a limited budget.

	'93	'94	'95	'96	'97
	$45	45	45	45	75

The Original Snow Village®

SNOWY HILLS HOSPITAL

ITEM #	INTRO	RETIRED	OSRP	GBTRU	↑
5448-8	1993	1996	$48	**$90**	20%

Particulars: A brick hospital with steps leading to double main entry doors. The roof of the Emergency entrance drive-up on the side is topped by a Christmas tree. Wreaths decorate the second story windows.

'93	'94	'95	'96	'97
$48	48	48	48	75

FISHERMAN'S NOOK RESORT

ITEM #	INTRO	RETIRED	OSRP	GBTRU	NO
5460-7	1994	CURRENT	$75	**$75**	CHANGE

Particulars: Building is office for cabin rental, store for bait and gas for boats, plus places for boats to tie up.

'94	'95	'96	'97
$75	75	75	75

FISHERMAN'S NOOK CABINS

ITEM #	INTRO	RETIRED	OSRP	GBTRU	NO
5461-5	1994	CURRENT	$50	**$50**	CHANGE

Particulars: Set of 2 includes *Fisherman's Nook Bass Cabin* and *Fisherman's Nook Trout Cabin*. Sold only as a set. Midyear release.

see below

'94	'95	'96	'97
$50	50	50	50

FISHERMAN'S NOOK BASS CABIN

ITEM #	INTRO	RETIRED	OSRP	GBTRU
5461-5	1994	CURRENT	*	*

Particulars: 1 of a 2-piece set. *Sold only as a set. See FISHERMAN'S NOOK CABINS. Midyear release. Each cabin named for fish–rustic wood cabin with wood pile and fireplace for heat.

FISHERMAN'S NOOK TROUT CABIN

ITEM #	INTRO	RETIRED	OSRP	GBTRU
5461-5	1994	CURRENT	*	*

Particulars: 1 of a 2-piece set. *Sold only as a set. See FISHERMAN'S NOOK CABINS. Midyear release. Each cabin named for fish–rustic wood cabin with wood pile and fireplace for heat.

SNOW VILLAGE® STARTER SET

ITEM #	INTRO	RETIRED	OSRP	GBTRU	↑
5462-3	1994	1996	$49.99	**$75**	7%

Particulars: Set of 6. Featured at Department 56, Inc. National Open Houses hosted by participating Gift Creation Concepts (GCC) retailers the first weekend in November 1994. Set includes *Shady Oak Church* building, *Sunday School Serenade* accessory, three assorted "bottle-brush" sisal trees, and a bag of Real Plastic Snow.

'94	'95	'96	'97
$49.99	50	50	70

WEDDING CHAPEL

ITEM #	INTRO	RETIRED	OSRP	GBTRU	NO
5464-0	1994	CURRENT	$55	**$55**	CHANGE

Particulars: A white clapboard church with a brick tower supporting a wooden steeple. A bell hangs in the tower above the door. The arched windows have green shutters. Attached snow covered tree.

'94	'95	'96	'97
$55	55	55	55

FEDERAL HOUSE

ITEM #	INTRO	RETIRED	OSRP	GBTRU	↑
5465-8	1994	1997	$50	**$70**	40%

Particulars: Stately symmetrical brick structure has a white portico and columns at the front door. Roof dormers and four chimneys complete the mirrored effect. The lower windows are decorated with wreaths. Attached snow covered tree. Part of the American Architecture Series.

'94	'95	'96	'97
$50	50	50	50

The Original Snow Village®

CARMEL COTTAGE

Item #	Intro	Retired	OSRP	GBTru	↑
5466-6	1994	1997	$48	**$65**	35%

Particulars: Cottage with stucco walls, a steep pitched roof, dormer on side and chimney at rear. Stone trims the door, side passage and windows.

'94	'95	'96	'97
$48	48	48	48

SKATE & SKI SHOP

Item #	Intro	Retired	OSRP	GBTru	NO
5467-4	1994	Current	$50	**$50**	CHANGE

Particulars: Chalet style shop has stone chimney and slate roof. Timber trims the windows and base.

'94	'95	'96	'97
$50	50	50	50

GLENHAVEN HOUSE

Item #	Intro	Retired	OSRP	GBTru	↑
5468-2	1994	1997	$45	**$60**	33%

Particulars: 2 ½-story home with bay windows on first floor. Small porch at entrance. House has formal look with an ornate pediment highlighting the attic windows on the front gable. Two trees attached at the right front corner.

'94	'95	'96	'97
$45	45	45	45

COCA–COLA® BRAND BOTTLING PLANT

Item #	Intro	Retired	OSRP	GBTru	↑
5469-0	1994	1997	$65	**$85**	31%

Particulars: Large, red Coca-Cola logo sign set on roof above entry doors. Vending machine sits at back of loading dock, two cases sit at front. Two smoke stacks rise from roof near skylights. Prototypes did not have cases of soda on loading dock.

'94	'95	'96	'97
$65	65	65	65

Marvel's Beauty Salon

Item #	Intro	Retired	OSRP	GBTru	↑
5470-4	1994	1997	$37.50	**$50**	33%

Particulars: Brick first story houses the Beauty Salon where a picture window displays styles. The stucco second story houses a Wig Shop. Named for Marvel Foster who worked for Department 56, Inc.

'94	'95	'96	'97
$37.50	37.50	37.50	37.50

Christmas Cove Lighthouse

Item #	Intro	Retired	OSRP	GBTru	No
5483-6	1995	Current	$60	**$60**	Change

Particulars: Ship beacon atop white block tower. Steps lead to brick home of keeper. Attached trees, Midyear release, 2-light socket cord. Lift-off top allows access to bulb in tower.

'95	'96	'97
$60	60	60

Coca-Cola® Brand Corner Drugstore

Item #	Intro	Retired	OSRP	GBTru	No
5484-4	1995	Current	$55	**$55**	Change

Particulars: Oversize Coke bottle and logo sign is advertisement for soda shop in drugstore. Stone trims the corner shop with bow windows and roof cornices. Midyear release.

'95	'96	'97
$55	55	55

Snow Carnival Ice Palace

Item #	Intro	Retired	OSRP	GBTru	No
54850	1995	Current	$95	**$95**	Change

Particulars: Set of 2. Turrets trim a fantasy frosty ice palace for festival King and Queen. Entry welcome gate with snowy trees leads to the magical creation built of blocks of ice. Northern American and Canadian cities often have Winter Holiday Festivals with grand ice buildings and sculptures.

'95	'96	'97
$95	95	95

PISA PIZZA

ITEM #	INTRO	RETIRED	OSRP	GBTRU	NO
54851	1995	CURRENT	$35	**$35**	CHANGE

Particulars: A replica of the Leaning Tower of Pisa, a landmark building in Italy, is central design on restaurant. Flanking doors and window have striped canopies.

'95	'96	'97
$36	35	35

PEPPERMINT PORCH DAY CARE

ITEM #	INTRO	RETIRED	OSRP	GBTRU	↑
5485-2	1995	1997	$45	**$70**	56%

Particulars: Day care center in white clapboard house. Mint candy theme on pillars and balcony. Boots, teddy bear on porch. Midyear release. Prototype had "Peppermint Place" as the name on the building.

'95	'96	'97
$45	45	45

VILLAGE POLICE STATION

ITEM #	INTRO	RETIRED	OSRP	GBTRU	NO
54853	1995	CURRENT	$48	**$48**	CHANGE

Particulars: The 56th Precinct is housed in a two-story brick building with stone coping capping off the roof edge. Arched windows accent the double entry design. There are awnings on the three upper windows with Department name above. Doughnut shop next door for a quick pick-me-up break.

'95	'96	'97
$48	48	48

HOLLY BROTHERS GARAGE

ITEM #	INTRO	RETIRED	OSRP	GBTRU	NO
54854	1995	CURRENT	$48	**$48**	CHANGE

Particulars: Gas station with two pumps. Coke machine, wall phone, repair stalls, tires, free air, office and rest rooms are housed in a white building. Owner's name above gas pumps.

'95	'96	'97
$48	48	48

RYMAN AUDITORIUM®

ITEM #	INTRO	RETIRED	OSRP	GBTRU	↑
54855	1995	1997	$75	**$90**	20%

Particulars: Nashville's country music auditorium. Featured acts are country western artists.

'95	'96	'97
$75	75	75

DUTCH COLONIAL

ITEM #	INTRO	RETIRED	OSRP	GBTRU	NO
54856	1995	1996	$45	**$70**	CHANGE

Particulars: Second story of colonial home is constructed as part of mansard roof that extends down to first floor level. Shuttered double windows frame front door two steps up from walk. One bedroom accesses an upper balustraded outdoor sitting area. Part of the American Architecture Series.

'95	'96	'97
$45	45	70

BEACON HILL VICTORIAN

ITEM #	INTRO	RETIRED	OSRP	GBTRU	NO
54857	1995	CURRENT	$60	**$60**	CHANGE

Particulars: Covered porch encloses turret structure that rises up entire height of house and features shuttered windows. Brick home with transverse roof has ornate wood molding trim on gables. Snowy fir trees on front corner.

'95	'96	'97
$60	60	60

BOWLING ALLEY

ITEM #	INTRO	RETIRED	OSRP	GBTRU	NO
54858	1995	CURRENT	$42	**$42**	CHANGE

Particulars: Bowling pins and ball atop brick building advertise sports activity within. Pins flank Village Lanes sign above archway of double entry doors. Snowy trees next to entrance.

'95	'96	'97
$42	42	42

Starbucks® Coffee

Item #	Intro	Retired	OSRP	GBTru	NO
54859	1995	Current	$48	**$48**	CHANGE

Particulars: Corner building features many varieties of coffee and baked treats. Stone structure with starred canopies over upper windows and larger awnings atop windows on street level. Store logo displayed on roof pediment.

'95	'96	'97
$48	48	48

Nick's Tree Farm

Item #	Intro	Retired	OSRP	GBTru	NO
54871	1996	Current	$40	**$40**	CHANGE

Particulars: Set of 10. Midyear release. Small wood hut provides office and warming area for Nick on a farm where he or you can select a live or cut tree. Nick pulls a cut tree on a sled.

'96	'97
$40	40

Smokey Mountain Retreat

Item #	Intro	Retired	OSRP	GBTru	NO
54872	1996	Current	$65	**$65**	CHANGE

Particulars: Midyear release. Log structure with two stone fireplaces has exposed log beams, covered entry and porch areas to hold sleds and outdoor gear. This building debuts a smoking chimney feature. A built-in Magic Smoking Element, powered by a separate transformer, heats a supplied nontoxic liquid causing it to smoke. See Trims, #52620 for refill *Village Magic Smoke*.

'96	'97
$65	65

Boulder Springs House

Item #	Intro	Retired	OSRP	GBTru	↑
54873	1996	1997	$60	**$70**	17%

Particulars: Midyear release. Clapboard house with 2 ½ stories has covered entry and front porch. Shutters frame front gable windows, attached tree behind side bow window.

'96	'97
$60	60

Reindeer Bus Depot

Item #	Intro	Retired	OSRP	GBTru	↑
54874	1996	1997	$42	**$60**	43%

Particulars: Depot is two stories with restaurant and waiting room flanking central entry topped by depot name and vertical bus sign. Midyear release.

'96	'97
$42	42

Rockabilly Records

Item #	Intro	Retired	OSRP	GBTru	NO
54880	1996	Current	$45	**$45**	CHANGE

Particulars: Art deco styled Rockabilly recording studio and business office. Roof sign created to look like vinyl record. Jukebox design on front building corners highlight coin operated record players found in soda fountains and entertainment areas. Light brick with barrel roll molding between the first and second floor.

'97
$45

Christmas Lake High School

Item #	Intro	Retired	OSRP	GBTru	NO
54881	1996	Current	$52	**$52**	CHANGE

Particulars: Variegated brick two-story school building has name above double entry doors with dedication date plaque in central roof gable. There are two chimneys where the side wings meet with the central portion of the building. Bell cupola above center gable. Basketball hoop by side entrance.

'97
$52

Birch Run Ski Chalet

Item #	Intro	Retired	OSRP	GBTru	NO
54882	1996	Current	$60	**$60**	CHANGE

Particulars: Peeled rough hewn logs used for ski lodge. Large fieldstone fireplace provides cozy lounge area after all day skiing. Chalet offers rooms, refreshments and even a first aid station for minor mishaps.

'97
$60

The Original Snow Village®

ROSITA'S CANTINA

ITEM #	INTRO	RETIRED	OSRP	GBTRU	NO
54883	1996	CURRENT	$50	$50	CHANGE

Particulars: Mexican restaurant in Southwest design to resemble smooth adobe with tile roof invites diners to taste the spicy food guaranteed to warm from the inside-out. El Loco Bar is tucked in at the side for those who want a beverage and a snack instead of dinner.

'97
$50

SHINGLE VICTORIAN

ITEM #	INTRO	RETIRED	OSRP	GBTRU	NO
54884	1996	CURRENT	$55	$55	CHANGE

Particulars: Bright blue and white 3-story home with wraparound porch. Top story features dormer windows. Formal living room has triple front window and a bow side window. Double entry doors with diamond shaped glass design. Saw-toothed roof ridge plus two chimneys. Part of the American Architecture Series.

'97
$55

THE SECRET GARDEN FLORIST

ITEM #	INTRO	RETIRED	OSRP	GBTRU	NO
54885	1996	CURRENT	$50	$50	CHANGE

Particulars: Canvas awning with silk-screened lettering protects front of shop that features display boxes of flower arrangements and plants. Bridal planning is also available upstairs from the shop.

'97
$50

HARLEY-DAVIDSON® MOTORCYCLE SHOP

ITEM #	INTRO	RETIRED	OSRP	GBTRU	NO
54886	1996	CURRENT	$65	$65	CHANGE

Particulars: Showroom and maintenance shop devoted to 'Hog' devotees. Cycle display on front entry reinforced canopy. Soda can and bottle ice chest and gas pump allow cyclist and cycle to fill-er-up. Repair area with roll up garage door and large disposal drums.

'97
$65

BACHMAN'S® FLOWER SHOP

ITEM #	INTRO	RETIRED	OSRP	GBTRU	↑
8802	1997	1997 ANNUAL	$50	$75	50%

Particulars: Personalized for Bachman's Village Gathering with a purple canvas awning with silk screened lettering. Company logo and year of establishment on front of shop. Display boxes with flower arrangements and plants. Bridal planning is also available upstairs.

'97
$50

RONALD MCDONALD HOUSE® (THE HOUSE THAT ♥ BUILT™)

ITEM #	INTRO	RETIRED	OSRP	GBTRU
8960	1997	SPECIAL	*	$465

Particulars: Two-story home with heart-trimmed tree and picket fence decorated with holly. These homes-away-from-home were created for the care and well-being of families of children undergoing treatment at nearby hospitals for very serious illnesses. This was a very limited piece available only to 1997 Homes For The Holidays participants. *The piece was not for retail sale. They were raffled at the Homes For The Holiday Event, with proceeds going to the Ronald McDonald Houses.

'97
$NE

MAINSTREET GIFT SHOP

ITEM #	INTRO	RETIRED	OSRP	GBTRU	↑
54887	1997	1997 ANNUAL	$50	$90	80%

Particulars: An actual Original Snow Village® house display is used as a focal point in the acrylic front window of the shop. Only available to Gift Creation Concepts (GCC) dealers to celebrate the 20th Anniversary of GCC. Two medallions came with the piece allowing display of the GCC Dealer logo or it could be personalized with the store name. A special GCC decal bottomstamp was added to the usual Department 56, Inc. embossed stamp.

'97
$50

THE ORIGINAL SNOW VILLAGE® START A TRADITION SET

ITEM #	INTRO	RETIRED	OSRP	GBTRU	NO
54902	1997	CURRENT	$75*	$100	CHANGE

Particulars: Set of 8. Two lighted buildings. *Kringles Toy Shop* has a revolving front door and acrylic windows. A jack-in-the-box decorates the front facade above the entry doors. A *Hot Chocolate Stand* is in the shape of a mug. Accessories include *Saturday Morning Downtown* where a little girl sips a mug of chocolate while a boy pulls a sled of presents and 2 trimmed trees in drum bases. A *Bag of Snow* and a *Cobblestone Road* complete the set which was first available at the Homes For The Holidays Event held 11/1/97 through 11/9/97. * Reduced to $75 during Event.

'97
$100

Old Chelsea Mansion

Item #	Intro	Retired	OSRP	GBTru	NO
54903	1997	Current	$85	**$85**	CHANGE

Particulars: Represents the New York home of Clement Clarke Moore the author of *A Visit From St. Nicholas.* Commemorates the 175th Anniversary of the poem. A 32-page hardcover, illustrated, full color book is included. The history of Moore, his home and the poem make this collector's book a Village "first." The brick three-story house has steps at the front entry and a door flanked by columns. Classical proportions produce a stately house.

'97
$85

New Hope Church

Item #	Intro	Retired	OSRP	GBTru	NO
54904	1997	Current	$60	**$60**	CHANGE

Particulars: Brick church with turret-like tower features acrylic stained glass windows. Community Bingo enthusiasts attend and enjoy an evening out in the company of friends.

'97
$60

Christmas Barn Dance

Item #	Intro	Retired	OSRP	GBTru
54910	1997	Current	$65	**$65**

Particulars: Red barn with double silo and mansard roof is site of holiday dance. Doors open to decorated area. Features many complex attachments, including metal ladder, lightning posts, weathervane, hanging lantern and pigeons.

Italianate Villa

Item #	Intro	Retired	OSRP	GBTru
54911	1997	Current	$55	**$55**

Particulars: American Architecture Series. Double entry door design is base for turret that rises up through roof in center of front facade. Windows feature molding and pediments. Ornate coping design highlights roof. Hanging porch swing. Sisal trees and metal lightning rod.

FARM HOUSE

ITEM #	INTRO	RETIRED	OSRP	GBTRU
54912	1997	CURRENT	$50	**$50**

Particulars: Porch protects front entry of 1 ½ story brick home. Roof line accented by two gables over shuttered windows. Large bay window on first floor with special glass wax stencils. Attached tree.

HERSHEY'S™ CHOCOLATE SHOP

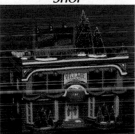

ITEM #	INTRO	RETIRED	OSRP	GBTRU
54913	1997	CURRENT	$55	**$55**

Particulars: Chocolate kisses decorate front store windows while lighted billboard on roof advertises candy bars. Red canopy over entry doors to sweet shop.

McDONALD'S®

ITEM #	INTRO	RETIRED	OSRP	GBTRU
54914	1997	CURRENT	$65	**$65**

Particulars: Golden Arches fast food restaurant circa the 1950s where burgers, fries and shakes are tops on the menu. Illuminated arches. Acrylic windows. Children sitting on bench are first time figurines have been used as an attachment.

GRACIE'S DRY GOODS & GENERAL STORE

ITEM #	INTRO	RETIRED	OSRP	GBTRU
54915	1997	CURRENT	$70	**$70**

Particulars: Set of 2. Columns flank front door and display windows. Upper story created as a flat wall to feature store name sign. Forerunner of supermarket and department store, this store had something for everyone. Separate gas pump allowed for a quick refill.

ROLLERAMA ROLLER RINK

ITEM #	INTRO	RETIRED	OSRP	GBTRU
54916	1997	CURRENT	$56	**$56**

Particulars: Oval 50's design skating rink is housed in building with domed roof similar to Quonset hut design. Boy and girl shadow design art work by front entry. Lights around marquis, acrylic signs and rooftop skylight illuminate.

LINDEN HILLS COUNTRY CLUB

ITEM #	INTRO	RETIRED	OSRP	GBTRU
54917	1997	CURRENT	$60	**$60**

Particulars: Set of 2. Brick and stone building with 2 ¹/₂-story gable over front entry doors houses restaurant and recreation facilities for member families. Pro Golf Shop on the side. Metal lanterns that light from within. Linden Hills is an area near downtown Minneapolis, close to Lake Harriet.

THE BRANDON BUNGALOW

ITEM #	INTRO	RETIRED	OSRP	GBTRU
54918	1997	CURRENT	$55	**$55**

Particulars: Stone and clapboard home. Stone fireplace chimney rises through roof. Family car sits in open garage. Evergreen shrubs set off front porch and railings. Named for a small resort town in Northern Minnesota.

BACHMAN'S® GREENHOUSE

ITEM #	INTRO	RETIRED	OSRP	GBTRU
2203	1998	1998 ANNUAL	$60	**$60**

Particulars: Exclusive created for the Bachman's Village Gathering. Companion piece to 1997 exclusive *Bachman's® Flower Shop*. "The design was inspired by a small greenhouse that once stood adjacent to Bachman's flagship store, and it is lit like no other piece. The unusual interior lights hang over the plant tables and they actually work. The piece also has see-through panes that duplicate the curved glass of the original greenhouse."- from *The Bachman's Village News*

RONALD McDONALD HOUSE® (THE HOUSE THAT ♥ BUILT™)

Item #	Intro	Retired	OSRP	GBTru
2210	1998	Ltd Ed 5,600	*	NE

Particulars: This is a very limited piece available to 1998 Homes For The Holidays participants. Two story bright and cheery yellow house carries out the heart motif. *The piece is not for retail sale. It will be raffled at the Event with proceeds going to the Ronald McDonald Houses. These homes-away-from-home were created for the care and well-being of families of children undergoing treatment at nearby hospitals for very serious illnesses.

ROCK CREEK MILL HOUSE

Item #	Intro	Retired	OSRP	GBTru
54932	1998	Current	$64	$64

Particulars: Midyear release. Large water wheel is two stories tall and actually turns to generate power to have a functioning mill. Stone foundation and chimney. Several attached trees.

CARNIVAL CAROUSEL

Item #	Intro	Retired	OSRP	GBTru
54933	1998	Current	$150	$150

Particulars: Midyear release. Colorfully painted and decorated building houses ornately carved carousel to delight children of all ages. Musical lighted piece plays 30 songs, has off/on switch and volume control. Motorized screen casts shadows. Has own adapter.

SNOWY PINES INN EXCLUSIVE GIFT SET

Item #	Intro	Retired	OSRP	GBTru
54934	1998	1998 Annual	$65	$65

Particulars: Set of 9. Gift Set is midyear release featured at Department 56, Inc. National Homes For The Holidays Open House Event 11/5/98 - 11/9/98. One lighted building–resort inn with facilities to rent rooms, dine, and enjoy winter recreation in the area. Accessory set of 2, entitled *Decorate the Tree,* has children trimming tree. 4 sisal trees, Brick Road, 1.5 oz. Bag Of Fresh Fallen Snow. Tinsel garland adds sparkle.

HAUNTED MANSION	ITEM #	INTRO	RETIRED	OSRP	GBTRU
	54935	1998	CURRENT	$110	**$110**

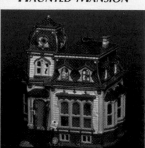

Particulars: Midyear release. Gothic looking house has front entry doors that hang open adding to haunted look. Building has no snow trim. Motorized screen projects ghosts, bats and witches on the windows. Comes with its own adapter.

NOTES: _____

_____

_____

_____

_____

_____

_____

_____

_____

_____

_____

_____

_____

_____

_____

_____

_____

_____

_____

_____

_____

_____

_____

5018-0	1990	Snowman With Broom
5038-5	1985	Scottie With Tree
5040-7	1988	Monks-A-Caroling
5053-9	1987	Singing Nuns
5056-3	1987	Snow Kids Sled, Skis
5057-1	1988	Family Mom/Kids, Goose/Girl
5059-8	1988	Santa/Mailbox
5064-1	1986	Carolers
5069-0	1986	Ceramic Car
5079-2	1986	Ceramic Sleigh
5094-6	1990	Kids Around The Tree
5095-4	1987	Girl/Snowman, Boy
5096-2	1988	Shopping Girls With Packages
5102-0	1988	3 Nuns With Songbooks
5103-9	1988	Praying Monks
5104-7	1989	Children In Band
5105-5	1990	Caroling Family
5107-1	1990	Christmas Children
5108-0	1989	For Sale Sign
5113-6	1990	Snow Kids
5116-0	1992	Man On Ladder Hanging Garland
5117-9	1990	Hayride
5118-7	1990	School Children
5129-2	1990	Apple Girl/ Newspaper Boy
5130-6	1991	Woodsman And Boy
5131-4	1992	Doghouse/Cat In Garbage Can
5133-0	1991	Water Tower
5134-9	1993	Kids Decorating The Village Sign
5136-5	1990	Woody Station Wagon
5137-3	1991	School Bus, Snow Plow
5146-2	1995	Village Gazebo
5147-0	1992	Choir Kids
5148-9	1990	Special Delivery
5158-6	1993	Down The Chimney He Goes
5159-4	1993	Sno-Jet Snowmobile
5160-8	1992	Sleighride
5161-6	1992	Here We Come A Caroling
5162-4	1992	Home Delivery
5163-2	1993	Fresh Frozen Fish
5164-0	1995	A Tree For Me
5165-9	1996	A Home For The Holidays
5168-3	1991	Kids Tree House
5169-1	1992	Bringing Home The Tree
5170-5	1991	Skate Faster Mom
5171-3	1996	Crack The Whip
5172-1	1991	Through The Woods
5173-0	1991	Statue Of Mark Twain
5174-8	1991	Calling All Cars
5179-9	1990	Mailbox
5180-2	1994	Village Birds
5197-7	1992	Special Delivery
5408-9	1994	Wreaths For Sale
5409-7	1993	Winter Fountain
5410-0	1994	Cold Weather Sports
5411-9	1992	Come Join The Parade
5412-7	1992	Village Marching Band
5413-5	1994	Christmas Cadillac
5414-3	1993	Snowball Fort
5415-1	1993	Country Harvest
5418-6	1994	Village Greetings
5428-3	1997	Village Used Car Lot
5430-5	1994	Nanny And The Preschoolers
5431-3	1995	Early Morning Delivery
5432-1	1996	Christmas Puppies
5433-0	1995	Round & Round We Go!
5435-6	1994	We're Going To A Christmas Pageant
5436-4	1995	Winter Playground
5440-2	1996	Spirit Of Snow Village Airplane
5449-6	1997	Safety Patrol
5450-0	1996	Christmas At The Farm
5451-8	1995	Check It Out Bookmobile
5452-6	1997	Tour The Village
5453-4	1996	Pint-Size Pony Rides
5455-0	1997	A Herd Of Holiday Heifers
5458-5	1996	Spirit Of Snow Village Airplane
5459-3	1996	Village News Delivery
5462-3	1996	Sunday School Seranade
5473-9	1997	Feeding The Birds
5474-7	1997	Mush!
5481-0	1997	Coca-Cola® brand Billboard
54860	1997	Frosty Playtime
54867	1997	Grand Ole Opry Carolers
54875	1997	A Ride On The Reindeer Lines
6459-9	1984	Monks-A-Caroling
8183-3	1991	Sisal Tree Lot

The Original Snow Village® Accessories—Retired

CAROLERS

ITEM #	INTRO	RETIRED	OSRP	GBT_{RU}	NO
5064-1	1979	1986	$12	**$125**	CHANGE

Particulars: Set of 4. Couple, girl, garlanded lamppost, snowman. First people in the Village and first non-lit accessory.

'91	'92	'93	'94	'95	'96	'97
$95	105	110	125	125	125	125

CERAMIC CAR

ITEM #	INTRO	RETIRED	OSRP	GBT_{RU}	NO
5069-0	1980	1986	$5	**$60**	CHANGE

Particulars: First vehicle, no other cars were available until 1985. Did not come in a box. Open roadster holds lap rugs, Christmas tree and wrapped presents.

'91	'92	'93	'94	'95	'96	'97
$20	42	48	52	50	55	60

CERAMIC SLEIGH

ITEM #	INTRO	RETIRED	OSRP	GBT_{RU}	↓
5079-2	1981	1986	$5	**$60**	8%

Particulars: Patterned after old-fashioned wood sleigh, holds Christmas tree and wrapped presents. Did not come in a box.

'91	'92	'93	'94	'95	'96	'97
$20	52	55	55	55	55	65

SNOWMAN WITH BROOM

ITEM #	INTRO	RETIRED	OSRP	GBT_{RU}	↑
5018-0	1982	1990	$3	**$15**	25%

Particulars: Snowman with top hat and red nose holds straw broom.

'91	'92	'93	'94	'95	'96	'97
$10	15	15	15	10	12	12

MONKS-A-CAROLING

ITEM #	INTRO	RETIRED	OSRP	GBTRU	↑
6460-2	1982	N/A	$6	**$205**	3%

Particulars: These original four friars singing carols were giftware adopted as a Original Snow Village® piece by collectors. The piece is unglazed, the Monks carry paper song books and have real cord for sashes.

'97
$200

MUNKS-A-CAROLING

ITEM #	INTRO	RETIRED	OSRP	GBTRU	NO
6459-9	1983	1984	$6	**$65**	CHANGE

Particulars: This is the 2nd *Monks-A-Caroling*. It was retired after one year due to the maker's inability to supply. This version is slightly smaller than the giftware piece, glazed, and the Monks carry ceramic songbooks and have painted-on ropes. The diffused rosy blush in the Monks' cheeks differentiate this piece from the 3rd version Monks (1984, Item #5040-7, from another supplier).

'91	'92	'93	'94	'95	'96	'97
$70	70	75	75	70	65	65

SCOTTIE WITH TREE

ITEM #	INTRO	RETIRED	OSRP	GBTRU	↑
5038-5	1984	1985	$3	**$175**	6%

Particulars: A black dog waits by a snow covered tree. Some pieces have a white star on top of the tree.

'91	'92	'93	'94	'95	'96	'97
$95	115	132	140	150	165	165

MONKS-A-CAROLING

ITEM #	INTRO	RETIRED	OSRP	GBTRU	↑
5040-7	1984	1988	$6	**$65**	30%

Particulars: Replaced the 1983 *Monks-A-Caroling*, Item #6459-9. On this piece the Monks have a distinct pink circle to give the cheeks blush.

'91	'92	'93	'94	'95	'96	'97
$25	25	30	38	40	38	50

The Original Snow Village® Accessories

SINGING NUNS

ITEM #	INTRO	RETIRED	OSRP	GBTRU	↓
5053-9	1985	1987	$6	**$130**	4%

Particulars: Four nuns in habits, sing carols.

'91	'92	'93	'94	'95	'96	'97
$65	75	85	105	125	130	135

AUTO WITH TREE— "SQUASHED"

ITEM #	INTRO	RETIRED	OSRP	GBTRU	↑
5055-5	1985	VARIATION	$5	**$90**	20%

Particulars: First version of red VW Beetle with sisal tree strapped to roof looks as if the tree's weight crushed the car. Approximately 3 3/8" long. Did not come in a box.

'97
$75

AUTO WITH TREE

ITEM #	INTRO	RETIRED	OSRP	GBTRU	NO
5055-5	1985	CURRENT	$5	**$6.50**	CHANGE

Particulars: Second version of red VW Beetle with sisal tree strapped to roof. Approximately 3" long. Did not come in a box.

'91	'92	'93	'94	'95	'96	'97
$6.50	6.50	6.50	6.50	6.50	6.50	6.50

SNOW KIDS SLED, SKIS

ITEM #	INTRO	RETIRED	OSRP	GBTRU	↓
5056-3	1985	1987	$11	**$50**	9%

Particulars: Set of 2. Three children on a toboggan and one child on skis. See *Snow Kids,* 1987, #5113-6, for these kids as part of a set of 4 in a scaled down size.

'91	'92	'93	'94	'95	'96	'97
$20	48	48	50	50	50	55

FAMILY MOM/KIDS, GOOSE/GIRL–"LARGE"

ITEM #	INTRO	RETIRED	OSRP	GBTRU	↑
5057-1	1985	1988	$11	**$50**	19%

Particulars: Set of 2. Mother holds hands of two children, one girl feeds corn to geese. First version. This is the original larger size. By 1987 the piece was downscaled.

'91	'92	'93	'94	'95	'96	'97
$30	35	35	45	45	48	42

FAMILY MOM/KIDS, GOOSE/GIRL–"SMALL"

ITEM #	INTRO	RETIRED	OSRP	GBTRU	↑
5057-1	1985	1988	$11	**$45**	7%

Particulars: Set of 2. Second version. This is the downscaled version. In addition to being smaller, there is more detail in the pieces.

'91	'92	'93	'94	'95	'96	'97
$30	35	35	45	45	48	42

SANTA/MAILBOX–"LARGE"

ITEM #	INTRO	RETIRED	OSRP	GBTRU	↓
5059-8	1985	1988	$11	**$55**	8%

Particulars: Set of 2. Santa with toy bag and girl mails letter to Santa as dog watches. First version. This is the original larger size. Girl has brown hair. By 1987 the piece was downscaled. 1997 was the first year we tracked secondary market performance separately.

'91	'92	'93	'94	'95	'96	'97
$25	40	46	48	50	53	60

SANTA/MAILBOX–"SMALL"

ITEM #	INTRO	RETIRED	OSRP	GBTRU	↓
5059-8	1985	1988	$11	**$50**	12%

Particulars: Set of 2. Second version. This is the downscaled version. In addition to being shorter, Santa and the girl are also trimmer. In this version the girl has blonde hair. 1997 was the first year we tracked secondary market performance separately.

'91	'92	'93	'94	'95	'96	'97
$25	40	46	48	50	53	57

The Original Snow Village® Accessories

KIDS AROUND THE TREE– "LARGE"

ITEM #	INTRO	RETIRED	OSRP	GBTRU	↑
5094-6	1986	1990	$15	**$60**	9%

Particulars: First version of *Kids Around The Tree*. This is the original larger size, 5 ³/₄" in height. By 1987 the piece was dramatically downscaled. Children join hands to make a ring around the snow covered tree with a gold star.

'91	'92	'93	'94	'95	'96	'97
$60	60	60	70	60	60	55

KIDS AROUND THE TREE– "SMALL"

ITEM #	INTRO	RETIRED	OSRP	GBTRU	↑
5094-6	1986	1990	$15	**$46**	15%

Particulars: Second version of *Kids Around The Tree*. This is the downscaled version, 4 ¹/₂" in height.

'91	'92	'93	'94	'95	'96	'97
$30	32	32	40	35	38	40

GIRL/SNOWMAN, BOY

ITEM #	INTRO	RETIRED	OSRP	GBTRU	↑
5095-4	1986	1987	$11	**$72**	11%

Particulars: Set of 2. Girl puts finishing touches on snowman as boy reaches to place decorated hat atop head. See *Snow Kids*, 1987, #5113-6, for these kids as part of a set of 4 in a scaled down size.

'91	'92	'93	'94	'95	'96	'97
$35	50	55	70	70	62	65

SHOPPING GIRLS WITH PACKAGES–"LARGE"

ITEM #	INTRO	RETIRED	OSRP	GBTRU	NO
5096-2	1986	1988	$11	**$50**	CHANGE

Particulars: Set of 2. Girls dressed toasty for shopping with hats, mittens, coats, boots, stand by some of their wrapped packages. First version. This is the original larger size–3" in height. By 1987 the piece was downscaled. 1997 was the first year we tracked secondary market performance separately.

'91	'92	'93	'94	'95	'96	'97
$25	35	38	44	45	48	50

SHOPPING GIRLS WITH PACKAGES—"SMALL"

ITEM #	INTRO	RETIRED	OSRP	GBT<small>RU</small>	↓
5096-2	1986	1988	$11	**$45**	4%

Particulars: Set of 2. Second version. This is the downscaled version—2 ³/₄" in height. 1997 was the first year we tracked secondary market performance separately.

'91	'92	'93	'94	'95	'96	'97
$25	35	38	44	45	40	47

SNOW VILLAGE HOUSE FOR SALE SIGN

ITEM #	INTRO	RETIRED	OSRP	GBT<small>RU</small>
NONE	1987	N/A	GIFT	NE

Particulars: This sign was given to dealers who attended trade shows and showrooms around the country. It was never intended for resale and is one of the rarest Original Snow Village® accessories. It came packed in a blister pack.

3 NUNS WITH SONGBOOKS

ITEM #	INTRO	RETIRED	OSRP	GBT<small>RU</small>	↑
5102-0	1987	1988	$6	**$140**	4%

Particulars: Three nuns in habits standing side-by-side carry songbooks to sing carols. Available for only one year.

'91	'92	'93	'94	'95	'96	'97
$50	75	95	115	125	128	135

PRAYING MONKS

ITEM #	INTRO	RETIRED	OSRP	GBT<small>RU</small>	↓
5103-9	1987	1988	$6	**$48**	4%

Particulars: Three monks, standing side-by-side, praying. Available for only one year.

'91	'92	'93	'94	'95	'96	'97
$30	32	42	42	40	44	50

The Original Snow Village® Accessories

CHILDREN IN BAND

ITEM #	INTRO	RETIRED	OSRP	GBTRU	↑
5104-7	1987	1989	$15	**$35**	17%

Particulars: One child conducts three band players: horn, drum and tuba.

'91	'92	'93	'94	'95	'96	'97
$25	35	28	24	25	32	30

CAROLING FAMILY

ITEM #	INTRO	RETIRED	OSRP	GBTRU	NO
5105-5	1987	1990	$20	**$35**	CHANGE

Particulars: Set of 3. Father holds baby, mother and son, and girl with pup.

'91	'92	'93	'94	'95	'96	'97
$25	35	30	32	30	28	35

TAXI CAB

ITEM #	INTRO	RETIRED	OSRP	GBTRU	NO
5106-3	1987	CURRENT	$6	**$6.50**	CHANGE

Particulars: Yellow Checker cab. Size is 3 ½" x 2".

'91	'92	'93	'94	'95	'96	'97
$6.50	6.50	6.50	6.50	6.50	6.50	6.50

CHRISTMAS CHILDREN

ITEM #	INTRO	RETIRED	OSRP	GBTRU	NO
5107-1	1987	1990	$20	**$35**	CHANGE

Particulars: Set of 4. Children at outdoor activities: girl and pup on sled, boy, girl holding wreath and girl feeding carrot to bunny.

'91	'92	'93	'94	'95	'96	'97
$25	35	35	30	30	35	35

FOR SALE SIGN

ITEM #	INTRO	RETIRED	OSRP	GBTRU	NO
5108-0	1987	1989	$3.50	**$10**	CHANGE

Particulars: First "For Sale Sign." This ceramic sign is trimmed with holly. See also *For Sale Sign,* 1989, #5166-7.

'91	'92	'93	'94	'95	'96	'97
$8	12	12	10	10	10	10

FOR SALE SIGN— "GCC BLANK"

ITEM #	INTRO	RETIRED	OSRP	GBTRU	↓
581-9	1987	PROMO	*	**$22**	12%

Particulars: Gift Creations Concepts (GCC) 1989 Christmas Catalog Exclusive, *free with any $100 Department 56 purchase. Holly trims blank sign for personalization.

'97
$25

SNOW KIDS

ITEM #	INTRO	RETIRED	OSRP	GBTRU	↑
5113-6	1987	1990	$20	**$56**	2%

Particulars: Set of 4 incorporates *Snow Kids Sled, Skis,* 1985, Item #5056-3, and *Girl/Snowman, Boy,* 1986, Item #5095 4, re-scaled to the smaller size. Three kids on toboggan, child on skis, boy and girl putting finishing touches on snowman.

'91	'92	'93	'94	'95	'96	'97
$30	52	52	48	45	50	55

MAN ON LADDER HANGING GARLAND

ITEM #	INTRO	RETIRED	OSRP	GBTRU	↑
5116-0	1988	1992	$7.50	**$19**	19%

Particulars: Man carries garland up ladder to decorate eaves of house. Man is ceramic, ladder is wooden, garland is sisal.

'91	'92	'93	'94	'95	'96	'97
$8	8	18	16	18	16	16

HAYRIDE

ITEM #	INTRO	RETIRED	OSRP	GBTRU	↑
5117-9	1988	1990	$30	**$68**	13%

Particulars: Farmer guides horse-drawn hay-filled sleigh with children as riders.

'91	'92	'93	'94	'95	'96	'97
$45	65	70	65	60	60	60

SCHOOL CHILDREN

ITEM #	INTRO	RETIRED	OSRP	GBTRU	↑
5118-7	1988	1990	$15	**$32**	7%

Particulars: Set of 3. Three children carrying school books.

'91	'92	'93	'94	'95	'96	'97
$20	30	25	28	25	25	30

APPLE GIRL/ NEWSPAPER BOY

ITEM #	INTRO	RETIRED	OSRP	GBTRU	↑
5129-2	1988	1990	$11	**$25**	14%

Particulars: Set of 2. Girl holds wood tray carrier selling apples for 5¢, newsboy sells the Village News.

'91	'92	'93	'94	'95	'96	'97
$20	25	20	22	20	22	22

WOODSMAN AND BOY

ITEM #	INTRO	RETIRED	OSRP	GBTRU	↑
5130-6	1988	1991	$13	**$36**	20%

Particulars: Set of 2. Man chops and splits logs and boy prepares to carry supply to fireplace.

'91	'92	'93	'94	'95	'96	'97
$13	26	22	25	30	30	30

DOGHOUSE/CAT IN GARBAGE CAN

Item #	Intro	Retired	OSRP	GBTRU	↑
5131-4	1988	1992	$15	**$30**	11%

Particulars: Set of 2. Dog sits outside doghouse decorated with wreath; cat looks at empty boxes and wrappings in garbage can.

'91	'92	'93	'94	'95	'96	'97
$15	15	30	30	25	27	27

FIRE HYDRANT & MAILBOX

Item #	Intro	Retired	OSRP	GBTRU	NO
5132-2	1988	Current	$6	**$6**	CHANGE

Particulars: Set of 2. Red fire hydrant and rural curbside mailbox on post. Sizes are 1 1/2" & 2 3/4", respectively.

'91	'92	'93	'94	'95	'96	'97
$6	6	6	6	6	6	6

WATER TOWER

Item #	Intro	Retired	OSRP	GBTRU	↑
5133-0	1988	1991	$20	**$90**	20%

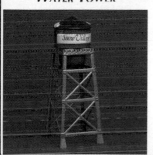

Particulars: 2 pieces. Metal scaffold base holds red ceramic Original Snow Village® water container with green top, ladder leads to top.

'91	'92	'93	'94	'95	'96	'97
$22	48	48	52	65	70	75

WATER TOWER— "JOHN DEERE"

Item #	Intro	Retired	OSRP	GBTRU	↓
2510-4	1988	Promo	$24	**$625**	10%

Particulars: Special piece, *John Deere Water Tower* is exactly the same as the *Original Snow Village® Water Tower* with the exception of it reads, "Moline Home of John Deere." It was offered for sale through the John Deere catalog.

'91	'92	'93	'94	'95	'96	'97
$125	125	150	395	650	675	695

The Original Snow Village® Accessories

NATIVITY

ITEM #	INTRO	RETIRED	OSRP	GBTRU	NO
5135-7	1988	CURRENT	$7.50	**$7.50**	CHANGE

Particulars: Holy Family, lamb, in crèche scene. Size is 2 ¼".

'91	'92	'93	'94	'95	'96	'97
$7.50	7.50	7.50	7.50	7.50	7.50	7.50

WOODY STATION WAGON

ITEM #	INTRO	RETIRED	OSRP	GBTRU	↑
5136-5	1988	1990	$6.50	**$35**	17%

Particulars: "Wood" paneled sides on station wagon.

'91	'92	'93	'94	'95	'96	'97
$12	20	22	30	25	25	30

SCHOOL BUS, SNOW PLOW

ITEM #	INTRO	RETIRED	OSRP	GBTRU	↑
5137-3	1988	1991	$16	**$67**	22%

Particulars: Set of 2. Yellow school bus and red sand gravel truck with snow plow.

'91	'92	'93	'94	'95	'96	'97
$16	25	25	55	50	57	55

TREE LOT

ITEM #	INTRO	RETIRED	OSRP	GBTRU	NO
5138-1	1988	CURRENT	$33.50	**$37.50**	CHANGE

Particulars: Christmas lights on tree lot's fence plus decorated shack and trees for sale. The shack is ceramic, the fence is wood and the trees are sisal. Size is 9 ½" x 5" x 4 ½".

'91	'92	'93	'94	'95	'96	'97
$37.50	37.50	37.50	37.50	37.50	37.50	37.50

SISAL TREE LOT

ITEM #	INTRO	RETIRED	OSRP	GBTRU	↓
8183-3	1988	1991	$45	**$90**	5%

Particulars: A variety of cut trees for sale at a street lot. Signs identify the trees in each row.

'91	'92	'93	'94	'95	'96	'97
$45	80	85	85	75	85	95

VILLAGE GAZEBO

ITEM #	INTRO	RETIRED	OSRP	GBTRU	↑
5146-2	1989	1995	$27	**$42**	5%

Particulars: Small, open, red roofed garden structure that will protect folks from rain and snow, or be a private place to sit.

'91	'92	'93	'94	'95	'96	'97
$27.50	28	30	30	30	42	40

CHOIR KIDS

ITEM #	INTRO	RETIRED	OSRP	GBTRU	↑
5147-0	1989	1992	$15	**$30**	7%

Particulars: Four kids in white and red robes with green songbooks caroling.

'91	'92	'93	'94	'95	'96	'97
$15	15	20	28	25	25	28

SPECIAL DELIVERY

ITEM #	INTRO	RETIRED	OSRP	GBTRU	↑
5148-9	1989	1990	$16	**$57**	14%

Particulars: Set of 2. Mailman and mailbag with his mail truck in USPO colors of red, white and blue with the eagle logo. Discontinued due to licensing problems with the U.S. Postal Service. Replaced with 1990, *Special Delivery*, Item #5197-7.

'91	'92	'93	'94	'95	'96	'97
$45	42	42	42	45	40	50

The Original Snow Village® Accessories

FOR SALE SIGN

ITEM #	INTRO	RETIRED	OSRP	GBTRU	NO
5166-7	1989	CURRENT	$4.50	**$4.50**	CHANGE

Particulars: Enameled metal sign can advertise "For Sale" or "SOLD" depending which side is displayed. Birds decorate and add color. Size is 3".

'91	'92	'93	'94	'95	'96	'97
$4.50	4.50	4.50	4.50	4.50	4.50	4.50

FOR SALE SIGN– "BACHMAN'S®"

ITEM #	INTRO	RETIRED	OSRP	GBTRU	NO
539-8	1989	PROMO	$4.50	**$25**	CHANGE

Particulars: Bachman's Exclusive for their Village Gathering in 1990. Enameled metal sign reads "Bachman's Village Gathering 1990". Birds decorate and add color. Size is 3".

'96	'97
$25	25

STREET SIGN

ITEM #	INTRO	RETIRED	OSRP	GBTRU	↑
5167-5	1989	1992	$7.50	**$12**	20%

Particulars: 6 pieces per package. Green metal street signs. Use the street names provided (Lake St., Maple Dr., Park Ave., River Rd., Elm St., Ivy Lane ...) or personalize to give each village street a unique name. Size: 4 1/4" tall.

'91	'92	'93	'94	'95	'96	'97
$7.50	7.50	NE	8	8	12	10

KIDS TREE HOUSE

ITEM #	INTRO	RETIRED	OSRP	GBTRU	↑
5168-3	1989	1991	$25	**$65**	8%

Particulars: Decorated club house built on an old dead tree. Steps lead up to the hideaway. Material is resin.

'91	'92	'93	'94	'95	'96	'97
$25	48	45	45	50	55	60

The Original Snow Village® Accessories

BRINGING HOME THE TREE

ITEM #	INTRO	RETIRED	OSRP	GBTRU	↑
5169-1	1989	1992	$15	**$28**	12%

Particulars: A man pulls a sled holding the tree as the girl watches to make sure it doesn't fall off. Tree is sisal.

'91	'92	'93	'94	'95	'96	'97
$15	15	20	22	25	27	25

SKATE FASTER MOM

ITEM #	INTRO	RETIRED	OSRP	GBTRU	↓
5170-5	1989	1991	$13	**$28**	7%

Particulars: Two children sit in the sleigh as their skating Mom pushes them across the ice.

'91	'92	'93	'94	'95	'96	'97
$13	30	28	24	20	28	30

CRACK THE WHIP

ITEM #	INTRO	RETIRED	OSRP	GBTRU	↓
5171-3	1989	1996	$25	**$30**	6%

Particulars: Set of 3. A fast moving line of skaters hold tightly to the person in front of them. The first person does slow patterns but as the line snakes out, the last people are racing to keep up and they whip out.

'91	'92	'93	'94	'95	'96	'97
$25	25	25	25	25	25	32

THROUGH THE WOODS

ITEM #	INTRO	RETIRED	OSRP	GBTRU	↑
5172-1	1989	1991	$18	**$30**	7%

Particulars: Set of 2. Children bring a tree and a basket of goodies to Grandma.

'91	'92	'93	'94	'95	'96	'97
$18	30	30	22	25	23	28

STATUE OF MARK TWAIN

ITEM #	INTRO	RETIRED	OSRP	GBTRU	↑
5173-0	1989	1991	$15	**$45**	13%

Particulars: A tribute to the author who wrote about lives of American folk.

'91	'92	'93	'94	'95	'96	'97
$15	28	28	30	30	35	40

CALLING ALL CARS

ITEM #	INTRO	RETIRED	OSRP	GBTRU	↑
5174-8	1989	1991	$15	**$70**	8%

Particulars: Set of 2. Police car and patrolman directing traffic.

'91	'92	'93	'94	'95	'96	'97
$15	32	30	30	35	35	65

MAILBOX

ITEM #	INTRO	RETIRED	OSRP	GBTRU	NO
5179-9	1989	1990	$3.50	**$20**	CHANGE

Particulars: Freestanding public mailbox in U.S.P.O. colors red, white and blue with logo. Discontinued due to licensing problems with the U.S. Postal Service. Replaced with *Mailbox,* 1990, Item #5198-5, page 99.

'91	'92	'93	'94	'95	'96	'97
$20	20	15	20	20	20	20

SNOW VILLAGE PROMOTIONAL SIGN

ITEM #	INTRO	RETIRED	OSRP	GBTRU	↑
9948-1	1989	DISC. '90	PROMO	**$25**	14%

Particulars: Earthenware sign intended to be used by Department 56, Inc. retailers as a promotional item. Sign displays the Original Snow Village® logo. Brickwork at the base supports the sign.

'95	'96	'97
$15	20	22

KIDS DECORATING THE VILLAGE SIGN

ITEM #	INTRO	RETIRED	OSRP	GBTRU	↑
5134-9	1990	1993	$12.50	**$26**	18%

Particulars: Two children place garland on a Original Snow Village® sign.

'91	'92	'93	'94	'95	'96	'97
$12.50	12.50	12.50	21	20	22	22

DOWN THE CHIMNEY HE GOES

ITEM #	INTRO	RETIRED	OSRP	GBTRU	NO
5158-6	1990	1993	$6.50	**$15**	CHANGE

Particulars: Santa with a big bag of toys enters chimney to make delivery on Christmas Eve. Chimney can be attached to a house rooftop.

'91	'92	'93	'94	'95	'96	'97
$6.50	6.50	6.50	14	14	15	15

SNO-JET SNOWMOBILE

ITEM #	INTRO	RETIRED	OSRP	GBTRU	↑
5159-4	1990	1993	$15	**$28**	12%

Particulars: Red and silver trimmed snowmobile with front ski runners and rear caterpillar treads.

'91	'92	'93	'94	'95	'96	'97
$15	15	15	24	24	25	25

SLEIGHRIDE

ITEM #	INTRO	RETIRED	OSRP	GBTRU	NO
5160-8	1990	1992	$30	**$60**	CHANGE

Particulars: Family rides in open old-fashioned green sleigh pulled by one horse.

'91	'92	'93	'94	'95	'96	'97
$30	30	52	54	55	50	60

The Original Snow Village® Accessories

HERE WE COME A CAROLING

ITEM #	INTRO	RETIRED	OSRP	GBTRU	↑
5161-6	1990	1992	$18	**$30**	7%

Particulars: Set of 3. Children and pet dog sing carols.

'91	'92	'93	'94	'95	'96	'97
$18	18	25	25	25	24	28

HOME DELIVERY

ITEM #	INTRO	RETIRED	OSRP	GBTRU	↑
5162-4	1990	1992	$16	**$38**	9%

Particulars: Set of 2. Milkman and milk truck.

'91	'92	'93	'94	'95	'96	'97
$16	16	30	30	30	33	35

FRESH FROZEN FISH

ITEM #	INTRO	RETIRED	OSRP	GBTRU	↑
5163-2	1990	1993	$20	**$44**	5%

Particulars: Set of 2. Ice fisherman and ice house.

'91	'92	'93	'94	'95	'96	'97
$20	20	20	35	35	36	42

A TREE FOR ME

ITEM #	INTRO	RETIRED	OSRP	GBTRU	↑
5164-0	1990	1995	$7.50	**$15**	25%

Particulars: 2 pieces per package. Ceramic snowman with top hat, corn cob pipe, and red muffler carries his own small snow covered sisal tree.

'91	'92	'93	'94	'95	'96	'97
$7.50	7.50	8	8	8	14	12

A HOME FOR THE HOLIDAYS

ITEM #	INTRO	RETIRED	OSRP	GBTRU	↑
5165-9	1990	1996	$6.50	**$12**	20%

Particulars: Birdhouse with blue bird sitting on roof. Pole is decorated with garland and there's a small snow covered evergreen. Size is 4" tall.

'91	'92	'93	'94	'95	'96	'97
$6.50	6.50	7	7	7	7	10

SPECIAL DELIVERY

ITEM #	INTRO	RETIRED	OSRP	GBTRU	↑
5197-7	1990	1992	$16	**$42**	17%

Particulars: Set of 2. Original Snow Village® postman and truck in red and green Snow Village Mail Service colors. "S.V. Mail Service" replaced the discontinued 1985 *Special Delivery*, Item #5148-9. (Postman remained the same, only the truck changed.)

'91	'92	'93	'94	'95	'96	'97
$16	16	22	38	35	36	36

VILLAGE MAIL BOX

ITEM #	INTRO	RETIRED	OSRP	GBTRU	NO
5198-5	1990	CURRENT	$3.50	**$3.50**	CHANGE

Particulars: Original Snow Village® mail receptacle in red and green S. V. Mail Service colors. Size is 2". S.V. Mail replaced the discontinued 1985 *Mailbox*, Item #5179-9, page 96.

'91	'92	'93	'94	'95	'96	'97
$3.50	3.50	3.50	3.50	3.50	3.50	3.50

CHRISTMAS TRASH CANS

ITEM #	INTRO	RETIRED	OSRP	GBTRU	NO
5209-4	1990	CURRENT	$6.50	**$7**	CHANGE

Particulars: Set of 2. Two galvanized refuse cans filled with holiday wrappings and garbage. Tops come off. Size is 1 ½".

'91	'92	'93	'94	'95	'96	'97
$6.50	7	7	7	7	7	7

The Original Snow Village® Accessories

WREATHS FOR SALE

ITEM #	INTRO	RETIRED	OSRP	GBTRU	↑
5408-9	1991	1994	$27.50	**$45**	13%

Particulars: Set of 4. Girl holds for sale sign, boy holds up wreaths, child pulls sled. Fence holds wreaths. Materials are ceramic, wood and sisal.

'91	'92	'93	'94	'95	'96	'97
$27.50	27.50	27.50	27.50	45	40	40

WINTER FOUNTAIN

ITEM #	INTRO	RETIRED	OSRP	GBTRU	↑
5409-7	1991	1993	$25	**$62**	13%

Particulars: Angel holds sea shell with water frozen as it flowed. Materials are ceramic and acrylic.

'91	'92	'93	'94	'95	'96	'97
$25	25	25	45	50	50	55

COLD WEATHER SPORTS

ITEM #	INTRO	RETIRED	OSRP	GBTRU	↓
5410-0	1991	1994	$27.50	**$42**	7%

Particulars: Set of 4. Three children play ice hockey.

'91	'92	'93	'94	'95	'96	'97
$27.50	27.50	27.50	27.50	45	45	45

COME JOIN THE PARADE

ITEM #	INTRO	RETIRED	OSRP	GBTRU	↓
5411-9	1991	1992	$12.50	**$20**	9%

Particulars: Two children carry parade banner.

'91	'92	'93	'94	'95	'96	'97
$12.50	12.50	22	18	20	20	22

VILLAGE MARCHING BAND

Item #	Intro	Retired	OSRP	GBTru	↑
5412-7	1991	1992	$30	**$67**	12%

Particulars: Set of 3. Drum Major, two horn players and two drummers.

'91	'92	'93	'94	'95	'96	'97
$30	30	68	45	50	55	60

CHRISTMAS CADILLAC

Item #	Intro	Retired	OSRP	GBTru	↑
5413-5	1991	1994	$9	**$18**	20%

Particulars: Pink car holds sisal tree and presents.

'91	'92	'93	'94	'95	'96	'97
$9	9	9	9	10	15	15

SNOWBALL FORT

Item #	Intro	Retired	OSRP	GBTru	↑
5414-3	1991	1993	$27.50	**$44**	10%

Particulars: Set of 3. One boy behind wall, one hides behind tree, one in open clearing, all with snowballs to throw.

'91	'92	'93	'94	'95	'96	'97
$27.50	27.50	27.50	40	40	40	40

COUNTRY HARVEST

Item #	Intro	Retired	OSRP	GBTru	↓
5415-1	1991	1993	$13	**$25**	7%

Particulars: Farm folk with market basket and pitchfork. Reminiscent of Grant Wood's *American Gothic* painting.

'91	'92	'93	'94	'95	'96	'97
$13	13	13	25	25	18	27

The Original Snow Village® Accessories

VILLAGE USED CAR LOT

ITEM #	INTRO	RETIRED	OSRP	GBTRU	↑
5428-3	1992	1997	$45	**$54**	20%

Particulars: Set of 5. Small office on a stone base with stone chimney. Attached tree. Free standing sign plus office sign advertises used cars and good terms. Three cars in the lot.

'92	'93	'94	'95	'96	'97
$45	45	45	45	45	45

VILLAGE PHONE BOOTH

ITEM #	INTRO	RETIRED	OSRP	GBTRU	NO
5429-1	1992	CURRENT	$7.50	**$7.50**	CHANGE

Particulars: Silver and red outdoor phone booth with accordion open/close doors. Size is 4" high.

'92	'93	'94	'95	'96	'97
$7.50	7.50	7.50	7.50	7.50	7.50

NANNY AND THE PRESCHOOLERS

ITEM #	INTRO	RETIRED	OSRP	GBTRU	↓
5430-5	1992	1994	$27.50	**$38**	5%

Particulars: Set of 2. Two girls and a boy hold onto Nanny's shopping basket as she pushes carriage with baby.

'92	'93	'94	'95	'96	'97
$27.50	27.50	27.50	30	38	40

EARLY MORNING DELIVERY

ITEM #	INTRO	RETIRED	OSRP	GBTRU	↑
5431-3	1992	1995	$27.50	**$42**	5%

Particulars: Set of 3. Village kids deliver morning newspaper. One tosses to house, one pushes sled, and Dalmatian holds next paper in mouth.

'92	'93	'94	'95	'96	'97
$27.50	27.50	27.50	27.50	34	40

CHRISTMAS PUPPIES

ITEM #	INTRO	RETIRED	OSRP	GBTRU	↑
5432-1	1992	1996	$27.50	**$42**	5%

Particulars: Set of 2. One girl hugs a pup as two kids take box of pups for a ride in red wagon.

'92	'93	'94	'95	'96	'97
$27.50	27.50	27.50	27.50	27.50	40

ROUND & ROUND WE GO!

ITEM #	INTRO	RETIRED	OSRP	GBTRU	↓
5433-0	1992	1995	$18	**$28**	7%

Particulars: Set of 2. Two kids go sledding on round saucer sleds.

'92	'93	'94	'95	'96	'97
$18	18	18	18	22	30

A HEAVY SNOW FALL

ITEM #	INTRO	RETIRED	OSRP	GBTRU	NO
5434-8	1992	CURRENT	$16	**$16**	CHANGE

Particulars: Set of 2. Girl stops to look at bird perched on handle of her shovel as boy shovels snow off the walkway.

'92	'93	'94	'95	'96	'97
$16	16	16	16	16	16

WE'RE GOING TO A CHRISTMAS PAGEANT

ITEM #	INTRO	RETIRED	OSRP	GBTRU	↑
5435-6	1992	1994	$15	**$25**	25%

Particulars: Children wear costumes of Santa, a decorated tree and a golden star.

'92	'93	'94	'95	'96	'97
$15	15	15	18	20	20

The Original Snow Village® Accessories

A HERD OF HOLIDAY HEIFERS

ITEM #	INTRO	RETIRED	OSRP	GBTRU	↑
5455-0	1993	1997	$18	**$27**	50%

Particulars: * Set of 3 Holstein cows.

'93	'94	'95	'96	'97
$18	18	18	18	18

CLASSIC CARS

ITEM #	INTRO	RETIRED	OSRP	GBTRU	NO
5457-7	1993	CURRENT	$22.50	**$22.50**	CHANGE

Particulars: Set of 3. Station wagon with roof rack, two-tone green sedan with tail fins, sedan with spare tire mounted outside trunk.

'93	'94	'95	'96	'97
$22.50	22.50	22.50	22.50	22.50

SPIRIT OF SNOW VILLAGE AIRPLANE

ITEM #	INTRO	RETIRED	OSRP	GBTRU	↑
5458-5	1993	1996	$12.50	**$28**	27%

Particulars: 2 Assorted–blue or yellow.
Size: 4 1/2" x 5 1/2" x 2 3/4". Propeller double strut winged planes.

'93	'94	'95	'96	'97
$12.50	12.50	12.50	12.50	22

VILLAGE NEWS DELIVERY

ITEM #	INTRO	RETIRED	OSRP	GBTRU	↑
5459-3	1993	1996	$15	**$28**	4%

Particulars: Set of 2. Driver carries newspaper from van to stores and home delivery children carriers.

'93	'94	'95	'96	'97
$15	15	15	15	27

The Original Snow Village® Accessories

CAROLING AT THE FARM

ITEM #	INTRO	RETIRED	OSRP	GBTRU	NO
5463-1	1994	Current	$35	**$35**	CHANGE

Particulars: Farmer drives tractor pulling carolers on hay covered wagon. One child pulls another onto the wagon. Midyear release. First ceramic accessory to be a midyear release.

'94	'95	'96	'97
$35	35	35	35

STUCK IN THE SNOW

ITEM #	INTRO	RETIRED	OSRP	GBTRU	NO
5471-2	1994	Current	$30	**$30**	CHANGE

Particulars: Set of 3. Dad pushes car, mom watches while son holds shovel and sand.

'94	'95	'96	'97
$30	30	30	30

PETS ON PARADE

ITEM #	INTRO	RETIRED	OSRP	GBTRU	NO
5472-0	1994	Current	$16.50	**$16.50**	CHANGE

Particulars: Set of 2. Two children walk dogs on cold wintry day.

'94	'95	'96	'97
$16.50	16.50	16.50	16.50

FEEDING THE BIRDS

ITEM #	INTRO	RETIRED	OSRP	GBTRU	↑
5473-9	1994	1997	$25	**$28**	12%

Particulars: Set of 3. Woman and children are feeding birds as other birds sit on frozen birdbath.

'94	'95	'96	'97
$25	25	25	25

The Original Snow Village® Accessories

MUSH!

	ITEM #	INTRO	RETIRED	OSRP	GBTRU	↑
	5474-7	1994	1997	$20	**$28**	40%

Particulars: Set of 2. A small child sits on a sled that is harnessed to a St. Bernard. An older child shouts to them from behind the mailbox.

'94	'95	'96	'97
$20	20	20	20

SKATERS & SKIERS

ITEM #	INTRO	RETIRED	OSRP	GBTRU	NO
5475-5	1994	CURRENT	$27.50	**$27.50**	CHANGE

Particulars: Set of 3. One child laces up her skates while another is happy to be able to stand. As one skier looks on, another goes BOOM!

'94	'95	'96	'97
$27.50	27.50	27.50	27.50

GOING TO THE CHAPEL

ITEM #	INTRO	RETIRED	OSRP	GBTRU	NO
5476-3	1994	CURRENT	$20	**$20**	CHANGE

Particulars: Set of 2. Family walks to the chapel with gifts and a wreath as a clergyman waits to greet them.

'94	'95	'96	'97
$20	20	20	20

SANTA COMES TO TOWN, 1995

ITEM #	INTRO	RETIRED	OSRP	GBTRU	↑
5477-1	1994	1995 ANNUAL	$30	**$47**	12%

Particulars: 1st in a Series of Dated Annual Santa pieces. Children circle Santa as he passes out presents. He is holding a sack of toys and a book dated "1995."

'94	'95	'96	'97
$30	30	34	42

MARSHMALLOW ROAST

ITEM #	INTRO	RETIRED	OSRP	GBTRU	NO
5478-0	1994	CURRENT	$32.50	**$32.50**	CHANGE

Particulars: Set of 3. Lighted–fire glows. Children take skating rest roasting marshmallows over log fire. Battery operated or can be used with Adapter, Item #5225-6.

'94	'95	'96	'97
$32.50	32.50	32.50	32.50

COCA–COLA® BRAND DELIVERY TRUCK

ITEM #	INTRO	RETIRED	OSRP	GBTRU	NO
5479-8	1994	CURRENT	$15	**$15**	CHANGE

Particulars: Red and white Coca-Cola delivery truck with large wreath on the back

'94	'95	'96	'97
$15	15	15	15

COCA–COLA® BRAND DELIVERY MEN

ITEM #	INTRO	RETIRED	OSRP	GBTRU	NO
5480-1	1994	CURRENT	$25	**$25**	CHANGE

Particulars: Set of 2. One man carries crates to truck as another stops to enjoy a Coke.

'94	'95	'96	'97
$25	25	25	25

COCA–COLA® BRAND BILLBOARD

ITEM #	INTRO	RETIRED	OSRP	GBTRU	↑
5481-0	1994	1997	$18	**$25**	39%

Particulars: Three lights shine on a billboard featuring Santa enjoying a Coke. Trees grow in the shade of the sign.

'94	'95	'96	'97
$18	18	18	18

The Original Snow Village® Accessories

A VISIT WITH SANTA

ITEM #	INTRO	RETIRED	OSRP	GBTRU	↓
VARIOUS	1995	1995 ANNUAL	$25	**$45**	25%

Particulars: Mother and children meet Santa on the street. Mother has shopping bag. Gifts are stacked on the snow. Piece was crafted for specific stores. The store's logo is on the shopping bag. The retailers chose the colors for the gift packages.

The stores and individual Item Numbers are as follows:

Bachman's .... #754-4
Fortunoff .... #767-6
Pine Cone Christmas Shop .... #773-0
Stat's .... #765-0
The Lemon Tree .... #768-4
The Limited Edition .... #764-1
William Glen .... #766-8
Young's Ltd. .... #769-2

'97
$60

FROSTY PLAYTIME

ITEM #	INTRO	RETIRED	OSRP	GBTRU	↑
54860	1995	1997	$30	**$37**	23%

Particulars: Set of 3. Child rides on playground bouncing deer as another holds a hula hoop. Boys make snow and ice houses.

'95	'96	'97
$30	30	30

POINSETTIAS FOR SALE

ITEM #	INTRO	RETIRED	OSRP	GBTRU	NO
54861	1995	CURRENT	$30	**$30**	CHANGE

Particulars: Set of 3. Vendor offers choice of plants to shoppers.

'95	'96	'97
$30	30	30

SANTA COMES TO TOWN, 1996

ITEM #	INTRO	RETIRED	OSRP	GBTru	↑
54862	1995	1996 ANNUAL	$32.50	$45	13%

Particulars: 2nd in a Series of Annual Dated Santas. Santa pulls sleigh loaded with gifts as children catch a ride.

'95	'96	'97
$32.50	32.50	40

CHOPPING FIREWOOD

ITEM #	INTRO	RETIRED	OSRP	GBTru	NO
54863	1995	CURRENT	$16.50	$16.50	CHANGE

Particulars: Set of 2. Father chops wood as son stacks into ventilated cords. Materials are ceramic and wood.

'95	'96	'97
$16.50	16.50	16.50

FIREWOOD DELIVERY TRUCK

ITEM #	INTRO	RETIRED	OSRP	GBTru	NO
54864	1995	CURRENT	$15	$15	CHANGE

Particulars: Holiday Farms truck loaded with firewood held in place by slatted wood panels.

'95	'96	'97
$15	15	15

SERVICE WITH A SMILE

ITEM #	INTRO	RETIRED	OSRP	GBTru	NO
54865	1995	CURRENT	$25	$25	CHANGE

Particulars: Set of 2. One attendant at car service station cleans windshield as other holds new tire.

'95	'96	'97
$25	25	25

The Original Snow Village® Accessories

PIZZA DELIVERY

ITEM #	INTRO	RETIRED	OSRP	GBT<small>RU</small>	NO
54866	1995	CURRENT	$20	**$20**	CHANGE

Particulars: Set of 2. Pisa Pizza green VW bug auto used for home delivery of fresh pizzas. Delivery person carries stacked boxed pies plus additional take-out.

'95	'96	'97
$20	20	20

GRAND OLD OPRY CAROLERS

ITEM #	INTRO	RETIRED	OSRP	GBT<small>RU</small>	↑
54867	1995	1997	$25	**$30**	20%

Particulars: Singer and musicians present carols country-style.

'95	'96	'97
$25	25	25

SNOW CARNIVAL ICE SCULPTURES

ITEM #	INTRO	RETIRED	OSRP	GBT<small>RU</small>	NO
54868	1995	CURRENT	$27.50	**$27.50**	CHANGE

Particulars: Set of 2. Mother and child get set to photograph an ice angel sculpture as the artist puts the final touches on penguins and snowflakes sculpture.

'95	'96	'97
$27.50	27.50	27.50

SNOW CARNIVAL KING & QUEEN

ITEM #	INTRO	RETIRED	OSRP	GBT<small>RU</small>	NO
54869	1995	CURRENT	$35	**$35**	CHANGE

Particulars: Ice carnival King and Queen arrive in sled-dog drawn sleigh.

'95	'96	'97
$35	35	35

The Original Snow Village® Accessories

STARBUCKS® COFFEE CART

ITEM #	INTRO	RETIRED	OSRP	GBTru	NO
54870	1995	CURRENT	$27.50	$27.50	CHANGE

Particulars: Set of 2. Woman stops to purchase hot coffee from vendor with mobile cart.

'95	'96	'97
$27.50	27.50	27.50

JUST MARRIED

ITEM #	INTRO	RETIRED	OSRP	GBTru	NO
54879	1995	CURRENT	$25	$25	CHANGE

Particulars: Set of 2. Groom carries bride. Car is decorated in congratulatory balloons, tin cans and banner.

'95	'96	'97
$25	25	25

Q & A

Q. What's the best (and safest) way to clean the buildings and accessories?

A. Collectors have used a variety of methods to clean their pieces. If all you need to do is remove dust, a feather duster is fine. It's soft enough not to scratch the surface of the pieces. If you want to be extremely safe, however, there's nothing better than air—compressed air in this case. You can purchase cans of compressed air at photo and computer shops. A quick burst of air will displace any dust that has settle on your buildings and accessories. One word of caution…hold on to the accessories when you "hit" them with a blast of air. Otherwise, they might be knocked over and broken.

Q. How can I find out how many of each building were made?

A. Unless it's a numbered limited edition, Department 56, Inc. generally does not announce how many pieces were produced for a particular design.

Q. Why do values for variations of some designs differ while those for variations of other pieces don't?

A. It's all up to collectors. For some unexplained reason, we—as a group—find particular variations very interesting and create a demand for them. Like most things in life, supply and demand have an effect on them. With other pieces, however, we have decided that the variations aren't worth getting excited over. This is one of the aspects that makes collecting intriguing and unpredictable.

the **Village Chronicle.**

The Original Snow Village® Accessories

Q & A

Q. What's the best way to store the small accessories such as fences that don't come in boxes?

A. There are many ways to store such items. Suggestions include storage boxes that are designed for Christmas ornaments. You can usually find these in stores during the holiday season. Another idea is to purchase the plastic storage containers that have individual compartments. These are actually intended to hold nuts, bots, screws, etc., but they're perfect for this use, too. These can be bought at hardware and home supply stores.

the **Village Chronicle.**

HERE COMES SANTA

ITEM #	INTRO	RETIRED	OSRP	GBTRU
VARIOUS	1996	1996 ANNUAL	$25	SEE BELOW

Particulars: Three children follow Santa; one carries a gift wrapped present.

The following retailers had this piece personalized for their store:

Bachman's	#07744	$55
Bronner's Wonderland	#07745	$45
Broughton Christmas Shoppe	#07748	$45
Calabash Nautical Gifts	#07753	$45
Carson Pirie Scott	#07763	$45
Dickens' Gift Shoppe	#07750	$45
European Imports	#07762	$45
Fibber Magee's	#07747	$45
Fortunoff	#07741	$75
Gustaf's	#07759	$45
Ingle's Nook	#07754	$45
North Pole City	#07742	$45
Pine Cone Christmas Shop	#07740	$45
Royal Dutch Collectibles	#07760	$45
Russ Country Gardens	#07756	$45
St. Nick's	#07757	$45
Seventh Avenue	#07758	$45
Stat's	#07749	$45
The Cabbage Rose	#07752	$45
The Calico Butterfly	#07751	$45
The Christmas Loft	#07755	$45
The Limited Edition	#07746	$45
William Glen	#07743	$45
Young's Ltd.	#07761	$45

A RIDE ON THE REINDEER LINES

ITEM #	INTRO	RETIRED	OSRP	GBTRU	↑
54875	1996	1997	$35	**$50**	43%

Particulars: Midyear release. Set of 3– Family ready to depart for the holidays. Child and Bus Driver and Reindeer Line Bus with racing deer on front and sides complete with large chrome bumper, wipers, and windows all around.

'96	'97
$35	35

TREETOP TREE HOUSE

ITEM #	INTRO	RETIRED	OSRP	GBTRU	NO
54890	1996	CURRENT	$35	**$35**	CHANGE

Particulars: Children's tree playhouse nestles in branches of a Jack Pine tree. A wooden ladder allows entry/exit and a mailbox is attached to the base of the tree. A tire swing hangs from a bare branch. Material is resin.

'97
$35

ON THE ROAD AGAIN

ITEM #	INTRO	RETIRED	OSRP	GBTRU	NO
54891	1996	CURRENT	$20	**$20**	CHANGE

Particulars: Set of 2. Station wagon carrying a canoe on roof rack hauls a trailer.

'97
$20

MOVING DAY

ITEM #	INTRO	RETIRED	OSRP	GBTRU	NO
54892	1996	CURRENT	$32.50	**$32.50**	CHANGE

Particulars: Set of 3. New owners help moving men carry household goods from the moving van into their new home in the village.

'97
$32.50

The Original Snow Village® Accessories

HOLIDAY HOOPS

ITEM #	INTRO	RETIRED	OSRP	GBTRU	NO
54893	1996	CURRENT	$20	**$20**	CHANGE

Particulars: Set of 3. Two students play one-on-one basketball.

'97
$20

MEN AT WORK

ITEM #	INTRO	RETIRED	OSRP	GBTRU	NO
54894	1996	CURRENT	$27.50	**$27.50**	CHANGE

Particulars: Set of 5. Village street and road repairs are handled by work crew and road vehicle.

'97
$27.50

TERRY'S TOWING

ITEM #	INTRO	RETIRED	OSRP	GBTRU	NO
54895	1996	CURRENT	$20	**$20**	CHANGE

Particulars: Set of 2. Track Compatible. Yellow tow truck hauls non-working cars to a service center.

'97
$20

CAROLING THROUGH THE SNOW

ITEM #	INTRO	RETIRED	OSRP	GBTRU	NO
54896	1996	CURRENT	$15	**$15**	CHANGE

Particulars: Track Compatible. Boy pushes carolers in sleigh.

'97
$15

HEADING FOR THE HILLS	ITEM # 54897	INTRO 1996	RETIRED CURRENT	OSRP $8.50	GBTRU **$8.50**	NO CHANGE

Particulars: Set of 2. Track Compatible. Car with ski carriers mounted to the car roof

'97
$8.50

A HARLEY-DAVIDSON® **HOLIDAY**	ITEM # 54898	INTRO 1996	RETIRED CURRENT	OSRP $22.50	GBTRU **$22.50**	NO CHANGE

Particulars: Set of 2. Father and child carry family presents to Harley-Davidson motorcycle and sidecar for trip home

'97
$22.50

SANTA COMES TO TOWN, **1997**	ITEM # 54899	INTRO 1996	RETIRED 1997 ANNUAL	OSRP $35	GBTRU **$42**	↑ 20%

Particulars: Third in a Series of Dated Annual Santas. Mayor presents Santa with a key to the Village as a children's band strikes up a tune.

'97
$35

HARLEY-DAVIDSON® FAT **BOY & SOFTAIL**	ITEM # 54900	INTRO 1996	RETIRED CURRENT	OSRP $16.50	GBTRU **$16.50**	NO CHANGE

Particulars: Set of 2. Two different popular motorcycle designs.

'97
$16.50

The Original Snow Village® Accessories

Harley-Davidson® Sign

Item #	Intro	Retired	OSRP	GBTru	
54901	1996	Current	$18	**$18**	NO CHANGE

Particulars: Motorcycle mounted on a sign advertises the location of Harley-Davidson® Motor Sales, Parts and Service business.

'97
$18

The Whole Family Goes Shopping

Item #	Intro	Retired	OSRP	GBTru	
54905	1997	Current	$25	**$25**	NO CHANGE

Particulars: Set of 3. Midyear release. Dad, Mom and children on a busy holiday shopping spree. Family Dalmatian joins in, hoping for a trip to the feed store for biscuits.

'97
$25

A Holiday Sleigh Ride Together

Item #	Intro	Retired	OSRP	GBTru
54921	1997	Current	$32.50	**$32.50**

Particulars: Track Compatible. Family goes for a sleigh ride in old fashioned sleigh pulled by a horse with bell trimmed harness.

Christmas Kids

Item #	Intro	Retired	OSRP	GBTru
54922	1997	Current	$27.50	**$27.50**

Particulars: Set of 5. Children carry gifts, shopping bags and holiday trim.

LET IT SNOW, LET IT SNOW

ITEM #	INTRO	RETIRED	OSRP	GBTRU
54923	1997	CURRENT	$20	**$20**

Particulars: Track Compatible. Father uses snow blower to clear sidewalk and little boy sweeps away blown snow.

KIDS LOVE HERSHEY'S™!

ITEM #	INTRO	RETIRED	OSRP	GBTRU
54924	1997	CURRENT	$30	**$30**

Particulars: Set of 2. Boy and girl wave at the Hershey's™ delivery truck.

McDONALD'S® ... LIGHTS UP THE NIGHT

ITEM #	INTRO	RETIRED	OSRP	GBTRU
54925	1997	CURRENT	$30	**$30**

Particulars: 15¢ hamburgers? Curbside Golden Arch lights up to let drivers know a fast food restaurant is open for business.

KIDS, CANDY CANES ... & RONALD McDONALD®

ITEM #	INTRO	RETIRED	OSRP	GBTRU
54926	1997	CURRENT	$30	**$30**

Particulars: Set of 3. Ronald and children with sled carrying candy canes.

The Original Snow Village® Accessories

HE LED THEM DOWN THE STREETS OF TOWN

ITEM #	INTRO	RETIRED	OSRP	GBTRU
54927	1997	CURRENT	$30	**$30**

Particulars: Set of 3. Snow Puff Marshmallow man carries store signboard as children dance around in delight.

EVERYBODY GOES SKATING AT ROLLERAMA

ITEM #	INTRO	RETIRED	OSRP	GBTRU
54928	1997	CURRENT	$25	**$25**

Particulars: Set of 2. Girls wearing 50's poodle skirts and boy in jeans carry skates and head to roller rink.

AT THE BARN DANCE, IT'S ALLEMANDE LEFT

ITEM #	INTRO	RETIRED	OSRP	GBTRU
54929	1997	CURRENT	$30	**$30**

Particulars: Set of 2. Hound dog keeps eye on fiddler as children do intricate square dance step.

HITCH-UP THE BUCKBOARD

ITEM #	INTRO	RETIRED	OSRP	GBTRU
54930	1997	CURRENT	$40	**$40**

Particulars: Track Compatible. Rancher drives horse drawn carriage for holiday visitors.

FARM ACCESSORY SET

ITEM #	INTRO	RETIRED	OSRP	GBTRU
54931	1997	CURRENT	$75	**$75**

Particulars: Set of 35. Trees, fences, hay, farm animals, watering trough & pump.

SAY IT WITH FLOWERS

ITEM #	INTRO	RETIRED	OSRP	GBTRU
2204	1998	1998 ANNUAL	$30	**$30**

Particulars: Set of 3. Created for Bachman's Village Gathering. Companion accessory to *Bachman's® Flower Shop* and *Bachman's® Greenhouse*. Includes Bachman's employee with purple wheelbarrow, a father and daughter with purple packages and a woman with purple wrapped flowers and wreath. Real paper is used on both packages.

SANTA COMES TO TOWN, 1998

ITEM #	INTRO	RETIRED	OSRP	GBTRU
54920	1998	1998 ANNUAL	$30	**$30**

Particulars: Santa and children decorate a Santa Snowman for the Village.

FIRST ROUND OF THE YEAR

ITEM #	INTRO	RETIRED	OSRP	GBTRU
54936	1998	CURRENT	$30	**$30**

Particulars: Set of 3. Midyear release. Track Compatible. Coordinates with Linden Hills Country Club. Man and woman golfers with golf cart.

The Original Snow Village® Accessories

TRICK OR TREAT KIDS	ITEM # 54937	INTRO 1998	RETIRED CURRENT	OSRP $33	GBTRU $33

Particulars: Set of 3. Midyear release. Children dressed in costume for Halloween festivities.

CARNIVAL TICKETS & COTTON CANDY	ITEM # 54938	INTRO 1998	RETIRED CURRENT	OSRP $30	GBTRU $30

Particulars: Set of 3. Midyear release. Vendor sells cotton candy and carousel tickets. Children buy cotton candy and balloons.

TWO FOR THE ROAD	ITEM # 54939	INTRO 1998	RETIRED CURRENT	OSRP $20 EACH	GBTRU $20/EA

Particulars: 3 Assorted. Midyear release. Softail Harley-Davidson® motorcycle with double riders offered in three different colors; blue, red or yellow.

Q & A

Q. Which village do the Heinz House and State Farm Main Street Memories belong to?

A. Actually, they don't belong to any village. They are part of the Department 56® Profiles™ Series. These buildings were designed and produced for use as promotional items by the H. J. Heinz Company and State Farm Insurance, respectively. The intention of the Profiles™ Series is to get buildings produced by Department 56, Inc. into the hands of people who had never seen nor heard of them. At that point, those people may decide to purchase village pieces.

the **Village Chronicle**.

THATCHED COTTAGE	ITEM #	INTRO	RETIRED	OSRP	GBTRU	↓
	5050-0	1979	1980	$30	**$645**	7%

Particulars: Small thatched cottage with attached tree. Chimney at rear of stucco and timber trim.

'96	'97
$725	690

COUNTRYSIDE CHURCH	ITEM #	INTRO	RETIRED	OSRP	GBTRU	↓
	5051-8	1979	1980	$25	**$510**	6%

Particulars: *Countryside Church* in a springtime setting. There's a large green tree against a simple white wood church with a steeple rising from the entry to the nave. For a snow version, see Original Snow Village® 1979, *Countryside Church*, Item #5058-3.

'96	'97
$685	545

ASPEN TREES (ACCESSORY)	ITEM #	INTRO	RETIRED	OSRP	GBTRU	↓
	5052-6	1979	1980	$16	**$200**	25%

Particulars: The trees that shiver and tremble in the wind. Small leaves on a hardwood tree.

'96	'97
NE	$265

SHEEP (ACCESSORY)	ITEM #	INTRO	RETIRED	OSRP	GBTRU	NO
	5053-4	1979	1980	$12	**NE**	CHANGE

Particulars: Set of 12 includes 9 white and 3 black sheep. The photograph shows one white sheep only.

'96	'97
NE	NE

Meadowland

Dickens' Village Series®

Dickens' Village Series® was introduced in 1984, and it wasn't long before it soared to its position as Department 56, Inc.'s most popular village. Featuring buildings and accessories based on Victorian England, it depicts the places and people we visualize when reading one of Charles Dickens' works.

Department 56 Inc.'s first porcelain series, Dickens' Village Series®, has experienced a popularity matched by few products in the collectible industry. The reasons for its success are varied, but they include the quality of the designs and production, the appeal of limited editions (there have been seven), and the fact that many collectors associate the entire village with *A Christmas Carol*, Dickens' most famous work and perhaps the most popular Christmas story ever.

In total, four of Dickens' stories have been the basis for the Village's designs. *A Christmas Carol, Nicholas Nickleby, David Copperfield,* and *Oliver Twist* have all been featured in porcelain. Though *The Old Curiosity Shop* is both a Dickens' story and a building in the Village, they are not the same.

The *Charles Dickens' Signature Series*, introduced in 1992, features buildings where Charles Dickens may have stayed while traveling. The last building in the Series, *Gad's Hill Place*, depicts his last home and was introduced in 1996. The buildings in the Series were each limited to one year of production.

In 1997, a new "sub-series" was introduced. Known as the *Historical Landmark Series™*, its first building was the *Tower Of London*. The second building in the Series is *The Old Globe Theatre*.

More than a decade since its introduction, and more than a century after the death of its namesake, Dickens' Village Series® is more popular than ever.

THE BOTTOM LINE:

Cost of all pieces introduced to Dickens' Village Series® through the 1998 midyear introductions, including variations: **$6,193**

GREENBOOK TruMarket Value of all pieces through the 1998 midyear introductions, including variations: **$25,450**

... NEW FOR SALE LISTINGS

MANCHESTER SQUARE STARTER SET - 1997

Consisting of G. Choir's Weights & Scales, Frogmore Chemist, Custom House (pictured), Lydby Trunk & Satchel Shop, a seven piece accessory set, trees, and snow, this is the largest starter set Department 56, Inc. has introduced to date.

EAST INDIES TRADING CO. - 1997

With the introduction of this building, the Dickens' Village Series® has a warehouse to go along with Fezziwig's Warehouse. (The Canadian Trading Co. is a similar building that is distributed in Canada only.)

LEACOCK POULTERER - 1997

This is an addition to the Christmas Carol Revisited Series. Could it be the poulterer he was referring to when Scrooge instructed the little boy outside his window to buy the large goose?

CROOKED FENCE COTTAGE - 1997

This quaint cottage design is a departure from the usual style of building in the Dickens' Village Series®.

ASHWICK LANE HOSE AND LADDER - 1997

The Dickens' Village Series® now has a fire station. Have you noticed the pun in its name?

THE OLD GLOBE THEATRE- 1997

The second building in the Historical Landmark Series™, this design depicts the Globe Theatre where Shakespeare performed.

THOMAS MUDGE TIMEPIECES - 1998

Named after the man who perfected the spring-driven watch, this building also features a separate entrance with a plaque stating that the works of Neilan Lund (Department 56, Inc.'s master architect) are inside.

SETON MORRIS SPICE MERCHANT GIFT SET - 1998

This set of ten includes both porcelain and resin features, and, therefore, offers a higher degree of detail than buildings of porcelain only.

5812-2 Great Denton Mill
5822-0 Giggelswick Mutton & Ham
5823-8 Hather Harness
58246 PORTOBELLO ROAD THATCHED COTTAGES, Set/3
  • 58247 Mr. & Mrs. Pickle
  • 58248 Cobb Cottage
  • 58249 Browning Cottage
58331 WRENBURY SHOPS, Set/3–Only 2 are Retired
  • 58332 Wrenbury Baker
  • 58333 The Chop Shop
5834-3 Dudden Cross Church

LIMITED EDITIONS

5585-9 Ruth Marion Scotch Woolens
        17,500 pcs
5586-7 Green Gate Cottage
        22,500 pcs
58336 Ramsford Palace
        27,500 pcs
5904-8 C. Fletcher Public House
        12,500 pcs
6502-1 Norman Church
        3,500 pcs
6519-6 Dickens' Village Mill
        2,500 pcs
6568-4 Chesterton Manor House
        7,500 pcs

CHARLES DICKENS SIGNATURE SERIES

Year	No.	Name
1992	5750-9	Crown & Cricket Inn
1993	5751-7	The Pied Bull Inn
1993	5809-2	Boarding & Lodging (#18)
1994	5752-5	Dedlock Arms
1995	5753-3	Sir John Falstaff Inn
1996	57534	The Grapes Inn
1997	57535	Gad's Hill Place

HISTORICAL LANDMARK SERIES™

Year	No.	Name
1997	58500	Tower Of London
1998	58501	The Old Globe Theatre

HOMES FOR THE HOLIDAYS

1995 5832-7
Dickens' Village Start A Tradition Set
  • Faversham Lamps & Oil
  • Morston Steak & Kidney Pie
  • Town Square Carolers

1997 58322
Dickens' Village Start A Tradition Set
  • Sudbury Church
  • Old East Rectory
  • The Spirit of Giving

1998 58308
Seton Morris Spice Merchant
Exclusive Gift Set
  • Seton Morris Spice Merchant
  • Christmas Apples

RETIRED BUILDINGS

5550-6	1992	DAVID COPPERFIELD
5550-6	1992	Mr. Wickfield Solicitor
5550-6	1992	Betsy Trotwood's Cottage
5550-6	1992	Peggotty's Seaside Cottage
5552-2	1995	Fagin's Hide-A-Way
5553-0	1993	OLIVER TWIST
5553-0	1993	Brownlow House
5553-0	1993	Maylie Cottage
5555-7	1995	Ashbury Inn
5557-3	1994	Nephew Fred's Flat
5562-0	1996	Old Michaelchurch
5567-0	1992	Bishops Oast House
5568-9	1996	KING'S ROAD
55690	1996	Tutbury Printer
55691	1996	C. H. Watt Physician
5582-4	1995	Knottinghill Church
5583-2	1991	Cobles Police Station
5584-0	1992	Theatre Royal
5800-9	1995	Hembleton Pewterer
5808-4	1996	PUMP LANE SHOPPES
58085	1996	Bumpstead Nye Cloaks & Canes
58086	1996	Lomas Ltd. Molasses
58087	1996	W. M. Wheat Cakes & Puddings
5811-4	1996	Kingsford's Brew House
5812-2	1997	Great Denton Mill
5822-0	1997	Giggelswick Mutton & Ham
5823-8	1997	Hather Harness
58246	1997	PORTOBELLO ROAD THATCHED COTTAGES
58247	1997	Mr. & Mrs. Pickle
58248	1997	Cobb Cottage
58249	1997	Browning Cottage
5832-7	1996	Start A Tradition Set
5832-7	1996	Faversham Lamps & Oil
5832-7	1996	Morston Steak & Kidney Pie
58332	1997	Wrenbury Baker
58333	1997	The Chop Shop
5834-3	1997	Dudden Cross Church
5900-5	1989	BARLEY BREE
5900-5	1989	Farmhouse
5900-5	1989	Barn
5902-1	1990	Counting House & Silas Thimbleton Barrister
5916-1	1988	Kenilworth Castle
5924-2	1990	COBBLESTONE SHOPS
5924-2	1990	The Wool Shop
5924-2	1990	Booter And Cobbler
5924-2	1990	T. Wells Fruit & Spice Shop
5925-0	1991	NICHOLAS NICKLEBY
5925-0	1991	Nicholas Nickleby Cottage
5925-0	1991	Wackford Squeers Boarding School
5926-9	1993	MERCHANT SHOPS
5926-9	1993	Poulterer
5926-9	1993	Geo. Weeton Watchmaker
5926-9	1993	The Mermaid Fish Shoppe
5926-9	1993	White Horse Bakery
5926-9	1993	Walpole Tailors
5927-7	1991	Ivy Glen Church
6500-5	1995	CHRISTMAS CAROL COTTAGES
6500-5	1995	Fezziwig's Warehouse
6500-5	1995	Scrooge & Marley Counting House
6500-5	1995	The Cottage of Bob Cratchit & Tiny Tim
6507-2	1989	DICKENS' LANE SHOPS
6507-2	1989	Thomas Kersey Coffee House
6507-2	1989	Cottage Toy Shop
6507-2	1989	Tuttle's Pub
6508-0	1990	Blythe Pond Mill House
6515-3	1988	THE ORIGINAL SHOPS OF DICKENS' VILLAGE
6515-3	1988	Crowntree Inn
6515-3	1988	Candle Shop
6515-3	1988	Green Grocer
6515-3	1988	Golden Swan Baker
6515-3	1988	Bean And Son Smithy Shop
6515-3	1988	Abel Beesley Butcher
6515-3	1988	Jones & Co. Brush & Basket Shop
6516-1	1989	Dickens' Village Church
6518-8	1988	DICKENS' COTTAGES
6518-8	1988	Thatched Cottage
6518-8	1988	Stone Cottage
6518-8	1988	Tudor Cottage
6528-5	1989	Chadbury Station And Train
6549-8	1989	Brick Abbey

What Goes Where?

Trying to decide which pieces to buy? Everyone has the same problem. But for newer collectors, deciding can be even more trying than for the experienced collectors. Why? Well, new collectors who want to or can only purchase a certain amount of buildings and accessories each year often want to complete series or stories within villages. But, how do you know what goes with what?

Here's a listing of what buildings and accessories are related. We've also included a short synopsis of each story.

A CHRISTMAS CAROL

Undoubtedly Charles Dickens' most famous work, *A Christmas Carol* was published in 1843. This would become his most requested story to "read" in public. Like many of his works, it deals with a man shaped by arrogance, ignorance, and to some degree, society. Again keeping with his design, Dickens demonstrates that a person can change, good can prosper, and the world can be a better place.

On Christmas Eve, Ebenezer Scrooge is visited by four people who are celebrating Christmas in their own generous manner. He would have nothing to do with their joyous Christmas spirit, and sends each on his way. This is typical of Scrooge's manner as we often see him dealing this way with Bob Cratchit, his clerk, the father of Tiny Tim.

That night he is again visited by four visions—the ghost of Marley, his departed partner; and the Spirits of Christmas Past, Present, and Future. These spirits warn him to change his ill-tempered ways or pay the price by being burdened throughout eternity. Each of the three Christmas spirits takes Scrooge on a journey showing him how he once celebrated Christmas, how others celebrate it, and how future Christmases will be.

After these journeys, Scrooge is convinced that he must change his ways and promising to do so, remains true to his word. This is witnessed by Scrooge giving Bob Cratchit a raise and becoming a second father to Tiny Tim.

BUILDINGS:

CHRISTMAS CAROL COTTAGES Set/3	6500-5	1986-1995
• Fezziwig's Warehouse		
• Scrooge & Marley Counting House		
• The Cottage of Bob Cratchit & Tiny Tim		
The Flat Of Ebenezer Scrooge	5587-5	1989-
Nephew Fred's Flat	5557-3	1991-1994
Boarding & Lodging School (#18)	5809-2	1993-1993
Boarding & Lodging School (#43)	5810-6	1994-
The Christmas Carol Cottage (Revisited)	58339	1996-
The Olde Camden Town Church (Revisited)	58346	1996-
The Melancholy Tavern (Revisited)	58347	1996-
Leacock Poulterer (Revisited)	58303	1997-

Christmas Carol Figures Set/3	6501-3	1986-1990
Fezziwig & Friends Set/3	5928-5	1988-1990
Christmas Carol Christmas Morning Figures Set/3	5588-3	1989-
Christmas Carol Christmas Spirits Figures Set/4	5589-1	1989-
Vision Of A Christmas Past Set/3	5817-3	1993-1996
Christmas Carol Holiday Trimming Set Set/21	5831-9	1994-1997
Caroling W/The Cratchit Family (Revisited) Set/3	58396	1996-
The Fezziwig Delivery Wagon (Revisited)	58400	1996-

DAVID COPPERFIELD

David Copperfield, published in 1850, was popular from the start, and has remained so even today. Different from his other classics, Dickens wrote this story in the first person. And why shouldn't he have? It was a sometimes thinly disguised autobiography combining his actual life experiences with the turns he wished his life had taken. Even the main character's name is a clue. The main character's initials are D. C., the reverse of Dickens' initials. Copperfield is sent away to school and works in a factory placing labels on bottles. Dickens also endured a similar fate. In the story, we find that Copperfield is infatuated with a woman whom he later marries but never really loves. The same was true for Dickens. The story ends with Copperfield becoming a successful, highly praised writer...Dickens' own story, once more.

David is brought up by his mother, and their housekeeper, Peggotty. His father had died before David's birth, and his mother marries Mr. Murdstone, a truly disagreeable man. Murdstone sends David to a school in London where he is very unhappy.

After his mother dies, Murdstone removes David from school and sends him to work in a factory, but he runs away to Dover where his aunt, Betsy Trotwood, lives. While attending a better school, he lives with a lawyer, Mr. Wickfield, and his daughter, Agnes. He later meets and marries his wife Dora, but a few years later, she dies.

David leaves the country, but eventually returns, and confesses to Agnes that she is the one he has always loved. They marry, and he becomes a successful writer.

BUILDINGS:

DAVID COPPERFIELD Set/3	5550-6	1989-1992
• Mr. Wickfield Solicitor		
• Betsy Trotwood's Cottage		
• Peggotty's Seaside Cottage		

ACCESSORIES:

David Copperfield Characters Set/5	5551-4	1989-1992

OLIVER TWIST

Published in 1838, *Oliver Twist* is considered the second most recognized work by Charles Dickens. This is due, in part, to the musical film *Oliver*, produced in the late 1960's.

The story chronicles the young life of a boy as he manages to escape life in a workhouse. The Artful Dodger introduces Oliver to a gang of young criminals headed by a life-long thief named Fagin. Fagin and a treacherous murderer, Bill Sikes, plan to corrupt Oliver Twist and lead him into a life of crime. During this time, Oliver's life becomes entwined with that of Mr. Brownlow whom he lives with for a short time before being brought back to Fagin's gang.

After a series of chance events and devious plots, Oliver is adopted by Mr. Brownlow who provides him with a loving and supportive home. His adventures that lead up to this include him being shot in Mrs. Maylie's home while being forced to burglarize it, Sikes accidently hanging himself and Fagin being tried and executed. It is not until the end of the novel that Oliver discovers who his parents were, and he inherits a portion of his father's estate.

BUILDINGS:

Fagin's Hide-A-Way	5552-2	1991-1995
OLIVER TWIST Set/2	5553-0	1991-1993
• Brownlow House		
• Maylie Cottage		

ACCESSORIES:

Oliver Twist Characters Set/3	5554-9	1991-1993

NICHOLAS NICKLEBY

Published in 1839, *Nicholas Nickleby* was written by Charles Dickens to bring attention to the practice of placing small children in boarding schools where they were "employed" as farmhands. This practice was not unusual in England, especially in Yorkshire.

After the death of his father, Nicholas Nickleby along with his mother and sister, moves to London to live with his uncle, Ralph. Not a pleasant arrangement in Ralph's eyes, he sends Nicholas off to school in Yorkshire where he becomes a student of a contemptuous schoolmaster, Wackford Squeers.

Nicholas runs away from the school, and after a brief stop in London, goes to Portsmouth where he acts in a traveling theater. He later returns to London and meets Madeline with whom he falls in love. His uncle plots to force Madeline to marry an acquaintance of his, but Nicholas thwarts the plan.

A family tragedy leads Ralph to kill himself. Squeers is jailed and his school is closed down. Nicholas finds happiness when he marries Madeline.

BUILDINGS:

NICHOLAS NICKLEBY Set/2	5925-0	1988-1991
• Nicholas Nickleby Cottage		
• Wackford Squeers Boarding School		

ACCESSORIES:

Nicholas Nickleby Characters Set/4	5929-3	1988-1991

Greenbook History List

| --- | --- | --- | --- | --- |
6515-3	THE ORIGINAL SHOPS OF DICKENS' VILLAGE, SET/7	1984	1988	1265.00
6515-3	Crowntree Inn	1984	1988	275.00
6515-3	Candle Shop	1984	1988	185.00
6515-3	Green Grocer	1984	1988	205.00
6515-3	Golden Swan Baker	1984	1988	185.00
6515-3	Bean And Son Smithy Shop	1984	1988	195.00
6515-3	Abel Beesley Butcher	1984	1988	135.00
6515-3	Jones & Co. Brush & Basket Shop	1984	1988	290.00
6516-1	Dickens' Village Church—White	1985	1989	425.00
6516-1	Dickens' Village Church—Cream	1985	1989	225.00
6516-1	Dickens' Village Church—Green	1985	1989	355.00
6516-1	Dickens' Village Church—Tan	1985	1989	195.00
6516-1	Dickens' Village Church—Dark	1985	1989	145.00
6518-8	DICKENS' COTTAGES, SET/3	1985	1988	925.00
6518-8	Thatched Cottage	1985	1988	180.00
6518-8	Stone Cottage—Tan	1985	1988	465.00
6518-8	Stone Cottage—Green	1985	1988	360.00
6518-8	Tudor Cottage	1985	1988	385.00
6519-6	Dickens' Village Mill	1985	Ltd Ed 2,500	5025.00
6500-5	CHRISTMAS CAROL COTTAGES, S/3	1986	1995	125.00
6500-5	Fezziwig's Warehouse	1986	1995	40.00
6500-5	Scrooge & Marley Counting House	1986	1995	45.00
6500-5	The Cottage of Bob Cratchit & Tiny Tim	1986	1995	60.00
6502-1	Norman Church	1986	Ltd Ed 3,500	3400.00
6507-2	DICKENS' LANE SHOPS, SET/3	1986	1989	580.00
6507-2	Thomas Kersey Coffee House	1986	1989	170.00
6507-2	Cottage Toy Shop	1986	1989	195.00
6507-2	Tuttle's Pub	1986	1989	225.00
6508-0	Blythe Pond Mill House—Correct	1986	1990	275.00
6508-0	Blythe Pond Mill House— By The Pond	1986	1990	125.00
6528-5	Chadbury Station And Train	1986	1989	385.00
5900-5	BARLEY BREE, SET/2	1987	1989	375.00
5900-5	Farmhouse	1987	1989	*NE
5900-5	Barn	1987	1989	*NE
5905-6	The Old Curiosity Shop	1987	Current	45.00
5916-1	Kenilworth Castle	1987	1988	675.00
6549-8	Brick Abbey	1987	1989	340.00
6568-4	Chesterton Manor House	1987	Ltd Ed 7,500	1445.00
5902-1	Counting House & Silas Thimbleton Barrister	1988	1990	90.00
5904-8	C. Fletcher Public House	1988	12,500*	525.00
5924-2	COBBLESTONE SHOPS, SET/3	1988	1990	365.00
5924-2	The Wool Shop	1988	1990	175.00
5924-2	Booter And Cobbler	1988	1990	120.00

ITEM #	NAME	ISSUED	RETIRED	GBT$_{RU}$$
5924-2	T. Wells Fruit & Spice Shop	1988	1990	95.00
5925-0	NICHOLAS NICKLEBY, SET/2	1988	1991	175.00
5925-0	Nicholas Nickleby Cottage	1988	1991	80.00
5925-0	Nic"k"olas Nickleby Cottage	1988	1991	115.00
5925-0	Wackford Squeers Boarding School	1988	1991	90.00
5926-9	MERCHANT SHOPS, SET/5	1988	1993	275.00
5926-9	Poulterer	1988	1993	60.00
5926-9	Geo. Weeton Watchmaker	1988	1993	55.00
5926-9	The Mermaid Fish Shoppe	1988	1993	70.00
5926-9	White Horse Bakery	1988	1993	60.00
5926-9	Walpole Tailors	1988	1993	55.00
5927-7	Ivy Glen Church	1988	1991	80.00
5550-6	DAVID COPPERFIELD, SET/3	1989	1992	195.00
5550-6	Mr. Wickfield Solicitor	1989	1992	95.00
5550-6	Betsy Trotwood's Cottage	1989	1992	60.00
5550-6	Peggotty's Seaside Cottage—Tan	1989	1992	120.00
5550-6	Peggotty's Seaside Cottage—Green	1989	1992	60.00
5574-3	Victoria Station	1989	Current	112.00
5582-4	Knottinghill Church	1989	1995	75.00
5583-2	Cobles Police Station	1989	1991	160.00
5584-0	Theatre Royal	1989	1992	80.00
5585-9	Ruth Marion Scotch Woolens	1989	Ltd Ed 17,500	360.00
5586-7	Green Gate Cottage	1989	Ltd Ed 22,500	250.00
5587-5	The Flat Of Ebenezer Scrooge— Taiwan/Panes	1989	Variation	90.00
5587-5	The Flat Of Ebenezer Scrooge— Taiwan/No Panes	1989	Variation	80.00
5587-5	The Flat Of Ebenezer Scrooge	1989	Current	37.50
5567-0	Bishops Oast House	1990	1992	80.00
5568-9	KING'S ROAD, SET/2	1990	1996	110.00
55690	Tutbury Printer	1990	1996	50.00
55691	C.H. Watt Physician	1990	1996	60.00
5552-2	Fagin's Hide-A-Way	1991	1995	85.00
5553-0	OLIVER TWIST, SET/2	1991	1993	135.00
5553-0	Brownlow House	1991	1993	75.00
5553-0	Maylie Cottage	1991	1993	60.00
5555-7	Ashbury Inn	1991	1995	75.00
5557-3	Nephew Fred's Flat	1991	1994	75.00
5562-0	Old Michaelchurch	1992	1996	60.00
5750-9	Crown & Cricket Inn	1992	1992 Annual	165.00
5800-9	Hembleton Pewterer	1992	1995	75.00
5801-7	King's Road Post Office	1992	Current	45.00
5751-7	The Pied Bull Inn	1993	1993 Annual	150.00
5808-4	PUMP LANE SHOPPES, SET/3	1993	1996	135.00
58085	Bumpstead Nye Cloaks & Canes	1993	1996	50.00
58086	Lomas Ltd. Molasses	1993	1996	45.00
58087	W.M. Wheat Cakes & Puddings	1993	1996	50.00
5809-2	Boarding & Lodging School (#18)	1993	1993 Annual	140.00
5811-4	Kingsford's Brew House	1993	1996	60.00

Dickens' Village Series®

ITEM #	NAME	ISSUED	RETIRED	GBTRU$
5812-2	Great Denton Mill	1993	1997	55.00
5752-5	Dedlock Arms	1994	1994 Annual	125.00
5810-6	Boarding & Lodging School (#43)	1994	Current	48.00
5821-1	Whittlesbourne Church	1994	Current	85.00
5822-0	Giggelswick Mutton & Ham	1994	1997	55.00
5823-8	Hather Harness	1994	1997	55.00
5824-6	PORTOBELLO ROAD			
	THATCHED COTTAGES, SET/3	1994	1997	130.00
58247	Mr. & Mrs. Pickle	1994	1997	45.00
58248	Cobb Cottage	1994	1997	45.00
58249	Browning Cottage	1994	1997	45.00
5753-3	Sir John Falstaff Inn	1995	1995 Annual	125.00
5832-7	Dickens' Village Start A Tradition Set	1995	1996	115.00
58328	J.D. Nichols Toy Shop	1995	Current	50.00
58329	Dursley Manor	1995	Current	55.00
58330	Blenham Street Bank	1995	Current	60.00
58331	WRENBURY SHOPS, SET/3	1995	*	*
58332	Wrenbury Baker	1995	1997	40.00
58333	The Chop Shop	1995	1997	42.00
58334	T. Puddlewick Spectacle Shop	1995	Current	35.00
5833-5	The Maltings	1995	Current	50.00
5834-3	Dudden Cross Church	1995	1997	55.00
57534	The Grapes Inn	1996	1996 Annual	135.00
58336	Ramsford Palace, Set/17	1996	Ltd Ed 27,500	475.00
58337	Butter Tub Farmhouse	1996	Current	40.00
58338	Butter Tub Barn	1996	Current	48.00
58339	The Christmas Carol Cottage (Revisited)	1996	Current	60.00
58344	Nettie Quinn Puppets & Marionettes	1996	Current	50.00
58345	Mulberrie Court Brownstones	1996	Current	90.00
58346	The Olde Camden Town Church			
	(Revisited)	1996	Current	55.00
58347	The Melancholy Tavern (Revisited)	1996	Current	45.00
58348	Quilly's Antiques	1996	Current	46.00
57535	Gad's Hill Place	1997	1997 Annual	120.00
58301	Manchester Square	1997	Current	250.00
58302	East Indies Trading Co.	1997	Current	65.00
58303	Leacock Poulterer (Revisited)	1997	Current	48.00
58304	Crooked Fence Cottage	1997	Current	60.00
58305	Ashwick Lane Hose & Ladder	1997	Current	54.00
58306	Canadian Trading Co.	1997	Current	65.00
58322	Dickens' Village Start A Tradition Set	1997	Current	100.00
58323	J. Lytes Coal Merchant	1997	Current	50.00
58324	Barmby Moor Cottage	1997	Current	48.00
58500	Tower Of London	1997	1997 Annual	345.00
58501	The Old Globe Theatre	1997	1998 Annual	175.00
58307	Thomas Mudge Timepieces	1998	Current	60.00
58308	Seton Morris Spice Merchant			
	Exclusive Gift Set	1998	1998 Annual	65.00
58309	Kensington Palace	1998	1998 Annual	195.00

𝔇ickens' 𝔙illage 𝔖eries®

THE ORIGINAL SHOPS OF DICKENS' VILLAGE

Item #	Intro	Retired	OSRP	GBTru	↓
6515-3	1984	1988	$175	**$1265**	3%

Particulars: Set of 7 includes *Crowntree Inn, Candle Shop, Green Grocer, Golden Swan Baker, Bean And Son Smithy Shop, Abel Beesley Butcher, Jones & Co. Brush & Basket Shop.*

see below

'91	'92	'93	'94	'95	'96	'97
$1200	1375	1295	1325	1295	1325	1310

CROWNTREE INN

Item #	Intro	Retired	OSRP	GBTru	↓
6515-3	1984	1988	$25	**$275**	8%

Particulars: 1 of the 7-piece set—THE ORIGINAL SHOPS OF DICKENS' VILLAGE. Large multi-paned windows run length of front of Inn with entry door decorated by wreath, second story stone, attic dormer.

'91	'92	'93	'94	'95	'96	'97
$375	350	335	320	300	305	300

CANDLE SHOP

Item #	Intro	Retired	OSRP	GBTru	↓
6515-3	1984	1988	$25	**$185**	5%

Particulars: 1 of the-7 piece set—THE ORIGINAL SHOPS OF DICKENS' VILLAGE. Timber framed windows, plaster on stone small house/store. Attic rental rooms, light over front entry. Variation in roof color—first ones shipped were gray followed by blue.

'91	'92	'93	'94	'95	'96	'97
$235	210	210	190	190	195	195

GREEN GROCER

Item #	Intro	Retired	OSRP	GBTru	↑
6515-3	1984	1988	$25	**$205**	5%

Particulars: 1 of the 7-piece set—THE ORIGINAL SHOPS OF DICKENS' VILLAGE. Thatched roof over timber two-story grocery/provisions store. Bay window for display. Attached storage room on side of store.

'91	'92	'93	'94	'95	'96	'97
$220	200	190	185	185	185	195

Golden Swan Baker

Item #	Intro	Retired	OSRP	GBTru	↑
6515-3	1984	1988	$25	**$185**	6%

Particulars: 1 of the 7-piece set THE ORIGINAL SHOPS OF DICKENS' VILLAGE. Painted sign with gold swan hangs above large bay window for display. Timbered building, brick chimney, light above entry door.

'91	'92	'93	'94	'95	'96	'97
$170	155	180	180	180	180	175

Bean And Son Smithy Shop

Item #	Intro	Retired	OSRP	GBTru	NO
6515-3	1984	1988	$25	**$195**	CHANGE

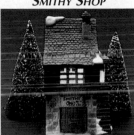

Particulars: 1 of the 7-piece set—THE ORIGINAL SHOPS OF DICKENS' VILLAGE. Double wood door, stone first story, second story set on stone with overhang. Steep curved roof with brick chimney.

'91	'92	'93	'94	'95	'96	'97
$185	185	185	190	195	190	195

Abel Beesley Butcher

Item #	Intro	Retired	OSRP	GBTru	↑
6515-3	1984	1988	$25	**$135**	4%

Particulars: 1 of the 7-piece set—THE ORIGINAL SHOPS OF DICKENS' VILLAGE. Timbered bottom half, second story plaster over stone, two chimneys.

'91	'92	'93	'94	'95	'96	'97
$175	145	130	120	125	130	130

Jones & Co. Brush & Basket Shop

Item #	Intro	Retired	OSRP	GBTru	↓
6515-3	1984	1988	$25	**$290**	3%

Particulars: 1 of the 7-piece set—THE ORIGINAL SHOPS OF DICKENS' VILLAGE. Cellar shop is a cobbler with small sign by his door to advertise, rest of building is for basketry, mats, and brush. Narrow staircase leads to entry.

'91	'92	'93	'94	'95	'96	'97
$325	355	355	335	300	290	300

Dickens' Village Series®

DICKENS' VILLAGE CHURCH—"WHITE"

ITEM #	INTRO	RETIRED	OSRP	GBTRU	↑
6516-1	1985	1989	$35	**$425**	6%

Particulars: There are five versions of the *Village Church:* "White," "Cream," "Green," "Tan" and "Dark." The variations in color affect GBTru$. "White" Church has off white to cream walls and brown roof matches brown cornerstones.

'91	'92	'93	'94	'95	'96	'97
$250	-	-	425	375	385	400

DICKENS' VILLAGE CHURCH—"CREAM"

ITEM #	INTRO	RETIRED	OSRP	GBTRU	↓
6516-1	1985	1989	$35	**$225**	21%

Particulars: "Cream" Church has cream walls with light yellow coloring in mortar between stones and a butter-scotch roof.

'91	'92	'93	'94	'95	'96	'97
$145	285	350	295	225	275	285

DICKENS' VILLAGE CHURCH—"GREEN"

ITEM #	INTRO	RETIRED	OSRP	GBTRU	↓
6516-1	1985	1989	$35	**$355**	8%

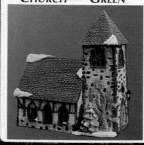

Particulars: "Green" Church has very light green tone on walls and a butterscotch roof.

'91	'92	'93	'94	'95	'96	'97
$225	350	415	350	330	325	385

DICKENS' VILLAGE CHURCH—"TAN"

ITEM #	INTRO	RETIRED	OSRP	GBTRU	↓
6516-1	1985	1989	$35	**$195**	3%

Particulars: "Tan" Church has tan walls and a butterscotch roof.

'91	'92	'93	'94	'95	'96	'97
$100	170	195	205	190	175	200

DICKENS' VILLAGE CHURCH—"DARK"

ITEM #	INTRO	RETIRED	OSRP	GBTRU	↓
6516-1	1985	1989	$35	**$145**	9%

Particulars: "Dark" Church or sometimes called "Butterscotch" has walls that are or nearly are the same color as the roof. This is the only sleeve to read "Village Church." All others read "Shops Of Dickens' Village."

'91	'92	'93	'94	'95	'96	'97
$-	155	160	155	155	150	160

DICKENS' COTTAGES

ITEM #	INTRO	RETIRED	OSRP	GBTRU	↓
6518-8	1985	1988	$75	**$925**	4%

Particulars: Set of 3 includes *Thatched Cottage, Stone Cottage, Tudor Cottage*. Early release to Gift Creations Concepts (GCC).

see below

'91	'92	'93	'94	'95	'96	'97
$875	1015	1015	1050	950	915	965

THATCHED COTTAGE

ITEM #	INTRO	RETIRED	OSRP	GBTRU	↓
6518-8	1985	1988	$25	**$180**	8%

Particulars: 1 of the 3-piece set—DICKENS' COTTAGES. Early release to Gift Creations Concepts (GCC). Double chimneys rise from thatched roof, second story plastered/timbered home with second story extending out on sides.

'91	'92	'93	'94	'95	'96	'97
$210	210	200	200	200	185	195

STONE COTTAGE—"TAN"

ITEM #	INTRO	RETIRED	OSRP	GBTRU	↑
6518-8	1985	1988	$25	**$465**	2%

Particulars: 1 of the 3-piece set—DICKENS' COTTAGES. There are two versions of the *Stone Cottage:* "Tan" and "Green." Tan variation is considered the first color shipped. The color change affects GBTru$. Early release to Gift Creations Concepts (GCC).

'91	'92	'93	'94	'95	'96	'97
$425	465	450	425	400	400	455

STONE COTTAGE— "GREEN"

	ITEM #	INTRO	RETIRED	OSRP	GBT_{RU}	↓
	6518-8	1985	1988	$25	**$360**	9%

Particulars: The "Green" version of the *Stone Cottage* is considered to be later shipments. Cottage has variegated fieldstone walls and roughhewn shingle roof.

'91	'92	'93	'94	'95	'96	'97
$425	380	375	425	400	400	395

TUDOR COTTAGE

	ITEM #	INTRO	RETIRED	OSRP	GBT_{RU}	NO CHANGE
	6518-8	1985	1988	$25	**$385**	

Particulars: 1 of the 3-piece set—DICKENS' COTTAGES. Early release to Gift Creations Concepts (GCC). Stone foundation with timbered/plastered walls forming a small house. Two chimneys for heating/cooking.

'91	'92	'93	'94	'95	'96	'97
$400	455	450	450	400	375	385

DICKENS' VILLAGE MILL

	ITEM #	INTRO	RETIRED	OSRP	GBT_{RU}	↑
	6519-6	1985	LTD ED 2,500	$35	**$5025**	1%

Particulars: Roughhewn stone makes up 3-section mill with large wooden mill wheel. Two sets double doors—one large set to allow carriage to be brought directly into building, smaller doors open into silo area. Early release to Gift Creations Concepts (GCC). Some sleeves read "Dickens' Village Cottage."

'91	'92	'93	'94	'95	'96	'97
$5550	5550	5550	5150	5000	4850	4995

CHRISTMAS CAROL COTTAGES

	ITEM #	INTRO	RETIRED	OSRP	GBT_{RU}	NO CHANGE
	6500-5	1986	1995	$75	**$125**	

Particulars: Set of 3 includes *Fezziwig's Warehouse*, *Scrooge & Marley Counting House*, *The Cottage Of Bob Cratchit & Tiny Tim*.

see next page

'91	'92	'93	'94	'95	'96	'97
$90	90	90	90	90	115	125

FEZZIWIG'S WAREHOUSE

Item #	Intro	Retired	OSRP	GBTru	NO
6500-5	1986	1995	$25	**$40**	CHANGE

Particulars: 1 of the 3-piece set—CHRISTMAS CAROL COTTAGES. Early pieces have panes cut out of front door (photo). Later pieces have a solid front door. This does not affect secondary market value. In *A Christmas Carol*, Fezziwig was young Scrooge's employer. On one day a year, Christmas Eve, Fezziwig held a high-spirited party for his staff and family in the warehouse.

'91	'92	'93	'94	'95	'96	'97
$30	30	30	30	30	40	40

SCROOGE & MARLEY COUNTING HOUSE

Item #	Intro	Retired	OSRP	GBTru	NO
6500-5	1986	1995	$25	**$45**	CHANGE

Particulars: 1 of the 3-piece set—CHRISTMAS CAROL COTTAGES. The office of Scrooge and his departed partner, Jacob Marley, in *A Christmas Carol*. A Counting House kept books and transacted business for different accounts–you would go to a Counting House to borrow money or repay a loan. Building is simple rectangular shape. Bottom brick, second story plastered with shuttered windows.

'91	'92	'93	'94	'95	'96	'97
$30	30	30	30	30	40	45

THE COTTAGE OF BOB CRATCHIT & TINY TIM

Item #	Intro	Retired	OSRP	GBTru	NO
6500-5	1986	1995	$25	**$60**	CHANGE

Particulars: 1 of the 3-piece set—CHRISTMAS CAROL COTTAGES. This is the tiny home in which Bob & Mary Cratchit raised their children—most notably Tiny Tim. Many scholars believe that Dickens fashioned the home after his own childhood home on Bayham Street in Camden Town.

'91	'92	'93	'94	'95	'96	'97
$30	30	30	30	30	50	60

NORMAN CHURCH

Item #	Intro	Retired	OSRP	GBTru	↑
6502-1	1986	Ltd Ed 3,500	$40	**$3400**	2%

Particulars: Solid four-sided tower used as both watch and bell tower. Doors and windows reflect the Romanesque rounded arches. The first pieces are light gray, the later pieces are darker gray. This does not affect secondary market value. Early release to Gift Creations Concepts (GCC).

'91	'92	'93	'94	'95	'96	'97
$3500	3500	3500	3600	3000	3250	3325

DICKENS' LANE SHOPS

	Item #	Intro	Retired	OSRP	GBTru	↓
	6507-2	1986	1989	$80	**$580**	6%

Particulars: Set of 3 includes *Thomas Kersey Coffee House, Cottage Toy Shop, Tuttle's Pub.*

see below

'91	'92	'93	'94	'95	'96	'97
$475	490	565	650	595	615	620

THOMAS KERSEY COFFEE HOUSE

	Item #	Intro	Retired	OSRP	GBTru	↓
	6507-2	1986	1989	$27	**$170**	11%

Particulars: 1 of the 3-piece set—DICKENS' LANE SHOPS. Unique roof set upon simple rectangular building rises up to central chimney with four flue pipes. Brick, plaster, and timber with tile or slate roof. Large multi-paned windows predominate front walls.

'91	'92	'93	'94	'95	'96	'97
$145	150	175	165	165	170	190

COTTAGE TOY SHOP

	Item #	Intro	Retired	OSRP	GBTru	↓
	6507-2	1986	1989	$27	**$195**	13%

Particulars: 1 of the 3-piece set—DICKENS' LANE SHOPS. Small thatched roof cottage. Shop has large bay windows for light and display. Outside side stair/entry for family to living quarters.

'91	'92	'93	'94	'95	'96	'97
$175	215	265	250	225	235	225

TUTTLE'S PUB

	Item #	Intro	Retired	OSRP	GBTru	↑
	6507-2	1986	1989	$27	**$225**	2%

Particulars: 1 of the 3-piece set—DICKENS' LANE SHOPS. Building rises three stories, ground level has pub for refreshments plus stable area for horse and carriages, second and third story jut out in step fashion. Travelers could rent rooms.

'91	'92	'93	'94	'95	'96	'97
$185	220	240	245	225	225	220

BLYTHE POND MILL HOUSE—"CORRECT"

ITEM #	INTRO	RETIRED	OSRP	GBTRU	↓
6508-0	1986	1990	$37	**$275**	7%

Particulars: Commonly referred to as the "correct" version, "Blythe Pond" is inscribed correctly on the bottom of the building. (The "Blythe Pond" sign above the door is correct in both versions.) Three-story timber house, fieldstone wing holds water wheel gears. Grinding stones rest next to house.

'91	'92	'93	'94	'95	'96	'97
$170	215	255	305	315	280	295

BLYTHE POND MILL HOUSE—"BY THE POND"

ITEM #	INTRO	RETIRED	OSRP	GBTRU	↓
6508-0	1986	1990	$37	**$125**	4%

Particulars: Commonly referred to as the "By The Pond" version because this is inscribed, in error, on the bottom of the building. (The "Blythe Pond" sign above the door is correct in both versions.) The error is more common than the correct piece.

'91	'92	'93	'94	'95	'96	'97
$95	105	125	135	135	135	130

CHADBURY STATION AND TRAIN

ITEM #	INTRO	RETIRED	OSRP	GBTRU	↑
6528-5	1986	1989	$65	**$385**	1%

Particulars: Set of 4. Three-car train. Station built of rough stone base and fieldstone. Columns support overhang to keep passengers dry. Indoor room warmed by fireplace. Wooden benches for waiting area. Early version of the station is ½" smaller than later version–no affect on secondary market value.

'91	'92	'93	'94	'95	'96	'97
$315	385	385	385	375	385	380

BARLEY BREE

ITEM #	INTRO	RETIRED	OSRP	GBTRU	↓
5900-5	1987	1989	$60	**$375**	1%

Particulars: Set of 2 includes *Farmhouse* and *Barn*. Unlike many sets, it is very unusual for *Barley Bree* to be sold or sought-after as individual pieces. Early versions have dark roofs, later versions have lighter roofs.

see next page

'91	'92	'93	'94	'95	'96	'97
$285	370	380	395	395	375	380

FARMHOUSE

ITEM #	INTRO	RETIRED	OSRP	GBTRU	NO
5900-5	1987	1989	$30	*NE	CHANGE

Particulars: 1 of the 2-piece set—BARLEY BREE. Thatched roof on small farmhouse with centralized chimney. Half-story tucked into steeply pitched roof. *Secondary market value not established for individual pieces in the set.

'91	'92	'93	'94	'95	'96	'97
NE	NE	NE	NE	NE	NE	NE

BARN

ITEM #	INTRO	RETIRED	OSRP	GBTRU	NO
5900-5	1987	1989	$30	*NE	CHANGE

Particulars: 1 of the 2-piece set—BARLEY BREE. Stone foundation, thatched roof, for livestock. *Secondary market value not established for individual pieces in the set.

'91	'92	'93	'94	'95	'96	'97
NE	NE	NE	NE	NE	NE	NE

THE OLD CURIOSITY SHOP

ITEM #	INTRO	RETIRED	OSRP	GBTRU	NO
5905-6	1987	CURRENT	$32	$45	CHANGE

Particulars: Generally thought to be designed after the Old Curiosity Shop on Portsmouth St. in London, as stated on the front of the actual building. However, many historians believe that this is not the building Dickens used for a model when writing *The Old Curiosity Shop*. Antiques corner shop is adjacent to rare book store. Curiosity shop has large display window and two chimneys. Book shop is taller and narrower.

'91	'92	'93	'94	'95	'96	'97
$37.50	37.50	40	40	42	42	45

KENILWORTH CASTLE

ITEM #	INTRO	RETIRED	OSRP	GBTRU	NO
5916-1	1987	1988	$70	$675	CHANGE

Particulars: Inspired by the remains of Kenilworth Castle, Warwickshire, England. A stronghold for Kings and Lords, it began in 1122 as a fortress, then passed to the Earl of Leicester in 1244. With living quarters it became a Medieval Palace, a favorite of Elizabeth I who visited as a guest of Robert Dudley. Early pieces are larger. It's not unusual for the Castle to have concave walls. Relatively straight walls can be found and are generally considered to be more valuable.

'91	'92	'93	'94	'95	'96	'97
$375	440	495	540	675	695	675

BRICK ABBEY

ITEM #	INTRO	RETIRED	OSRP	GBTRU	↓
6549-8	1987	1989	$33	**$340**	9%

Particulars: Two spires flank front doors, rose window above entry oak doors. Example of a stage of Gothic architecture. Many pieces have spires that lean inward. Those with straight spires are considered to be premiere pieces and usually command a higher price. An abbey is a church that belongs or once belonged to a monastery or convent.

'91	'92	'93	'94	'95	'96	'97
$350	400	380	405	395	375	375

CHESTERTON MANOR HOUSE

ITEM #	INTRO	RETIRED	OSRP	GBTRU	↓
6568-4	1987	LTD ED 7,500	$45	**$1445**	8%

Particulars: Known as a Great House, countryside home with many acres of land. Stone facade, slate roof, plaster and half timber, open pediment above wood entry door with double gable roof design. Early release to Gift Creations Concepts (GCC). Box and bottomstamp read "Manor."

'91	'92	'93	'94	'95	'96	'97
$1800	1875	1825	1725	1650	1665	1575

COUNTING HOUSE & SILAS THIMBLETON BARRISTER

ITEM #	INTRO	RETIRED	OSRP	GBTRU	NO CHANGE
5902-1	1988	1990	$32	**$90**	

Particulars: Square, 3-story, 3-chimney, offices. Equal angle gables create 4-section roof. Attached plaster/timbered 3-story building is smaller and narrower. Lamps in initial shipments had natural porcelain panes. Later shipments had yellow panes. Box reads "Silas Thimbleton Barrister," bottomstamp reads "Counting House."

'91	'92	'93	'94	'95	'96	'97
$95	95	90	90	85	90	90

C. FLETCHER PUBLIC HOUSE

ITEM #	INTRO	RETIRED	OSRP	GBTRU	↓
5904-8	1988	LTD ED 12,500*	$35	**$525**	9%

Particulars: *Plus Proof Editions. Market Price for Proofs is not established. Pub windows wrap around corner. Wood ribs support wider/longer 2nd story. Sweet Shop tucks in next to pub, is plaster/timber design. Early release to Gift Creations Concepts (GCC).

'91	'92	'93	'94	'95	'96	'97
$725	700	645	590	575	545	580

MERCHANT SHOPS

Item #	Intro	Retired	OSRP	GBTru	↑
5926-9	1988	1993	$150	**$275**	6%

Particulars: Set of 5 includes *Poulterer, Geo. Weeton Watchmaker, The Mermaid Fish Shoppe, White Horse Bakery, Walpole Tailors.*

see below

'91	'92	'93	'94	'95	'96	'97
$175	175	180	230	255	245	260

POULTERER

Item #	Intro	Retired	OSRP	GBTru	NO
5926-9	1988	1993	$32.50	**$60**	CHANGE

Particulars: 1 of the 5-piece set—MERCHANT SHOPS. Three-story stone block and timber, fresh geese hang outside front door.

'91	'92	'93	'94	'95	'96	'97
$35	35	36	60	55	55	60

GEO. WEETON WATCHMAKER

Item #	Intro	Retired	OSRP	GBTru	NO
5926-9	1988	1993	$32.50	**$55**	CHANGE

Particulars: 1 of the 5-piece set—MERCHANT SHOPS. All brick, rounded bay window, slate roof, fan light window in oak front door.

'91	'92	'93	'94	'95	'96	'97
$35	35	36	60	55	55	55

THE MERMAID FISH SHOPPE

Item #	Intro	Retired	OSRP	GBTru	↓
5926-9	1988	1993	$32.50	**$70**	7%

Particulars: 1 of the 5-piece set—MERCHANT SHOPS. Roadside fish bins, bay windows, angled doors and walls, wooden trap door in roof.

'91	'92	'93	'94	'95	'96	'97
$35	35	36	70	65	70	75

WHITE HORSE BAKERY

	ITEM #	INTRO	RETIRED	OSRP	GBTRU	↓
	5926-9	1988	1993	$32.50	**$60**	14%

Particulars: 1 of the 5 piece set MERCHANT SHOPS. Two large windows to display baked goods, roof is hipped and gabled with scalloped shingles.

'91	'92	'93	'94	'95	'96	'97
$35	35	36	55	55	55	70

WALPOLE TAILORS

	ITEM #	INTRO	RETIRED	OSRP	GBTRU	NO
	5926-9	1988	1993	$32.50	**$55**	CHANGE

Particulars: 1 of the 5-piece set—MERCHANT SHOPS. Stone and brick covered by stucco. Large first floor windows have wood panels under sills. 2nd floor has bow window.

'91	'92	'93	'94	'95	'96	'97
$35	35	36	55	55	55	55

IVY GLEN CHURCH

	ITEM #	INTRO	RETIRED	OSRP	GBTRU	↓
	5927-7	1988	1991	$35	**$80**	6%

Particulars: Square-toothed parapet tops stone turret by front entry of a thatched roof church. Curved timber design above door is repeated on bell chamber of turret. Arched windows. This church has a chimney.

'91	'92	'93	'94	'95	'96	'97
$37.50	80	85	80	85	80	85

DAVID COPPERFIELD

	ITEM #	INTRO	RETIRED	OSRP	GBTRU	↑
	5550-6	1989	1992	$125	**$195**	8%
			w/TAN PEGOTTY'S		**$250**	↑6%

Particulars: Set of 3 includes *Mr. Wickfield Solicitor, Betsy Trotwood's Cottage, Peggotty's Seaside Cottage.* Early release to Showcase Dealers, 1989.

see next page

Set w/original Tan Pegotty's	'91	'92	'93	'94	'95	'96	'97
	$220	220	310	250	225	230	235

	'91	'92	'93	'94	'95	'96	'97
	$125	125	230	190	175	165	180

RUTH MARION SCOTCH WOOLENS

ITEM #	INTRO	RETIRED	OSRP	GBTRU	↓
5585-9	1989	LTD ED 17,500*	$65	**$360**	9%

Particulars: *Plus Proof Editions. Proofs have "Proof" stamped on the bottom of the piece instead of a number. **GBTru for Proof is $350.** Herringbone brick design between timbers decorates front of 1 ½-story shops and home. Small flower shop tucked onto one side. Named for the wife of Department 56, Inc. artist, Neilan Lund. Early release to Gift Creations Concepts (GCC).

'91	'92	'93	'94	'95	'96	'97
$350	405	380	405	385	390	395

GREEN GATE COTTAGE

ITEM #	INTRO	RETIRED	OSRP	GBTRU	↓
5586-7	1989	LTD ED 22,500*	$65	**$250**	9%

Particulars: *Plus Proof Editions. Proofs have "Proof" stamped on the bottom of the piece instead of a number. **GBTru for Proof is $245.** 3-story home. Repeated vault design on chimney, dormers, and third-story windows. Balcony above door. Fenced courtyard and 2 doors give impression of 2 homes. Small part has steep roof, crooked chimney, and ornamental molding.

'91	'92	'93	'94	'95	'96	'97
$300	340	280	275	275	270	275

THE FLAT OF EBENEZER SCROOGE—"TAIWAN/PANES"

ITEM #	INTRO	RETIRED	OSRP	GBTRU	↑
5587-5	1989	VARIATION	$37.50	**$90**	6%

Particulars: There are three variations of *The Flat Of Ebenezer Scrooge* that affect secondary market value. The First Version was made in Taiwan, has yellow panes in the windows and the far left shutter on the 4th floor is slightly open allowing light to shine through. Early release to National Association Of Limited Edition Dealers (NALED), 1989. Addition to *Christmas Carol* grouping.

'91	'92	'93	'94	'95	'96	'97
$-	-	-	135	100	95	85

THE FLAT OF EBENEZER SCROOGE—"TAIWAN/NO PANES"

ITEM #	INTRO	RETIRED	OSRP	GBTRU	↑
5587-5	1989	VARIATION	$37.50	**$80**	7%

Particulars: The Second Version was made in Taiwan but doesn't have panes in the windows.

'91	'92	'93	'94	'95	'96	'97
$-	115	-	85	60	65	75

THE FLAT OF EBENEZER SCROOGE

ITEM #	INTRO	RETIRED	OSRP	GBTRU	NO
5587-5	1989	CURRENT	$37.50	**$37.50**	CHANGE

Particulars: The latest version is back to panes in the windows and is made in the Philippines or China.

'91	'92	'93	'94	'95	'96	'97
$-	-	-	37.50	37.50	37.50	37.50

BISHOPS OAST HOUSE

ITEM #	INTRO	RETIRED	OSRP	GBTRU	↑
5567-0	1990	1992	$45	**$80**	7%

Particulars: Large attached barn, round cobblestone oasts contain a kiln for drying malt or hops to produce ale. Exterior finished as a roughcast surface over brick. Oast houses are located throughout the Kent countryside. Many, however, have been converted to private homes.

'91	'92	'93	'94	'95	'96	'97
$45	48	85	85	75	80	75

Make the Most of Your Oast

When Department 56, Inc. introduced *Bishops Oast House* in 1990, few collectors realized what it was, and fewer cared. They just didn't like it. On more than one occasion collectors were heard to wonder aloud why a Bishop would live in such a house—not realizing that Bishop was the occupant's last name.

This building may take on a completely different meaning if you ever have the opportunity to visit the Kentish countryside in England. There you will see the peculiar shaped buildings dotting the land. Some have been converted into actual homes, but others remain, performing their daily routine of drying or roasting hops for use in beer.

Hop vines flourish in hop yards throughout the Kent countryside. Growing to a length of eight to ten feet or more, a hop vine produces flowers arranged in a cone-shaped spike. These flowers, the hops, contain a bitter oil. It is this characteristic that, after the flower is dried, gives beer its bitter flavor. Depending on the type of beer, more or less hops are used in its brewing. Bitters, one of England's favorite types of beer, requires a greater amount of hops than most others.

After hops are picked, they are taken to the oast house and spread across a grid. A fire is lit under the grid, and the smoke rises up through the hops. The smoke kills any insects contained in the leaves and escapes through the opening at the top of the oast's inverted cone. Hours later, after the hops have dried out, they are put into hop pockets or sacks. They stay here until purchased by a merchant who will use them himself to produce beer or sell them to a brewery.

Bishops Oast House was around on the primary market for a fairly short time (1990-1992) which indicates that it didn't sell very well. This short retail life, however, may ultimately lead to a popular life on the secondary market, especially as more Dickens' Village Series® collectors learn about its history and how it is utilized.

I wonder if the *Oast House* would have been more popular when it was available at retailers if Department 56, Inc. made a wagon full of hops being delivered to or taken from the oast house. I think this would have helped convey the function of an oast. Maybe then its reception by collectors would have been better…instead of bitter.

the Village Chronicle.

NEPHEW FRED'S FLAT

ITEM #	INTRO	RETIRED	OSRP	GBTRU	↑
5557-3	1991	1994	$35	$75	7%

Particulars: Addition to *Christmas Carol* grouping. Taiwan piece is darker in color and approx. $\frac{1}{4}$" shorter than pieces from China. Four-story home with 3-story turret-like bow windows. Planters flank front door. Overhang window above side door with crow stepped coping in gable rising to two chimneys. Ivy grows up corner area—garlands, wreath, and Christmas greetings decorate facade.

'91	'92	'93	'94	'95	'96	'97
$35	35	36	36	65	65	70

OLD MICHAELCHURCH

ITEM #	INTRO	RETIRED	OSRP	GBTRU	NO
5562-0	1992	1996	$42	$60	CHANGE

Particulars: Stone base with lath and plaster filling space between timbered upper portion. Tower rises up front facade with heavy solid look, a simple four sided structure. Double wood doors at rear of church. Early release to Showcase Dealers and Gift Creations Concepts (GCC).

'92	'93	'94	'95	'96	'97
$42	46	46	48	48	60

CROWN & CRICKET INN

ITEM #	INTRO	RETIRED	OSRP	GBTRU	↓
5750-9	1992	1992 ANNUAL	$100	$165	3%

Particulars: 1st Edition in the Charles Dickens' Signature Series. Special collector box and hang tag. Three-story brick and stone with pillars flanking covered formal entry. Curved canopy roof on Golden Lion Arms Pub. Wrought iron balustrade outlines triple window on second floor. Dressed stone edges walls. Mansard roof with decorative trim and molding. The trim on the early pieces was light; later pieces had a darker gray trim.

'92	'93	'94	'95	'96	'97
$100	165	175	175	145	170

HEMBLETON PEWTERER

ITEM #	INTRO	RETIRED	OSRP	GBTRU	↓
5800-9	1992	1995	$72	$75	6%

Particulars: Timber framed with plaster in Elizabethan style. Bay windows create two-story front facade. Chimney Sweep shop with steep pitched roof hugs one side of the pewterer. Early issue has two small additions on right side, later issue has one large addition.

'92	'93	'94	'95	'96	'97
$72	72	72	72	75	80

KING'S ROAD POST OFFICE

ITEM #	INTRO	RETIRED	OSRP	GBTru	NO
5801-7	1992	CURRENT	$45	**$45**	CHANGE

Particulars: Simple four-sided stone three-story building with semicircular turret-like two-story rise out of window area. Entrance door surmounted by pediment just below post office sign. Triple flue chimney rises off back of building.

'92	'93	'94	'95	'96	'97
$45	45	45	45	45	45

THE PIED BULL INN

ITEM #	INTRO	RETIRED	OSRP	GBTru	NO
5751-7	1993	1993 ANNUAL	$100	**$150**	CHANGE

Particulars: 2nd Edition in the Charles Dickens' Signature Series. Special collector box and hang tag. Elizabethan style with wood and plaster upper stories and stone and brick lower levels. Front entry at side of Inn allows public rooms to be of good size to service guests and local folk.

'93	'94	'95	'96	'97
$100	160	145	150	150

PUMP LANE SHOPPES

ITEM #	INTRO	RETIRED	OSRP	GBTru	↓
5808-4	1993	1996	$112	**$135**	7%

Particulars: Set of 3 includes *Bumpstead Nye Cloaks & Canes*, #58085, *Lomas Ltd. Molasses*, #58086 and *W.M. Wheat Cakes & Puddings*, #58087.

see below

'93	'94	'95	'96	'97
$112	112	112	112	145

BUMPSTEAD NYE CLOAKS & CANES

ITEM #	INTRO	RETIRED	OSRP	GBTru	↑
58085	1993	1996	$37.50	**$50**	11%

Particulars: 1 of the 3-piece set—PUMP LANE SHOPPES. Tall narrow shop with timbered 2nd story. Front gable has design etched into trim. Shop was noted for cloaks and capes as well as canes and walking sticks.

'93	'94	'95	'96	'97
$37.50	37.50	27.50	37.50	45

GIGGELSWICK MUTTON & HAM

Item #	Intro	Retired	OSRP	GBTru	↑
5822-0	1994	1997	$48	**$55**	15%

Particulars: Midyear release. The town of Giggleswick is located in North Yorkshire. Butcher shop concentrates on meats from sheep and pigs. Smokehouse on side cures meat and adds special flavoring. Shop has corner wraparound windows.

'94	'95	'96	'97
$48	48	48	48

HATHER HARNESS

Item #	Intro	Retired	OSRP	GBTru	↑
5823-8	1994	1997	$48	**$55**	15%

Particulars: Stone, brick and stucco 3-story shop and family home. Double doors allow entry of horses, oxen, carriages and wagons to be fixed.

'94	'95	'96	'97
$48	48	48	48

PORTOBELLO ROAD THATCHED COTTAGES

Item #	Intro	Retired	OSRP	GBTru	↑
5824-6	1994	1997	$120	**$130**	8%

Particulars: Set of 3 includes *Mr. & Mrs. Pickle*, #58247, *Cobb Cottage*, #58248 and *Browning Cottage*, #58249.

see below

'94	'95	'96	'97
$120	120	120	120

MR. & MRS. PICKLE

Item #	Intro	Retired	OSRP	GBTru	↑
58247	1994	1997	$40	**$45**	13%

Particulars: 1 of the 3-piece set—PORTOBELLO ROAD THATCHED COTTAGES. Timbered stucco home with attached Antique Store. Home sign highlights a pickle.

'94	'95	'96	'97
$40	40	40	40

COBB COTTAGE

ITEM #	INTRO	RETIRED	OSRP	GBTRU	↑
58248	1994	1997	$40	**$45**	13%

Particulars: 1 of the 3 piece set—PORTOBELLO ROAD THATCHED COTTAGES. The thatched roof is being completed on a stucco, timber and brick home. First Heritage Village Collection® house without snow on the roof. Unique L-shape with ornate roof ridges.

'94	'95	'96	'97
$40	40	40	40

BROWNING COTTAGE

ITEM #	INTRO	RETIRED	OSRP	GBTRU	↑
58249	1994	1997	$40	**$45**	13%

Particulars: 1 of the 3-piece set—PORTOBELLO ROAD THATCHED COTTAGES. 2-story brick, timber and stucco home. Original thatch roof replaced by slate to denote increase in family's wealth. Dutch door entry.

'94	'95	'96	'97
$40	40	40	40

SIR JOHN FALSTAFF INN

ITEM #	INTRO	RETIRED	OSRP	GBTRU	↓
5753-3	1995	1995 ANNUAL	$100	**$125**	4%

Particulars: 4th Edition in the Charles Dickens' Signature Series. Special collector box and hang tag. This is based on the inn still located across the street from Gad's Hill Place, Dickens' last home. Three-story Inn of stucco, timber and brick with slate roof. Two-story bay windows frame front entry.

'95	'96	'97
$100	130	130

DICKENS' VILLAGE START A TRADITION SET

ITEM #	INTRO	RETIRED	OSRP	GBTRU	↓
5832-7	1995	1996	$85	**$115**	4%

Particulars: Set of 13. Starter Set was midyear release featured at National Homes For The Holidays Open House Event—Oct/Nov 1995. Special packaging for promotion. Set was also available during Event week of November 7–11, 1996. Set includes: *Faversham Lamps & Oil*—2-story shop/home w/stone trim on arched door/windows. Crowstepped roof edges. *Morston Steak And Kidney Pie*—Meat pies prepared in small 1 ½-story shop/home. *Town Square Carolers* accessory, 6 assorted sisal trees, Cobblestone Road & Bag of Real Plastic Snow.

'95	'96	'97
$85	85	120

J.D. NICHOLS TOY SHOP

ITEM #	INTRO	RETIRED	OSRP	GBTRU	
58328	1995	CURRENT	$48	**$50**	NO CHANGE

Particulars: Brightly lit front window, topped by ledge carrying store name, and trimmed with 3 potted trees, highlights toy shop. Tall front gables feature timber design. Brick chimneys rise from steeply pitched roof.

'95	'96	'97
$48	50	50

DURSLEY MANOR

ITEM #	INTRO	RETIRED	OSRP	GBTRU	
58329	1995	CURRENT	$50	**$55**	NO CHANGE

Particulars: Two plaques above entry state building name and year cornerstone placed. Brick with stone trim at windows, carriage portico, roof edging and the 3 chimneys.

'95	'96	'97
$50	50	55

BLENHAM STREET BANK

ITEM #	INTRO	RETIRED	OSRP	GBTRU	
58330	1995	CURRENT	$60	**$60**	NO CHANGE

Particulars: Many windows bring light and openness to squared building design. Strength and fortress-like solidarity promoted by use of stone, columns, and arches above windows. Double entry doors topped by fanlight window arch.

'95	'96	'97
$60	60	60

WRENBURY SHOPS

ITEM #	INTRO	RETIRED	OSRP	GBTRU
58331	1995	*	$100	*

Particulars: Set of 3 includes *Wrenbury Baker*, #58332, *The Chop Shop*, #58333 and *T. Puddlewick Spectacle Shop*, #58334. *Set is split between Current and Retired–2 out of the 3 from this set–*Wrenbury Baker* and *The Chop Shop* were retired in 1997.

see next page

'95	'96	'97
$100	100	100

WRENBURY BAKER

ITEM #	INTRO	RETIRED	OSRP	GBTRU	↑
58332	1995	1997	$35	**$40**	14%

Particulars: 1 of the 3-piece set—WRENBURY SHOPS. Cottage shop houses baker. 1 ½-story with roof line coming down to first floor. Single chimney rises through hand hewn roof. Sign outside by entry.

'95	'96	'97
$35	35	35

THE CHOP SHOP

ITEM #	INTRO	RETIRED	OSRP	GBTRU	↑
58333	1995	1997	$35	**$42**	20%

Particulars: 1 of the 3-piece set WRENBURY SHOPS. Large chimney with 4 flue pots rises through rough shingle roof. Sign outside entry advertises wares. Stucco facade.

'95	'96	'97
$35	35	35

T. PUDDLEWICK SPECTACLE SHOP

ITEM #	INTRO	RETIRED	OSRP	GBTRU	
58334	1995	CURRENT	$35	**$35**	NO CHANGE

Particulars: 1 of the 3-piece set—WRENBURY SHOPS. Ornate timber tudor style shop selling glasses, lorgnettes, looking glasses, monocles, and spyglasses. Sign outside advertises product.

'95	'96	'97
$35	35	35

THE MALTINGS

ITEM #	INTRO	RETIRED	OSRP	GBTRU	
5833-5	1995	CURRENT	$50	**$50**	NO CHANGE

Particulars: Midyear release. Home, shop and bridge in one construct of stone, stucco and wood. Large doors allow carts to enter. A malting is a building used to roast or malt barley for brewing beer and ale.

'95	'96	'97
$50	50	50

DUDDEN CROSS CHURCH

ITEM #	INTRO	RETIRED	OSRP	GBTRU	↑
5834-3	1995	1997	$45	**$55**	22%

Particulars: Midyear release. Brick church with stone coping. Bell tower rises on one side through roof. Stone archway to courtyard on other side near entry door.

'95	'96	'97
$45	45	45

THE GRAPES INN

ITEM #	INTRO	RETIRED	OSRP	GBTRU	NO
57534	1996	1996 ANNUAL	$120	**$135**	CHANGE

Particulars: 5th Edition in Charles Dickens' Signature Series. Inn on the waterfront supplies food, drink and lodging for weary travelers. Rowboats are tied up to rear unloading dock. Two staircases outside lead to inn or to pub and dining areas. Located in Limehouse, this Inn is said to be used as the model for the "Porters" in *Our Mutual Friend*.

'96	'97
$120	135

RAMSFORD PALACE

ITEM #	INTRO	RETIRED	OSRP	GBTRU	↓
58336	1996	LTD ED 27,500	$175	**$475**	4%

Particulars: Midyear release. Set of 17 includes *Ramsford Palace* and Accessories: *Palace Guards, Set/2, Palace Gate, Palace Fountain, Wall Hedge, Set/8, Corner Wall Topiaries, Set/4*. The building is modeled after Castle Howard in York. The mansion, built by the Earl of Carlisle, was begun in 1700. The south facade comprises a central block surmounted by a dome, between two wings. Corinthian pilasters accentuate the height.

'96	'97
$175	495

BUTTER TUB FARMHOUSE

ITEM #	INTRO	RETIRED	OSRP	GBTRU	NO
58337	1996	CURRENT	$40	**$40**	CHANGE

Particulars: Midyear release. Three steeply pitched red roof heights set off tall narrow chimneys. Door and windows have wood frames. High gables match roof heights on front facade. Butter Tub refers to a pass in Yorkshire where cool pools of water known as buttertubs form in potholes.

'96	'97
$40	40

BUTTER TUB BARN	ITEM # 58338	INTRO 1996	RETIRED CURRENT	OSRP $48	GBTRU $48	NO CHANGE

Particulars: Midyear release. Two separate barn areas share one steep roof. Wagons can enter through double wood doors or into central loading area.

	'96	'97
	$48	48

THE CHRISTMAS CAROL COTTAGE (REVISITED)	ITEM # 58339	INTRO 1996	RETIRED CURRENT	OSRP $60	GBTRU $60	NO CHANGE

Particulars: Midyear release. An addition to the *Christmas Carol Revisited Series*. A new expanded version of home of Bob and Mary Cratchit. Roof has 2 dormer windows. Two fireplaces now heat the house. A log pile against a large chimney holds a built-in Magic Smoking Element powered by a separate transformer that heats a supplied nontoxic liquid allowing smoke to rise out of the chimney.

	'96	'97
	$60	60

Why Butter Tub?

When the *Butter Tub Farmhouse and Barn* were introduced last year, they were well accepted— especially the barn because of its unique center passage. The quaint name of this piece also seems to fit nicely and to add to its popularity. But have you ever wondered why the pieces are named Butter Tub? It wasn't simply a cute name that the designer dreamed up in the middle of the night and gave to it the next morning, but actually has a story behind it.

Buttertubs (spelled as one word with an "s" as opposed to Department 56, Inc.'s two word, no "s" version) refers to an area in the hills of northwest Yorkshire, England. It's best described in a letter we received from Ed & Jean Rahn of Cincinnati.

In May/June of 1996, we were thrilled to have the opportunity to visit England as part of a Charles Dickens Tour. We extended the trip a few days for we had always wanted to visit the James Herriot country in Yorkshire.

Our one day bus tour in Yorkshire took us along many beautiful moors and dales. As our bus traveled northward out of Hawes into the moors and hills, we learned that in earlier days farm ladies traveled this route, taking their dairy products from their farms to the urbanized areas. This is the way those folks earned their "pin" money, so to speak.

The rugged terrain included numerous depressions in the mountain rock, brought about by the wind and rain over the centuries. These depressions were like bowls or tubs in which cold mountain water collected. When the travelers stopped in the area for a little food or rest, they placed their dairy products into these cold water tubs, leading to the name Buttertubs Pass.

Ed & Jean

the **Village Chronicle**.

NETTIE QUINN PUPPETS & MARIONETTES

ITEM #	INTRO	RETIRED	OSRP	GBTRU	NO
58344	1996	CURRENT	$50	**$50**	CHANGE

Particulars: Front of store features a puppet/marionette stage for performances to passing village folk. Decorations on stage and front facade of 3-story building advertise the wood carving craftsman's talents. This is the first Heritage Village Collection® building to feature multiple weathervanes.

'97
$50

MULBERRIE COURT BROWNSTONES

ITEM #	INTRO	RETIRED	OSRP	GBTRU	NO
58345	1996	CURRENT	$90	**$90**	CHANGE

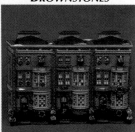

Particulars: Three identical attached town houses, #5, #6, #7 are three-story brick residences. Each entry door features a glass fanlight and each has a bow window on 1st & 2nd story. Individual room fireplace chimneys are grouped into one roof structure. Railing with gate separates home from passing strollers.

'97
$90

THE OLDE CAMDEN TOWN CHURCH (REVISITED)

ITEM #	INTRO	RETIRED	OSRP	GBTRU	NO
58346	1996	CURRENT	$55	**$55**	CHANGE

Particulars: An addition to the *Christmas Carol Revisited Series.* This is the church where Bob Cratchit and Tiny Tim spent Christmas morning in *A Christmas Carol.* Dickens may have used St. Stephen's Church in Camden as a model. Piece comes with a miniature storybook created and written by designers which sets scene for piece.

'97
$55

THE MELANCHOLY TAVERN (REVISITED)

ITEM #	INTRO	RETIRED	OSRP	GBTRU	NO
58347	1996	CURRENT	$45	**$45**	CHANGE

Particulars: An addition to the *Christmas Carol Revisited Series.* Tavern where Scrooge ate in *A Christmas Carol.* It is believed that Dickens developed his idea for the tavern from Baker's Chop Shop that once stood along Change Alley in London. Tall narrow timbered tavern offers brew and meals. Piece comes with a miniature storybook created and written by designers which sets scene for piece.

'97
$45

QUILLY'S ANTIQUES

ITEM #	INTRO	RETIRED	OSRP	GBTRU	NO
58348	1996	CURRENT	$46	**$46**	CHANGE

Particulars: Small town shop with entry and display window built out from front wall. Family lives in cramped upper floor quarters. Walkway crowded with antique objects and small items. Access to side yard through wood door.

'97
$46

GAD'S HILL PLACE

ITEM #	INTRO	RETIRED	OSRP	GBTRU	↑
57535	1997	1997 ANNUAL	$98	**$120**	22%

Particulars: 6th Edition in the Charles Dickens' Signature Series. Located in Kent, this was the last home of Dickens and the only one he ever owned. Three-story red brick home in Queen Anne period style. Balance established by center hall entry highlighted by pediment. Each side of home equals the other in rooms and window treatment. One chimney, bell tower and an attached gazebo displaying Christmas tree.

'97
$98

MANCHESTER SQUARE

ITEM #	INTRO	RETIRED	OSRP	GBTRU
58301	1997	CURRENT	$250	**$250**

Particulars: Set of 25. Four lighted buildings: *G. Choir's Weights & Scales, Frogmore Chemist, Custom House, Lydby Trunk & Satchel Shop.* Also included: Manchester Square Accessories, Set of 7, 12 Trees, Road and Snow. The *Custom House* features the first circular staircase with detailed metal rails and, in early shipments, had a bottomstamp that read "Dickens' Village Seires." (Only *Custom House* pictured.)

EAST INDIES TRADING CO.

ITEM #	INTRO	RETIRED	OSRP	GBTRU
58302	1997	CURRENT	$65	**$65**

Particulars: Three story brick and plaster trading company plus attached warehouse. Features an acrylic skylight. The original East India Company was a British trading company incorporated in 1600. Their primary business was exporting English woolen cloth and importing the products of the East Indies. **Canadian** Trading Co., #58306, (with a change of color and name) is a variation only available in Canada.

LEACOCK POULTERER (REVISITED)

ITEM #	INTRO	RETIRED	OSRP	GBTRU
58303	1997	CURRENT	$48	**$48**

Particulars: An addition to the *Christmas Carol Revisited Series*. Fresh game hangs outside front window to advertise shop. Stone chimneys rise on sides of tudor timber and plaster building.

CROOKED FENCE COTTAGE

ITEM #	INTRO	RETIRED	OSRP	GBTRU
58304	1997	CURRENT	$60	**$60**

Particulars: Thatched cottage with large stone fireplace chimney. Hanging metal birdcage and kitten are featured. Small crooked fence gave cottage its name. Before towns used a numbering system, houses and buildings were known by their unique architectural details. Early shipments had bottomstamp that read "Dickens' Village Seires."

ASHWICK LANE HOSE & LADDER

ITEM #	INTRO	RETIRED	OSRP	GBTRU
58305	1997	CURRENT	$54	**$54**

Particulars: Brick and stone 2 1/2-story firehouse has ornate coping design on front tower turret. Rails designed to have a swayed look surround top of tower and second story building area.

CANADIAN TRADING CO.

ITEM #	INTRO	RETIRED	OSRP	GBTRU
58306	1997	CURRENT	$65	**$65**

Particulars: Three story brick and plaster trading company plus attached warehouse. Features an acrylic skylight. Similar to *East Indies Trading Co.* with a change of color and name. This will only be available in Canada.

DICKENS' VILLAGE START A TRADITION SET

ITEM #	INTRO	RETIRED	OSRP	GBTRU	NO
58322	1997	CURRENT	$75*	**$100**	CHANGE

Particulars: Set of 13. Starter Set is midyear release featured at Department 56, Inc. National Homes For The Holidays Open House Event—11/1/97 to 11/9/97. *SRP reduced to $75 for the Event. Includes 2 lighted buildings: *Sudbury Church* and *Old East Rectory*. An accessory Set of 3, *The Spirit Of Giving*, a young lady and girl giving gift baskets of food for the poor to the Rector, a Cobblestone Road, 6 sisal trees and Real Plastic Snow complete the set .

'97
$100

J. LYTES COAL MERCHANT

ITEM #	INTRO	RETIRED	OSRP	GBTRU	NO
58323	1997	CURRENT	$50	**$50**	CHANGE

Particulars: Midyear release. A very tall building housing a coal merchant. Coverings for the upper windows are metal plates hinged to the window instead of glass panes. Original shipments had bottomstamps that read "Dickens' Vallage."

'97
$50

BARMBY MOOR COTTAGE

ITEM #	INTRO	RETIRED	OSRP	GBTRU	NO
58324	1997	CURRENT	$48	**$48**	CHANGE

Particulars: Midyear release. House is 1 ½-story built of stones from the moor. Front of home has one large gable highlighted by a carved barge-board. Above front door are two small gabled dormer windows. Barmby Moor is a village located east of York.

'97
$48

TOWER OF LONDON

ITEM #	INTRO	RETIRED	OSRP	GBTRU	↑
58500	1997	1997 ANNUAL	$165	**$345**	109%

Particulars: 1st Edition in Historical Landmark Series. Midyear release. Set of 5. Lighted main structure, non-lighted gate/tower, sign, raven master with 2 ravens, wall with 4 ravens. This, the White Tower, is one of the many towers that comprise the actual Tower Of London. Famous for housing a royal prison as well as the Crown Jewels. Legend says six ravens must be kept at the tower to preserve the monarchy.

'97
$165

NEW ENGLAND VILLAGE®

The second porcelain village to be introduced by Department 56, Inc. was New England Village® in 1986. It immediately captured the spirit and character of the six-state region. The coastline, farmlands, mountains, and valleys were all represented.

Throughout the years, there has been only one limited edition, *Smythe Woolen Mill*. Surprisingly, there have been introductions inspired by areas other than New England itself. These include two Pennsylvania farms, Jannes Mullet and A. Bieler; and the New York-based story, *The Legend Of Sleepy Hollow*. Most recently, the well-received designs of coastal homes and businesses have propelled New England Village's popularity to an all-time high.

THE BOTTOM LINE:

Cost of all pieces introduced to New England Village® through the 1998 midyear introductions, including variations: **$2,203**

GREENBOOK TruMarket Value of all pieces through the 1998 midyear introductions, including variations: **$7,855**

NEW ENGLAND VILLAGE® SINCE WE LAST MET...

... NEW FOR SALE LISTINGS

EAST WILLET POTTERY - 1997

There's another addition to foundry buildings that have been popping up in the Village during the past few years. Crocks and jars are the specialty of this firing house.

STEEN'S MAPLE HOUSE (SMOKING HOUSE) - 1997

This is the New England Village's® first smoking building. Here the Steen's make and sell syrup, candy and related products.

SEMPLE'S SMOKEHOUSE - 1997

If you found an old smokehouse in the mountains of northern New England, you would expect it to look like this "wood and stone" structure. Notice that there is very little snow on the building.

THE EMILY LOUISE - 1998

This impressive cargo ship that lights up has real string for its ropes and lines. A well-stocked dock completes the set of two.

... NO LONGER ON THE MARKET

5647-2	Blue Star Ice Co.
5651-0	Arlington Falls Church
5657-0	BREWSTER BAY COTTAGES, Set of 2
	• 56568 Jeremiah Brewster House
	• 56569 Thomas T. Julian House

WHAT GOES WHERE

THE LEGEND OF SLEEPY HOLLOW

Considered by many to be America's first highly praised writer, Washington Irving is best remembered for two tales that take place in the Hudson Valley, "Rip Van Winkle" and "The Legend Of Sleepy Hollow." Both of these stories appeared in Irving's *The Sketch Book* published in 1819.

"The Legend Of Sleepy Hollow" is often incorrectly referred to as "The Legend Of The Headless Horseman." This is because it is the mysterious rider who, with his head perched on the pommel of his saddle, sticks in the mind of the reader, not the main character, Ichabod Crane.

The story follows Crane, a schoolmaster from Connecticut, teaching in the nearby town in New York. This tall, lanky fellow had aspirations to wed Katrina Van Tassel, or more accurately, the wealth she would inherit. Crane had competition, however, in the likes of Brom Bones, a worthy suitor, indeed.

After attending a party at the Van Tassel farmhouse, Ichabod heads home in the dark of night. Along the way, just where it is said that goblins can be encountered, he is confronted by the headless horseman. A chase ensues, and, just as Ichabod reaches the point where the ghosts do not pass, he is knocked from his horse by a pumpkin that hits him in the head. Ichabod was never seen again, and the reason for his disappearance was never learned. Was it a mysterious ghost or Brom Bones?

Buildings:

SLEEPY HOLLOW, Set of 3	5954-4	1990-1993
• Sleepy Hollow School		
• Van Tassel Manor		
• Ichabod Crane's Cottage		
Sleepy Hollow Church	5955-2	1990-1993

Accessories:

Sleepy Hollow Characters, Set of 3	5956-0	1990-1992

NEW ENGLAND VILLAGE®

RETIRED BUILDINGS

5640-5	1995	McGrebe-Cutters & Sleighs
5642-1	1996	Bluebird Seed And Bulb
5643-0	1995	Yankee Jud Bell Casting
5644-8	1995	Stoney Brook Town Hall
5647-2	1997	Blue Star Ice Co.
5648-0	1996	A. BIELER FARM
56481	1996	Pennsylvania Dutch Farmhouse
56482	1996	Pennsylvania Dutch Barn
5651-0	1997	Arlington Falls Church
56568	1997	Jeremiah Brewster House
56569	1997	Thomas T. Julian House
5657-0	1997	BREWSTER BAY COTTAGES
5930-7	1994	Craggy Cove Lighthouse
5931-5	1989	Weston Train Station
5939-0	1990	CHERRY LANE SHOPS
5939-0	1990	Ben's Barbershop
5939-0	1990	Otis Hayes Butcher Shop
5939-0	1990	Anne Shaw Toys
5940-4	1991	Ada's Bed And Boarding House
5942-0	1991	Berkshire House
5943-9	1992	Jannes Mullet Amish Farm House
5944-7	1992	Jannes Mullet Amish Barn
5946-3	1994	Shingle Creek House
5947-1	1996	Captain's Cottage
5954-4	1993	SLEEPY HOLLOW
5954-4	1993	Sleepy Hollow School
5954-4	1993	Van Tassel Manor
5954-4	1993	Ichabod Crane's Cottage
5955-2	1993	Sleepy Hollow Church
6530-7	1989	NEW ENGLAND VILLAGE
6530-7	1989	Apothecary Shop
6530-7	1989	General Store
6530-7	1989	Nathaniel Bingham Fabrics
6530-7	1989	Livery Stable & Boot Shop
6530-7	1989	Steeple Church
6530-7	1989	Brick Town Hall
6530-7	1989	Red Schoolhouse
6538-2	1989	Jacob Adams Farmhouse And Barn
6539-0	1990	Steeple Church
6544-7	1990	Timber Knoll Log Cabin

LIMITED EDITION

6543-9	Smythe Woolen Mill	7,500

QUIKREFERENCE

GREENBOOK HISTORY LIST

ITEM #	NAME	ISSUED	RETIRED	GBTRU$
6530-7	NEW ENGLAND VILLAGE, Set/7	1986	1989	1150.00
6530-7	Apothecary Shop	1986	1989	100.00
6530-7	General Store	1986	1989	295.00
6530-7	Nathaniel Bingham Fabrics	1986	1989	170.00
6530-7	Livery Stable & Boot Shop	1986	1989	150.00
6530-7	Steeple Church—First Version	1986	1989	175.00
6530-7	Steeple Church—Second Version	1986	1989	105.00
6530-7	Brick Town Hall	1986	1989	200.00
6530-7	Red Schoolhouse	1986	1989	290.00
6538-2	Jacob Adams Farmhouse & Barn	1986	1989	555.00
5930-7	Craggy Cove Lighthouse	1987	1994	70.00
5931-5	Weston Train Station	1987	1989	275.00
6543-9	Smythe Woolen Mill	1987	Ltd Ed 7,500	1050.00
6544-7	Timber Knoll Log Cabin	1987	1990	180.00
5932-3	Old North Church	1988	Current	48.00
5939-0	CHERRY LANE SHOPS, Set/3	1988	1990	310.00
5939-0	Ben's Barbershop	1988	1990	110.00
5939-0	Otis Hayes Butcher Shop	1988	1990	95.00
5939-0	Anne Shaw Toys	1988	1990	170.00
5940-4	Ada's Bed & Boarding House—V. 1	1988	1991	295.00
5940-4	Ada's Bed & Boarding House—V. 2	1988	1991	140.00
5940-4	Ada's Bed & Boarding House—V. 3	1988	1991	125.00
5942-0	Berkshire House—Original Blue	1989	1991	155.00
5942-0	Berkshire House—Teal	1989	1991	100.00
5942-0	Berkshire House—Forest Green	1989	1991	90.00
5943-9	Jannes Mullet Amish Farm House	1989	1992	110.00
5944-7	Jannes Mullet Amish Barn	1989	1992	95.00
6539-0	Steeple Church	1989	1990	95.00
5946-3	Shingle Creek House	1990	1994	55.00
5947-1	Captain's Cottage	1990	1996	60.00
5954-4	SLEEPY HOLLOW, Set/3	1990	1993	205.00
5954-4	Sleepy Hollow School	1990	1993	95.00
5954-4	Van Tassel Manor	1990	1993	55.00
5954-4	Ichabod Crane's Cottage	1990	1993	55.00
5955-2	Sleepy Hollow Church	1990	1993	60.00
5640-5	McGrebe-Cutters & Sleighs	1991	1995	60.00
5642-1	Bluebird Seed And Bulb	1992	1996	55.00
5643-0	Yankee Jud Bell Casting	1992	1995	55.00
5644-8	Stoney Brook Town Hall	1992	1995	60.00
5647-2	Blue Star Ice Co.	1993	1997	55.00
5648-0	A. BIELER FARM, Set/2	1993	1996	110.00
56481	Pennsylvania Dutch Farmhouse	1993	1996	60.00
56482	Pennsylvania Dutch Barn	1993	1996	65.00

ITEM #	NAME	ISSUED	RETIRED	GBT$_{RU}$$
5651-0	Arlington Falls Church	1994	1997	50.00
5652-9	Cape Keag Fish Cannery	1994	Current	48.00
5653 7	Pigeonhead Lighthouse	1994	Current	50.00
5657-0	BREWSTER BAY COTTAGES, S/2	1995	1997	115.00
56568	Jeremiah Brewster House	1995	1997	60.00
56569	Thomas T. Julian House	1995	1997	60.00
56571	Chowder House	1995	Current	40.00
56572	Woodbridge Post Office	1995	Current	40.00
56573	Pierce Boat Works	1995	Current	55.00
56172	Apple Valley School	1996	Current	35.00
56574	J. Hudson Stoveworks	1996	Current	60.00
56575	Navigational Charts & Maps	1996	Current	48.00
56576	Bobwhite Cottage	1996	Current	50.00
56577	Van Guilder's Ornamental Ironworks	1997	Current	50.00
56578	East Willet Pottery	1997	Current	45.00
56579	Steen's Maple House	1997	Current	60.00
56580	Semple's Smokehouse	1997	Current	45.00
56581	The Emily Louise	1998	Current	70.00

NEW ENGLAND VILLAGE®

NEW ENGLAND VILLAGE

	ITEM #	INTRO	RETIRED	OSRP	GBTRU	↓
	6530-7	1986	1989	$170	**$1150**	10%

Particulars: Set of 7 includes *Apothecary Shop, General Store, Nathaniel Bingham Fabrics, Livery Stable & Boot Shop, Steeple Church, Brick Town Hall* and *Red Schoolhouse.* *In 1994, Set of 7 could be purchased for approximately 15% less than the sum of the individual pieces.

see below

'91	'92	'93	'94	'95	'96	'97
$650	950	1125	*	1250	1225	1275

APOTHECARY SHOP

	ITEM #	INTRO	RETIRED	OSRP	GBTRU	↓
	6530-7	1986	1989	$25	**$100**	5%

Particulars: 1 of the 7-piece set—NEW ENGLAND VILLAGE. Variegated fieldstone with white wood bay window. Gable and lean-to are blue clapboard.

'91	'92	'93	'94	'95	'96	'97
$70	80	88	92	100	100	105

GENERAL STORE

	ITEM #	INTRO	RETIRED	OSRP	GBTRU	↓
	6530-7	1986	1989	$25	**$295**	14%

Particulars: 1 of the 7-piece set—NEW ENGLAND VILLAGE. Round columns support full length covered porch. Two small dormers on roof with central chimney.

'91	'92	'93	'94	'95	'96	'97
$185	250	360	360	350	325	345

NATHANIEL BINGHAM FABRICS

	ITEM #	INTRO	RETIRED	OSRP	GBTRU	↑
	6530-7	1986	1989	$25	**$170**	6%

Particulars: 1 of the 7-piece set—NEW ENGLAND VILLAGE. Clapboard saltbox design fabric store and Post Office. Each shop has own chimney. Living quarters above larger fabric store.

'91	'92	'93	'94	'95	'96	'97
$85	125	150	150	150	160	160

LIVERY STABLE & BOOT SHOP

ITEM #	INTRO	RETIRED	OSRP	GBTRU	↓
6530-7	1986	1989	$25	**$150**	3%

Particulars: 1 of the 7-piece set—NEW ENGLAND VIL-LAGE. Two-story painted clapboard house with wood planked wing contains tannery and livery stable. Stable has stone chimney, double doors.

'91	'92	'93	'94	'95	'96	'97
$70	105	112	142	145	150	155

STEEPLE CHURCH— "FIRST VERSION"

ITEM #	INTRO	RETIRED	OSRP	GBTRU	↓
6530-7	1986	1989	$25	**$175**	3%

Particulars: 1 of the 7-piece set—NEW ENGLAND VIL-LAGE. Variations in this piece affect GBTru$. This is the First Version where the tree is attached with porcelain slip. Reissued in 1989 as #6539-0 when #6530-7 retired with the rest of the Original NEW ENGLAND VILLAGE Set.

'91	'92	'93	'94	'95	'96	'97
$65	130	155	175	175	185	180

STEEPLE CHURCH— "SECOND VERSION"

ITEM #	INTRO	RETIRED	OSRP	GBTRU	↑
6530-7	1986	1989	$25	**$105**	5%

Particulars: 1 of the 7-piece set—NEW ENGLAND VIL-LAGE. This is the Second Version where the tree is attached with glue. Building is a white clapboard church w/tier-2 steeple. Windows have molding above and below. Simple design.

'91	'92	'93	'94	'95	'96	'97
$-	-	100	100	95	100	

Left to right: Second Version, First Version. When viewed straight on, the First Version's tree does not touch the ground and appears level with first step.

NEW ENGLAND VILLAGE®

BRICK TOWN HALL

ITEM #	INTRO	RETIRED	OSRP	GBTRU	↓
6530-7	1986	1989	$25	**$200**	11%

Particulars: 1 of the 7-piece set—NEW ENGLAND VIL-LAGE. Mansard roof over two-story Town Hall. Cupola is centered on roof ridge between two brick chimneys. Windows trimmed with ornamental molding.

'91	'92	'93	'94	'95	'96	'97
$150	190	212	215	210	220	225

RED SCHOOLHOUSE

ITEM #	INTRO	RETIRED	OSRP	GBTRU	↑
6530-7	1986	1989	$25	**$290**	4%

Particulars: 1 of the 7-piece set—NEW ENGLAND VIL-LAGE. Red one-room wood school with stone chimney and open belfry. Generally heated by wood stove. Hand powered water pump by front door.

'91	'92	'93	'94	'95	'96	'97
$150	210	240	270	260	255	280

JACOB ADAMS FARMHOUSE

ITEM #	INTRO	RETIRED	OSRP	GBTRU	↓
6538-2	1986	1989	$65	**$555**	2%

Particulars: Set of 5. Two buildings–Farmhouse and Barn, 3 animals. Buildings light. Red multilevel wood barn atop a stone foundation. Stone silo attached. Home features front porch, small front bay window, butter churn by door, simple design. It is very unusual for these buildings to be sold separately. Because the animals were simply wrapped and placed in the box with no separate compartments, they are often damaged.

'91	'92	'93	'94	'95	'96	'97
$250	375	510	575	575	525	565

JACOB ADAMS BARN

CRAGGY COVE LIGHTHOUSE

ITEM #	INTRO	RETIRED	OSRP	GBTRU	NO CHANGE
5930-7	1987	1994	$35	$70	

Particulars: Keeper lives in small white clapboard home attached to lighthouse. Front porch of home features holiday decorated columns. Stone house foundation, whitewashed brick light tower.

'91	'92	'93	'94	'95	'96	'97
$44	45	45	45	60	60	70

WESTON TRAIN STATION

ITEM #	INTRO	RETIRED	OSRP	GBTRU	↓ 2%
5931-5	1987	1989	$42	$275	

Particulars: Luggage ramps lead to platform, where you purchase tickets and wait inside or on benches outside. Wheeled luggage cart stands on side of building. This station looks very much like the now-dilapidated station in Weston, MA.

'91	'92	'93	'94	'95	'96	'97
$165	215	248	265	275	260	280

SMYTHE WOOLEN MILL

ITEM #	INTRO	RETIRED	OSRP	GBTRU	↓ 3%
6543-9	1987	LTD ED 7,500	$42	$1050	

Particulars: Fabric woven for manufacturing into clothing, yard goods. Hydro powered by water wheel. Stone base with wood upper stories. Bales of wool stacked outside office door. Lower windows each with shutter.

'91	'92	'93	'94	'95	'96	'97
$1100	1235	1255	1255	1150	1050	1085

TIMBER KNOLL LOG CABIN

ITEM #	INTRO	RETIRED	OSRP	GBTRU	↑ 3%
6544-7	1987	1990	$28	$180	

Particulars: Two stone chimneys and fireplace provide heat and cooking facilities for rustic log cabin. Wood shakes comprise roof. One wing rises two stories.

'91	'92	'93	'94	'95	'96	'97
$75	95	130	150	165	165	175

NEW ENGLAND VILLAGE®

OLD NORTH CHURCH

ITEM #	INTRO	RETIRED	OSRP	GBTRU	NO
5932-3	1988	CURRENT	$40	**$48**	CHANGE

Particulars: This design is based on the famous historic landmark, Christ Church in Boston, where sexton Robert Newman hung lanterns in its steeple to warn colonists in Charlestown that the British were on their way to Lexington and Concord. Red brick church. First- and second-floor windows feature sunburst and/or spoke tops. Steeple rises from main entry. Belfry has tiered design.

'91	'92	'93	'94	'95	'96	'97
$42	44	45	45	45	45	48

CHERRY LANE SHOPS

ITEM #	INTRO	RETIRED	OSRP	GBTRU	↓
5939-0	1988	1990	$80	**$310**	10%

Particulars: Set of 3 includes *Ben's Barbershop, Otis Hayes Butcher Shop* and *Anne Shaw Toys.*

see below

'91	'92	'93	'94	'95	'96	'97
$175	215	275	NE	325	330	345

BEN'S BARBERSHOP

ITEM #	INTRO	RETIRED	OSRP	GBTRU	↓
5939-0	1988	1990	$27	**$110**	4%

Particulars: 1 of the 3-piece set—CHERRY LANE SHOPS. A barber pole hangs from front house corner next to a bench for customers. Water tower on roof supplies the shop's needs. Upstairs office used by a lawyer.

'91	'92	'93	'94	'95	'96	'97
$60	75	85	85	95	110	115

OTIS HAYES BUTCHER SHOP

ITEM #	INTRO	RETIRED	OSRP	GBTRU	↑
5939-0	1988	1990	$27	**$95**	6%

Particulars: 1 of the 3-piece set—CHERRY LANE SHOPS. Dutch door entry, stone side walls, brick front. Small size and thick walls plus river/lake ice helped keep meat fresh.

'91	'92	'93	'94	'95	'96	'97
$55	65	68	75	75	80	90

ANNE SHAW TOYS

ITEM #	INTRO	RETIRED	OSRP	GBTRU	↓
5939-0	1988	1990	$27	**$170**	3%

Particulars: 1 of the 3 piece set—CHERRY LANE SHOPS. Large front windows with window boxes allow a look at toys for sale. Molding beneath floor edge and squared shape give roof a turret look and feel.

'91	'92	'93	'94	'95	'96	'97
$80	115	125	150	160	155	175

ADA'S BED AND BOARDING HOUSE—"VERSION 1"

ITEM #	INTRO	RETIRED	OSRP	GBTRU	↑
5940-4	1988	1991	$36	**$295**	4%

Particulars: There are three color and mold variations that affect GBTru$. The first version is lemon yellow in color, the rear steps are part of the building's mold, and there are alternating yellow panes on the second-story windows. Building is a large family home converted to a bed and breakfast for travelers. Double chimneys. Central cupola and wraparound front porch.

'91	'92	'93	'94	'95	'96	'97
$37.50	310	300	300	325	310	285

ADA'S BED AND BOARDING HOUSE—"VERSION 2"

ITEM #	INTRO	RETIRED	OSRP	GBTRU	↓
5940-4	1988	1991	$36	**$140**	10%

Particulars: The second version is a paler yellow but the same mold as Version 1–the rear steps are part of the building's mold.

'91	'92	'93	'94	'95	'96	'97
$37.50	150	160	195	150	165	155

ADA'S BED AND BOARDING HOUSE—"VERSION 3"

ITEM #	INTRO	RETIRED	OSRP	GBTRU	↓
5940-4	1988	1991	$36	**$125**	4%

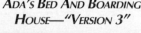

Particulars: The third version is pale yellow in color and a different mold where the rear steps are an add on—not part of the the building's mold. In this version the second-story windows have yellow panes in the top half only.

'91	'92	'93	'94	'95	'96	'97
$37.50	85	105	125	125	125	130

NEW ENGLAND VILLAGE®

BERKSHIRE HOUSE— "ORIGINAL BLUE"

ITEM #	INTRO	RETIRED	OSRP	GBTRU	↓
5942-0	1989	1991	$40	**$155**	3%

Particulars: Variations in color affect GBTru$: "Original Blue," "Teal," or "Forest Green." This is the "Original Blue." Building is a Dutch colonial inn with two front entries, half porch, five dormered windows on front, second-story mansard roof.

'91	'92	'93	'94	'95	'96	'97
$40	125	140	150	150	160	160

BERKSHIRE HOUSE— "TEAL"

ITEM #	INTRO	RETIRED	OSRP	GBTRU	↓
5942-0	1989	1991	$40	**$100**	9%

Particulars: This is the "Teal" house.

'91	'92	'93	'94	'95	'96	'97
$40	95	95	95	100	110	110

BERKSHIRE HOUSE— "FOREST GREEN"

ITEM #	INTRO	RETIRED	OSRP	GBTRU	
5942-0	1989	1991	$40	**$90**	NO CHANGE

Particulars: This is the "Forest Green" house.

'91	'92	'93	'94	'95	'96	'97
-	-	-	-	NE	NE	NE

JANNES MULLET AMISH FARM HOUSE

ITEM #	INTRO	RETIRED	OSRP	GBTRU	↓
5943-9	1989	1992	$32	**$110**	4%

Particulars: White frame house, fenced yard on side, two chimneys, gutter and leader to barrel to collect rain water. Along with the *Jannes Mullet Amish Barn,* this is the first "non-New England" piece to be added to the New England Village®.

'91	'92	'93	'94	'95	'96	'97
$32	32	85	100	110	110	115

JANNES MULLET AMISH BARN

ITEM #	INTRO	RETIRED	OSRP	GBTRU	NO
5944-7	1989	1992	$48	**$95**	CHANGE

Particulars: Wood and fieldstone with attached sheds and silo, Amish family black buggy stands at barn entrance. Along with the *Jannes Mullet Amish Farm House,* this is the first "non-New England" piece to be added to the New England Village®.

'91	'92	'93	'94	'95	'96	'97
$48	48	86	98	90	90	95

STEEPLE CHURCH

ITEM #	INTRO	RETIRED	OSRP	GBTRU	↑
6539-0	1989	1990	$30	**$95**	19%

Particulars: Reissue—see 1986 *Steeple Church,* #6530-7. White clapboard church with steeple. Windows have molding above and below. Simple design.

'91	'92	'93	'94	'95	'96	'97
$65	85	85	85	90	90	80

SHINGLE CREEK HOUSE

ITEM #	INTRO	RETIRED	OSRP	GBTRU	↓
5946-3	1990	1994	$37.50	**$55**	8%

Particulars: Saltbox design with chimney rising from mid-roof. Windows have shutters and molding on top and base. Attached shed on one side, with storm cellar doors and fenced side entrance. Early release to Showcase Dealers and the National Association Of Limited Edition Dealers (NALED).

'91	'92	'93	'94	'95	'96	'97
$37.50	40	40	40	45	55	60

CAPTAIN'S COTTAGE

ITEM #	INTRO	RETIRED	OSRP	GBTRU	↑
5947-1	1990	1996	$40	**$60**	9%

Particulars: 2 ½-story has balcony full length of 2nd story. Enclosed staircase on house side to second floor. A connected double dormer is centered on front roof between two ridge chimneys.

'91	'92	'93	'94	'95	'96	'97
$40	40	42	42	44	45	55

NEW ENGLAND VILLAGE®

STONEY BROOK TOWN HALL

ITEM #	INTRO	RETIRED	OSRP	GBTRU	NO
5644-8	1992	1995	$42	**$60**	CHANGE

Particulars: Rectangular brick building serves as meeting hall for town governance. Side entry with a latch gate, cellar windows with shutters, roof dormers and two chimneys, and many windows on long sides of building complete structure.

'92	'93	'94	'95	'96	'97
$42	42	42	42	60	60

BLUE STAR ICE CO.

ITEM #	INTRO	RETIRED	OSRP	GBTRU	↑
5647-2	1993	1997	$45	**$55**	15%

Particulars: Stone 1st story with insulated wood upper storage level. Wooden chute enabled ice block to be pulled up where sawdust or salt hay insulated each block.

'93	'94	'95	'96	'97
$45	45	48	48	48

A. BIELER FARM

ITEM #	INTRO	RETIRED	OSRP	GBTRU	↓
5648-0	1993	1996	$92	**$110**	4%

Particulars: Set of 2 includes *Pennsylvania Dutch Farmhouse*, #56481 and *Pennsylvania Dutch Barn*, #56482.

see below

'93	'94	'95	'96	'97
$92	92	95	95	115

PENNSYLVANIA DUTCH FARMHOUSE

ITEM #	INTRO	RETIRED	OSRP	GBTRU	↓
56481	1993	1996	$42	**$60**	8%

Particulars: 1 of the 2-piece set—A. BIELER FARM. Two-story clapboard home. Many windowed to let in light, colorful trim on all windows, roof and wall moldings.

'93	'94	'95	'96	'97
$42	42	43.50	43.50	65

PENNSYLVANIA DUTCH BARN

Item #	Intro	Retired	OSRP	GBTru	NO
56482	1993	1996	$50	**$65**	CHANGE

Particulars: 1 of the 2-piece set A. BIELER FARM. Red barn with green mansard roof. Two stone silos on one corner. Double door entry reached by stone supported ramp. Hex signs hung on barn outer walls.

'93	'94	'95	'96	'97
$50	50	51.50	51.50	65

ARLINGTON FALLS CHURCH

Item #	Intro	Retired	OSRP	GBTru	↑
5651-0	1994	1997	$40	**$50**	19%

Particulars: Midyear release. Wood church with steeple rising in tiers above main entry. Pillars at front doors are wrapped in garlands. Double tier of windows on side of church to let in daylight. Simple structure with a country look.

'94	'95	'96	'97
$40	42	42	42

CAPE KEAG FISH CANNERY

Item #	Intro	Retired	OSRP	GBTru	NO
5652-9	1994	CURRENT	$48	**$48**	CHANGE

Particulars: Lobster pots, buoys are stacked on wharf along building front. Brick tower rising on side of factory cannery allows visual check of fishing boats.

'95	'96	'97
$48	48	48

PIGEONHEAD LIGHTHOUSE

Item #	Intro	Retired	OSRP	GBTru	NO
5653-7	1994	CURRENT	$50	**$50**	CHANGE

Particulars: Light shines from porthole windows. Tower connects to keeper's home. Steps lead down from rocks to water.

'95	'96	'97
$50	50	50

NEW ENGLAND VILLAGE®

BREWSTER BAY COTTAGES

Item #	Intro	Retired	OSRP	GBTRU	↑
5657-0	1995	1997	$90	**$115**	28%

Particulars: Set of 2 includes *Jeremiah Brewster House,* #56568 and *Thomas T. Julian House,* #56569.

see below

	'95	'96	'97
	$90	90	90

THOMAS T. JULIAN HOUSE

Item #	Intro	Retired	OSRP	GBTRU	↑
56569	1995	1997	$45	**$60**	33%

Particulars: 1 of the 2-piece set—BREWSTER BAY COTTAGES. Midyear release. Central chimney rises where 4 gabled roof meets. 2-story bay windowed turret next to covered porch entry. The boxes of the first pieces shipped read "Jeremiah Brewster House." When the mistake was noticed, Department 56, Inc. applied a sticker with the correct name over the incorrect one. Later shipments have the correct name printed directly on the box.

	'95	'96	'97
	$45	45	45

JEREMIAH BREWSTER HOUSE

Item #	Intro	Retired	OSRP	GBTRU	↑
56568	1995	1997	$45	**$60**	33%

Particulars: 1 of the 2-piece set—BREWSTER BAY COTTAGES. Midyear release. Shed roof side addition attached to main square 2-story house. Shuttered windows, widow's walk on roof. The boxes of the first pieces shipped read "Thomas T. Julian House." When the mistake was noticed, Department 56, Inc. applied a sticker with the correct name over the incorrect one. Later shipments have the correct name printed directly on the box.

	'95	'96	'97
	$45	45	45

CHOWDER HOUSE

Item #	Intro	Retired	OSRP	GBTRU	
56571	1995	Current	$40	**$40**	NO CHANGE

Particulars: Small cozy eating establishment sits on fieldstone base. Small boats can tie up to one side while another entry serves walk-ins. Blue clapboard with a mansard roof.

	'95	'96	'97
	$40	40	40

WOODBRIDGE POST OFFICE

Item #	Intro	Retired	OSRP	GBTru	NO
56572	1995	Current	$40	**$40**	CHANGE

Particulars: Two-story brick post office serves village for mail, stamps, parcels and postal cards. Windows flank double entry doors.

'95	'96	'97
$40	40	40

PIERCE BOAT WORKS

Item #	Intro	Retired	OSRP	GBTru	NO
56573	1995	Current	$55	**$55**	CHANGE

Particulars: Boats for lobstermen and fishermen are built at the boat works. Wooden building with double doors allow boats to be pulled or rolled down ramp. Rowboat held on winch and pulley rig on side of building.

'95	'96	'97
$55	55	55

APPLE VALLEY SCHOOL

Item #	Intro	Retired	OSRP	GBTru	NO
56172	1996	Current	$35	**$35**	CHANGE

Particulars: Midyear release. Small squared brick and stone village school. Tall central chimney connects to stove to keep schoolrooms heated. Bell tower in front gable.

'96	'97
$35	35

J. HUDSON STOVEWORKS

Item #	Intro	Retired	OSRP	GBTru	NO
56574	1996	Current	$60	**$60**	CHANGE

Particulars: Manufacturer of stoves combines shop and foundry. Stone and brick factory attached to office. Stoves are on display outside front door. Foundry is powered by coal and wood furnaces.

'97
$60

NEW ENGLAND VILLAGE®

NAVIGATIONAL CHARTS & MAPS

ITEM #	INTRO	RETIRED	OSRP	GBTRU	
56575	1996	CURRENT	$48	**$48**	NO CHANGE

Particulars: Business provides information for sea and river vessels to travel the waterways safely. 2 1/2-story with stone base and clapboard upper levels. Double stairs hug front facade with door entry on second story. Seagulls rest on roof which also has weathervane

'97
$48

BOBWHITE COTTAGE

ITEM #	INTRO	RETIRED	OSRP	GBTRU	
56576	1996	CURRENT	$50	**$50**	NO CHANGE

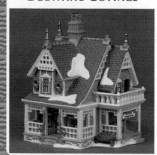

Particulars: 1 1/2-story home with front and side porches. Porch design features square and octagonal fretwork. Steep pitched roof has front dormer. Upper side bedroom has door to sun porch protected by balustrade railing. The house is named for a North American Quail or Partridge native to this area.

'97
$50

VAN GUILDER'S ORNA-MENTAL IRONWORKS

ITEM #	INTRO	RETIRED	OSRP	GBTRU	
56577	1997	CURRENT	$50	**$50**	NO CHANGE

Particulars: Midyear release. Third building in the village that pertains to metal craftsmanship. A sign on the front of the building announces that weathervanes are available. It is the first New England Village® building with multiple weathervanes.

'97
$50

EAST WILLET POTTERY

ITEM #	INTRO	RETIRED	OSRP	GBTRU
56578	1997	CURRENT	$45	**$45**

Particulars: Shop with an attached kiln to fire pottery. Assorted pottery containers are displayed on ground in front of shop windows.

STEEN'S MAPLE HOUSE

ITEM #	INTRO	RETIRED	OSRP	GBTRU
56579	1997	CURRENT	$60	**$60**

Particulars: Cottage shop sells products made from maple tree sap boiled into syrup on the premises. Stone foundation supports a clapboard building. Cast iron burner produces the valued product. With magic smoking element to produce smoke.

SEMPLE'S SMOKEHOUSE

ITEM #	INTRO	RETIRED	OSRP	GBTRU
56580	1997	CURRENT	$45	**$45**

Particulars: Stone and wood shop that specializes in slow cooking and curing of meats by burning different woods to create special smoky flavors in the finished product. Cords of firewood stacked outside.

THE EMILY LOUISE

ITEM #	INTRO	RETIRED	OSRP	GBTRU
56581	1998	CURRENT	$70	**$70**

Particulars: Set of 2. Midyear release. Ship is inspired by cargo-carrying packet ships popular in the 1800's. Double masted with tiny rope used to create the rigging. Dock is second piece of the set. (Ship is lighted.)

Insuring Your Collection

Whether it is a *clink,* a *crack,* or a *crash,* there are very few sounds that will strike fear into the heart of a collector like these will. The first thought is "no, it couldn't have happened!" Then you see it...it's over...it's gone. One of the most cherished pieces you own has been broken. What are you going to do? How can you ever replace it?

Replacing a piece, be it a building or accessory, is relatively easy. But, you must take the proper precautions <u>before</u> anything happens.

continued page 192

NEW ENGLAND VILLAGE®

Insuring Your Collection

continued from 191

Many collectors do not see the need to have a separate rider with their insurance company just to cover their collections. Others have such a vast number of retired pieces that they would not dare have them uninsured any more than they would not have their car, home, or other highly valuable object insured.

When or if you do look into insuring your collection, meet with the agent so you can show him photos and price guides. This will help him understand what it is you are talking about. Remember, most agents have never heard of Department 56, Inc. Many collectors have had good luck using the analogy of baseball cards or older, more well-known collectibles such as Hummels to assist the agents in understanding the product.

Discuss with the agent the manner in which the pieces retire, rise and fall in value (mostly rise) and are traded, bought and sold. Don't forget to include the subjects of swap & sells and room hops. If you will be bringing collectibles to other locations to sell them, will they be covered?

What happens if a piece is merely chipped? Is the piece insured if *you* break it? What if just the box and sleeve get damaged? Ask these and every other question you can think of that pertains to how you collect now and how you think you may collect in the future. When the agent says that you are covered or will be covered for a particular circumstance, ask where in the policy it is stated. This will confirm that the agent understands your needs and that you are covered in case of a loss. Many insurance companies have a "fine arts" rider that will be useful for covering collectibles, and other companies are now offering "collectible riders."

Once you are covered, you will be responsible for updating the values of the insured items. Do this once a year or sooner if a piece experiences a substantial increase in value. A good time for this is when your annual payment is due, in January, or any date that you will easily remember each year.

The more evidence you have of your collection, the better it will be if you need to make a claim. Take photos or videotape your collection. If using a camcorder, take advantage of its audio capabilities and elaborate about the article you are taping, i.e. variation, edition number, where and when you purchased or received it, original cost, and current value. If you have numbered limited editions, record the numbers. Photograph them individually as well as in their setting in your house. Make duplicates of the photos or video. Keep one set in the house for reference and one off-site, perhaps in a safe deposit box. Keep receipts with the second set, if possible.

If you do insure your collection, we hope it is a precaution that will never have to be called upon. If you are unfortunate and have to turn to this solution, however, remember that there is often a silver lining.

We have seen photos of a couple's display that is very unusual. The most attention-grabbing part of their display is the result of their house burning. Many of their pieces were broken, but one in particular was badly charred, yet unbroken. When they were able to create a display again, they placed that charred piece right in with the rest. They took the firefighters and engine from the Christmas In The City Series® and placed them on the scene of their "fire." With a flickering bulb lit inside the charred building, and cotton "smoke" flowing from the tops of the windows, the couple can sit back, watch a building burn, and enjoy it this time.

the **Village Chronicle.**

ALPINE VILLAGE SERIES™

Alpine Village Series™, the third porcelain village, was introduced in 1986. It represents a Bavarian town featuring businesses, farms, and homes that dot the mountainsides and valleys throughout the Alps.

This slow-to-grow village has never had a limited edition. In fact, it wasn't until 1997 that it first received a midyear introduction. The attractiveness of its latest introductions, as well as its slow growth, has captured the interest of many collectors.

THE BOTTOM LINE:

Cost of all pieces introduced to the Alpine Village Series™ through the 1998 midyear introductions, including variations: **$791**

GREENBOOK TruMarket Value of all pieces through the 1998 midyear introductions, including variations: **$2,358**

ALPINE VILLAGE SERIES™ SINCE WE LAST MET...

... NEW FOR SALE LISTINGS

SPIELZEUG LADEN (TOY STORE) - 1997

Children of the Village now have a store to buy toys and games. It features a whimsical FAO Schwarz-type clock on its tower.

FEDERBETTEN UND STEPPDECKEN (FEATHER BEDS & QUILTS) - 1997

What would an alpine village be without those overstuffed feather beds and colorful quilts? This shop will be supplying them to the villagers.

... NO LONGER ON THE MARKET

56190 Metterniche Wurst
5953-6 Grist Mill
65407 Apotheke
65408 E. Staubr Backer

RETIRED BUILDINGS

5615-4	Bahnhof
56190	Metterniche Wurst
5952-8	Josef Engel Farmhouse
5953-6	Grist Mill
6540-4	ALPINE VILLAGE, Set of 5
65405	• Besson Bierkeller
65406	• Gasthof Eisl
65407	• Apotheke
65408	• E. Staubr Backer
65409	• Milch-Kase
6541-2	Alpine Church

GREENBOOK HISTORY LIST

ITEM #	NAME	ISSUED	RETIRED	GBTru$
6540-4	ALPINE VILLAGE, Set/5	1986	96 & 97	210.00
65405	Besson Bierkeller	1986	1996	45.00
65406	Gasthof Eisl	1986	1996	40.00
65407	Apotheke	1986	1997	45.00
65408	E. Staubr Backer	1986	1997	45.00
65409	Milch-Kase	1986	1996	45.00
5952-8	Josef Engel Farmhouse	1987	1989	995.00
6541-2	Alpine Church—White Trim	1987	1991	375.00
6541-2	Alpine Church—Dark Trim	1987	1991	175.00
5953-6	Grist Mill	1988	1997	45.00
5615-4	Bahnhof	1990	1993	80.00
5617-0	St. Nikolaus Kirche	1991	Current	37.50
5618-9	ALPINE SHOPS, Set/2	1992	*	*
56190	Metterniche Wurst	1992	1997	45.00
56191	Kukuck Uhren	1992	Current	37.50
5612-0	Sport Laden	1993	Current	50.00
5614-6	Bakery & Chocolate Shop	1994	Current	37.50
56171	Kamm Haus	1995	Current	42.00
56173	Danube Music Publisher	1996	Current	55.00
56174	Bernhardiner Hundchen	1997	Current	50.00
56192	Spielzeug Laden	1997	Current	65.00
56176	Federbetten Und Steppdecken	1998	Current	48.00

ALPINE VILLAGE SERIES™

ALPINE CHURCH— "DARK TRIM"

	ITEM #	INTRO	RETIRED	OSRP	GBTRU	↑
	6541-2	1987	1991	$32	**$175**	9%

Particulars: This is the "Dark Trim."

'91	'92	'93	'94	'95	'96	'97
$36	85	112	155	165	155	160

GRIST MILL

	ITEM #	INTRO	RETIRED	OSRP	GBTRU	NO
	5953-6	1988	1997	$42	**$45**	CHANGE

Particulars: Irregular shingle roofing tops the mill that grinds corn and wheat into meal and flour.

'91	'92	'93	'94	'95	'96	'97
$44	45	45	45	45	45	45

BAHNHOF

	ITEM #	INTRO	RETIRED	OSRP	GBTRU	↓
	5615-4	1990	1993	$42	**$80**	6%

Particulars: (Train Station) Stucco upper wall atop tiled lower wall. Ticket window in base of tower rises through roof and repeats tile design. The first pieces have gilded trim. Subsequent pieces have a yellow/mustard trim.

'91	'92	'93	'94	'95	'96	'97
$42	42	42	85	70	70	85

ST. NIKOLAUS KIRCHE

	ITEM #	INTRO	RETIRED	OSRP	GBTRU	NO
	5617-0	1991	CURRENT	$37.50	**$37.50**	CHANGE

Particulars: Designed after Church Of St. Nikolaus in Oberndorf, Austria. Bell tower rises above front entry, topped by onion dome. Set-in rounded arched windows accent nave sides. Pebble-dash finish on surface walls. The home of the Christmas hymn "Silent Night, Holy Night."

'91	'92	'93	'94	'95	'96	'97
$37.50	37.50	37.50	37.50	37.50	37.50	37.50

ALPINE SHOPS

	Item #	Intro	Retired	OSRP	GBTru
	5618-9	1992	*	$75	*

Particulars: Set of 2 includes *Metterniche Wurst,* #56190 and *Kukuck Uhren,* #56191. *Set is split between Current and Retired–*Metterniche Wurst* was retired in 1997.

see below

'92	'93	'94	'95	'96	'97
$75	75	75	75	75	75

METTERNICHE WURST

	Item #	Intro	Retired	OSRP	GBTru	↑
	56190	1992	1997	$37.50	**$45**	20%

Particulars: 1 of the 2-piece set—ALPINE SHOPS. (Sausage Shop) Stucco over stone and brick with steeply pitched roof coming down to first floor on sides. Front facade framed by ornamental curved coping.

'92	'93	'94	'95	'96	'97
$37.50	37.50	37.50	37.50	37.50	37.50

KUKUCK UHREN

	Item #	Intro	Retired	OSRP	GBTru	NO
	56191	1992	Current	$37.50	**$37.50**	CHANGE

Particulars: 1 of the 2-piece set—ALPINE SHOPS. (Clock Shop) Franc Schiller displays his trademark clock on shop sign above recessed entry door. Small shop has wood timbers that outline the stone, brick and stucco exterior.

'92	'93	'94	'95	'96	'97
$37.50	37.50	37.50	37.50	37.50	37.50

SPORT LADEN

	Item #	Intro	Retired	OSRP	GBTru	NO
	5612-0	1993	Current	$50	**$50**	CHANGE

Particulars: Shop for skiing and winter sports equipment. Small shop tucked away on one side. Roof overhangs protect facade and chimneys are capped to keep out snow, ice and rain.

'93	'94	'95	'96	'97
$50	50	50	50	50

BAKERY & CHOCOLATE SHOP

ITEM #	INTRO	RETIRED	OSRP	GBTRU	NO
5614-6	1994	CURRENT	$37.50	**$37.50**	CHANGE

Particulars: (Konditorei Schokolade) Garland and banners hang down from the second-story balcony. The extended eaves protect the building from heavy snows.

'94	'95	'96	'97
$37.50	37.50	37.50	37.50

KAMM HAUS

ITEM #	INTRO	RETIRED	OSRP	GBTRU	NO
56171	1995	CURRENT	$42	**$42**	CHANGE

Particulars: "House On The Crest" is the translation of this Alpine building's name. Long stairs lead up to the main balcony and front door of the skiers' inn. Roof overhangs offer protection from icing. Large fireplace at rear of roof has a cap to keep snow from falling in.

'95	'96	'97
$42	42	42

DANUBE MUSIC PUBLISHER

ITEM #	INTRO	RETIRED	OSRP	GBTRU	NO
56173	1996	CURRENT	$55	**$55**	CHANGE

Particulars: The Donau Musik Verlag continues onion dome roof motif on store facade and attached music studio which announces violin lessons. Dressed stone outlines windows, doorways and corners on main facade while pargeting carved in ornamental patterns highlights studio.

'97
$55

BERNHARDINER HUNDCHEN

ITEM #	INTRO	RETIRED	OSRP	GBTRU	NO
56174	1997	CURRENT	$50	**$50**	CHANGE

Particulars: Midyear release. Kennels and training center for St. Bernard puppies and dogs. The breed is known for endurance and ability to track and rescue people lost or injured in snowy mountainous regions.

'97
$50

ALPINE VILLAGE SERIES™

SPIELZEUG LADEN

ITEM #	INTRO	RETIRED	OSRP	GBTRU
56192	1997	CURRENT	$65	**$65**

Particulars. Two story toy shop trimmed with gingerbread design cutouts on railing, door and clock tower.

FEDERBETTEN UND STEPPDECKEN

ITEM #	INTRO	RETIRED	OSRP	GBTRU
56176	1998	CURRENT	$48	**$48**

Particulars: Midyear release. Featherbeds and quilts are the products of this shop with some of the wares on display on the railings and front fence. Goose down and feathers are used in product design to provide toasty sleeping on wintry nights.

Working With Brokers

Buying and selling retired pieces through established secondary market brokers can be a fun and rewarding experience. There are a few things you should keep in mind, however, to ensure that your venture is a successful one.

By selling collectibles through a secondary market broker, collectors have very little involvement in the actual selling process. Collectors simply contact the broker, tell him which items that they want to have listed and wait for a call. The broker places the items in listings that he sends out to collectors. When the broker sells a piece, he calls the seller to have the piece sent to the broker's office. The broker then checks the piece for damage, and if all is fine, sends it to the buyer. After the transaction is completed, the broker forwards a check to the seller, less the broker's commission.

Before working with a broker, there are a few things that you will want to discuss together. What commission rate does the brokerage use? Is there a charge, other than the commission, for listing a piece? How long after sending the piece to the broker can you expect to have your check?

One thing that you have to take into consideration when listing something with a broker is how much money you want to receive when the item is sold. Realize that if a piece currently has a secondary value of $300, for example, you more than likely will not be receiving all of that $300. The broker will be taking a commission from that money leaving you with slightly less. It is well worth the difference when you factor in what it would cost you in time and phone bills to complete the transaction yourself.

continued page 202

ALPINE VILLAGE SERIES™

Working With Brokers

continued from 201

Continuing with this same scenario, if you ask to receive $300, after the broker adds in the commission, the final selling price of your piece will be higher than what others are selling their pieces for. This is much like selling an actual house through a real estate agent. If houses in your neighborhood are selling for $100,000, you will receive approximately $94,000 once the agent's commission is deducted. If you raise your selling price to $106,000 to cover the commission, you may price yourself out of the market.

Another fact that you should know when dealing with brokers is how they price their listings. Some list the price before their commission, and you must add in their percentage and shipping fees yourself in order to determine the final price. Most brokers, however, show the final prices in their listings. All you have to do is add the shipping fees. You must remember these important details when it comes to comparing prices of two or more brokers.

Simply listing a piece with a broker is no guarantee that it will sell. A broker sells lowest priced pieces first. If your listing is higher priced than the other listings of like pieces, yours may sit unsold for quite awhile. You will do yourself justice if you ask the broker for advice when setting a selling price.

When listing with a broker, there is generally no obligation to sell the piece through that particular broker. This being the case, you still can try to sell your items through other means—including other brokers. One thing brokers do ask is that if you do sell an item that you have listed with them, you contact them and let them know that it has been sold. Doing this enables them to remove your piece from their listings and avoid disappointing a collector who is interested in your piece.

When making your purchases through secondary brokers, you may not be able to inspect the piece before deciding to buy it, however the broker is inspecting it for you. You also have the opportunity to inspect it once you receive it. Do not overlook this point! The ultimate responsibility of ensuring your new piece is in good condition is yours.

Once the piece arrives, check it immediately. Run your finger around the edges to feel for a small chip. If it is a building you are inspecting, go to a dark room, put the light inside the building, turn it on and look at the piece closely once again. Then put it aside, but not away. Check the piece in the same manner the next day. This is when problems are often found. If there is something that you are not comfortable with, call the person or company who sold you the piece and inform him about your finding. He will then let you know how to go about resolving the problem.

Don't let it get to this point before knowing how you can resolve such problems. Before agreeing to purchase a piece, always ask the broker what the policy is should you not like the condition of the piece once it arrives. By keeping yourself informed about the broker's policies, you can be confident that you will be satisfied in the end.

the **Village Chronicle**.

CHRISTMAS IN THE CITY®

The hustle and bustle of Christmas In the big city was made available to collectors when Department 56, Inc. introduced its fourth porcelain village, Christmas In The City®, in 1987. This representation of a large city instantly brought collectors back to the days of holiday shopping before the advent of sprawling suburban malls. Many collectors imagined that Christmas In The City® represented New York City, but Department 56, Inc. never confirmed this, not until 1996, anyway. It was then that *Grand Central Railway Station* was introduced.

Christmas In The City® has had two limited editions, *Dorothy's Dress Shop* and the *Cathedral Church Of St. Mark*. It was the *Cathedral Church Of St. Mark* that drew attention when its planned production of 17,500 was curtailed at 3,024 due to production problems.

THE BOTTOM LINE:

Cost of all pieces introduced to Christmas In The City® through the 1998 midyear introductions, including variations: **$2,582**

GREENBOOK TruMarket Value of all pieces through the 1998 midyear introductions, including variations: **$8,345**

CHRISTMAS IN THE CITY® SINCE WE LAST MET...

... NEW FOR SALE LISTINGS

JOHNSON'S GROCERY & DELI - 1997

This colorful building features foods and breads in bins outside the store. This is the second corner grocer for the Series.

THE CAPITOL - 1997

Did you ever realize that the City is a capital? Well, it is. This stately government building is the perfect addition or alternative to City Hall.

RIVERSIDE ROW SHOPS - 1997

This dinimutive row of three businesses is the answer for those who are seeking smaller buildings. It includes a bank, barber shop, and stationary store.

THE GRAND MOVIE THEATER - 1998

Memories of seeing movies on the big screen will come to you when you see this tall, thin movie house. Its semi-circular ticket booth features a gold roof.

Scottie's Toy Shop Gift Set - 1998

This ten piece set features a die-cast window with three-dimensional toys inside. Its characters have been designed so they are able to be looking in the window.

...NO LONGER ON THE MARKET

5534-4 Hollydale's Department Store
5881-5 Brokerage House
5882-3 First Metropolitan Bank
5887-4 Ivy Terrace Apartments

RETIRED BUILDINGS		
5531-0	1996	UPTOWN SHOPPES
55311	1996	Haberdashery
55312	1996	Music Emporium
55313	1996	City Clockworks
5534-4	1997	Hollydale's Department Store
5536-0	1995	Red Brick Fire Station
5537-9	1994	Wong's In Chinatown
5538-7	1995	"Little Italy" Ristorante
5543-3	1993	Arts Academy
5544-1	1994	The Doctor's Office
5880-7	1996	WEST VILLAGE SHOPS
58808	1996	Potter's Tea Seller
58809	1996	Spring St. Coffee House
5881-5	1997	Brokerage House
5882-3	1997	First Metropolitan Bank
5887-4	1997	Ivy Terrace Apartments
5961-7	1989	Sutton Place Brownstones
5962-5	1990	The Cathedral
5963-3	1989	Palace Theatre
5968-4	1991	Chocolate Shoppe
5969-2	1991	City Hall
5970-6	1992	Hank's Market
5972-2	1990	Variety Store
5973-0	1994	Ritz Hotel
5977-3	1992	5607 Park Avenue Townhouse
5978-1	1992	5609 Park Avenue Townhouse
6512-9	1990	CHRISTMAS IN THE CITY
6512-9	1990	Toy Shop And Pet Store
6512-9	1990	Bakery
6512-9	1990	Tower Restaurant

LIMITED EDITIONS

5549-2 Cathedral Church Of St. Mark
          3,024
5974-9 Dorothy's Dress Shop
          12,500

QUIKREFERENCE

GREENBOOK HISTORY LIST

ITEM #	NAME	ISSUED	RETIRED	GBTᴿᵤ$
5961-7	Sutton Place Brownstones	1987	1989	895.00
5962-5	The Cathedral	1987	1990	350.00
5963-3	Palace Theatre	1987	1989	940.00
6512-9	CHRISTMAS IN THE CITY, Set/3	1987	1990	625.00
6512-9	Toy Shop And Pet Store	1987	1990	250.00
6512-9	Bakery	1987	1990	125.00
6512-9	Tower Restaurant	1987	1990	285.00
5968-4	Chocolate Shoppe	1988	1991	150.00
5969-2	City Hall—Proof	1988	1991	200.00
5969-2	City Hall	1988	1991	185.00
5970-6	Hank's Market	1988	1992	90.00
5972-2	Variety Store	1988	1990	185.00
5973-0	Ritz Hotel	1989	1994	80.00
5974-9	Dorothy's Dress Shop	1989	Ltd Ed 12,500	390.00
5977-3	5607 Park Avenue Townhouse	1989	1992	90.00
5978-1	5609 Park Avenue Townhouse	1989	1992	90.00
5536-0	Red Brick Fire Station	1990	1995	85.00
5537-9	Wong's In Chinatown	1990	1994	80.00
5534-4	Hollydale's Department Store	1991	1997	90.00
5538-7	"Little Italy" Ristorante	1991	1995	85.00
5542-5	All Saints Corner Church	1991	Current	110.00
5543-3	Arts Academy	1991	1993	80.00
5544-1	The Doctor's Office	1991	1994	80.00
5549-2	Cathedral Church Of St. Mark	1991	Ltd Ed 3,024	2050.00
5531-0	UPTOWN SHOPPES, Set/3	1992	1996	185.00
55311	Haberdashery	1992	1996	60.00
55312	Music Emporium	1992	1996	70.00
55313	City Clockworks	1992	1996	70.00
5880-7	WEST VILLAGE SHOPS, Set/2	1993	1996	120.00
58808	Potter's Tea Seller	1993	1996	65.00
58809	Spring St. Coffee House	1993	1996	65.00
5881-5	Brokerage House	1994	1997	60.00
5882-3	First Metropolitan Bank	1994	1997	75.00
5883-1	Heritage Museum Of Art	1994	Current	96.00
5887-4	Ivy Terrace Apartments	1995	1997	70.00
58875	Holy Name Church	1995	Current	96.00
58876	Brighton School	1995	Current	52.00
58877	BROWNSTONES ON THE SQUARE, Set/2	1995	Current	90.00
58878	Beekman House	1995	Current	45.00
58879	Pickford Place	1995	Current	45.00
58880	Washington Street Post Office	1996	Current	52.00
58881	Grand Central Railway Station	1996	Current	90.00
58882	Cafe Caprice French Restaurant	1996	Current	45.00

CHRISTMAS IN THE CITY®

ITEM #	NAME	ISSUED	RETIRED	GBTRU$
58883	The City Globe	1997	Current	65.00
58884	Hi-De-Ho Nightclub	1997	Current	52.00
58886	Johnson's Grocery & Deli	1997	Current	60.00
58887	The Capitol	1997	Current	110.00
58888	Riverside Row Shops	1997	Current	52.00
58870	The Grand Movie Theater	1998	Current	50.00
58871	Scottie's Toy Shop			
	Exclusive Gift Set	1998	1998 Annual	65.00

CHRISTMAS IN THE CITY®

SUTTON PLACE BROWNSTONES

Item #	Intro	Retired	OSRP	GBTru	↑
5961-7	1987	1989	$80	**$895**	2%

Particulars: Three multistoried homes, attached via shared common walls. Three shops occupy semi-below ground-level space. Attic dormer windows have iron grillwork. "Sutton Place Rowhouse" is inscribed on the bottom, not "Sutton Place Brownstones." It's common for a piece to have a concave back wall, however, one with a relatively straight wall can be found and is generally considered to be more valuable.

	'91	'92	'93	'94	'95	'96	'97
	$425	760	775	825	825	845	875

THE CATHEDRAL

Item #	Intro	Retired	OSRP	GBTru	↓
5962-5	1987	1990	$60	**$350**	1%

Particulars: Twin spires, early Gothic design and decorated windows set this Cathedral apart. Stone church incorporates a fortress-like solidness. The first version is smaller, darker, and has snow on the steps. The second version is larger, lighter, and has no snow on the steps.

	'91	'92	'93	'94	'95	'96	'97
	$220	285	305	330	335	340	355

PALACE THEATRE

Item #	Intro	Retired	OSRP	GBTru	↑
5963-3	1987	1989	$45	**$940**	1%

Particulars: Mask of Comedy & Tragedy are bas-reliefs on brick building featuring Christmas Show of Nutcracker. Stage entrance on side of building. The first version is smaller and has more snow on the roof. The first version has gilded trim; the second version has yellow/mustard trim. It's not unusual for a piece to have concave or convex walls, however, a piece with relatively straight walls can be found and is generally considered to be more valuable.

	'91	'92	'93	'94	'95	'96	'97
	$450	1100	1025	925	925	890	935

CHRISTMAS IN THE CITY

Item #	Intro	Retired	OSRP	GBTru	↑
6512-9	1987	1990	$112	**$625**	6%

Particulars: Set of 3 includes *Toy Shop And Pet Store, Bakery* and *Tower Restaurant.*

see next page

	'91	'92	'93	'94	'95	'96	'97
	$250	290	335	375	475	565	590

TOY SHOP AND PET STORE

ITEM #	INTRO	RETIRED	OSRP	GBTRU	↓
6512-9	1987	1990	$37.50	**$250**	9%

Particulars: 1 of the 3-piece set—CHRISTMAS IN THE CITY. Side by side Pet Store and Toy Shop. Tucked in at side is Tailor Shop. Ground floor has extra high ceiling with half circle windows. Individual pieces may vary in color. The earlier pieces are very dark, later ones are lighter.

'91	'92	'93	'94	'95	'96	'97
$85	115	120	150	220	235	275

BAKERY

ITEM #	INTRO	RETIRED	OSRP	GBTRU	↑
6512-9	1987	1990	$37.50	**$125**	9%

Particulars: 1 of the 3-piece set—CHRISTMAS IN THE CITY. Four-story building with Bakery on first two levels. Iron grill work for safety and decor on smaller windows. Two different height chimneys. Individual pieces may vary in color. The earlier pieces are light, later ones are darker.

'91	'92	'93	'94	'95	'96	'97
$80	80	95	95	95	100	115

TOWER RESTAURANT

ITEM #	INTRO	RETIRED	OSRP	GBTRU	↑
6512-9	1987	1990	$37.50	**$285**	4%

Particulars: 1 of the 3-piece set—CHRISTMAS IN THE CITY. Multisided tower structure is integral part of residential building. Double door entry to restaurant/cafe. Iron grillwork on upper tower windows. Individual pieces may vary in color. The earlier pieces are very dark, later one are lighter. Box reads "Tower Cafe," bottom has no name.

'91	'92	'93	'94	'95	'96	'97
$110	130	165	175	200	235	275

CHOCOLATE SHOPPE

ITEM #	INTRO	RETIRED	OSRP	GBTRU	NO
5968-4	1988	1991	$40	**$150**	CHANGE

Particulars: Paneled roof between first and second story extends to shop signs. Building over Shoppe rises three stories plus attic. Above Brown Brothers Bookstore is one short story plus attic. Stone facade has heart panels at base while bookstore has sign and canopy over window. Individual pieces may vary in color. The earlier pieces are dark, later ones are lighter. The roof of the attached bookstore is most often not level. None of the variations affect GBTru$.

'91	'92	'93	'94	'95	'96	'97
$45	90	90	110	100	135	150

CHRISTMAS IN THE CITY®

CITY HALL—"PROOF"

ITEM #	INTRO	RETIRED	OSRP	GBTRU	↑
5969-2	1988	1991	$65	**$200**	3%

Particulars: This piece is smaller than the regular City Hall. It came in a foam box with no sleeve or light cord.

'91	'92	'93	'94	'95	'96	'97
$	225	215	200	185	195	195

CITY HALL

ITEM #	INTRO	RETIRED	OSRP	GBTRU	↑
5969-2	1988	1991	$65	**$185**	9%

Particulars: Imposing fortress with four towers at corners plus repeat design on clock tower. Broad steps plus large columns establish entry doors. Stone arches accent first-floor windows plus tower window. Planters with evergreens on either side of steps.

'91	'92	'93	'94	'95	'96	'97
$75	150	150	150	155	160	170

HANK'S MARKET

ITEM #	INTRO	RETIRED	OSRP	GBTRU	↑
5970-6	1988	1992	$40	**$90**	6%

Particulars: This piece is also referred to as "Corner Grocer." Boxes and barrels of produce are on display. Rolled awnings over sign. Brick building with painted brick on upper sections of second story. Two upper windows are multi-paned with half-circle sunburst, other window has awning. Two chimneys on steeply pitched roof.

'91	'92	'93	'94	'95	'96	'97
$45	45	78	78	80	85	85

VARIETY STORE

ITEM #	INTRO	RETIRED	OSRP	GBTRU	↑
5972-2	1988	1990	$45	**$185**	3%

Particulars: The mold used for this building is the same one used for the *Drugstore*, #672-6, in the Bachman's Hometown Series. The design was based on a building in Stillwater, MN. Corner store in two-story brick building. Garland decorated awnings extend out to shelter display windows and shoppers. Separate door for upper story. Next door shop is barbershop with striped pole outside. Small eyeglass shop completes trio.

'91	'92	'93	'94	'95	'96	'97
$100	105	108	135	150	165	180

RITZ HOTEL

ITEM #	INTRO	RETIRED	OSRP	GBTRU	NO
5973-0	1989	1994	$55	**$80**	CHANGE

Particulars: Red doors complete columned entryway, red window canopy over each second story French window. Stone, block, and brick building. Cupola on attic window. Slate roof.

'91	'92	'93	'94	'95	'96	'97
$55	55	55	55	65	75	80

DOROTHY'S DRESS SHOP

ITEM #	INTRO	RETIRED	OSRP	GBTRU	↑
5974-9	1989	LTD ED 12,500	$70	**$390**	3%

Particulars: Bright green door and awning, bay windows on first and second floor, mansard roof.

'91	'92	'93	'94	'95	'96	'97
$350	355	370	370	350	375	380

5607 PARK AVENUE TOWNHOUSE

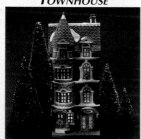

ITEM #	INTRO	RETIRED	OSRP	GBTRU	↑
5977-3	1989	1992	$48	**$90**	6%

Particulars: Four stories with ground floor card and gift shop, curved corner turret, blue canopy over double French door entry. Earlier pieces had gilded trim at top of building, later production had dull gold colored paint. This does not affect secondary market value.

'91	'92	'93	'94	'95	'96	'97
$48	50	78	81	80	80	85

5609 PARK AVENUE TOWNHOUSE

ITEM #	INTRO	RETIRED	OSRP	GBTRU	↑
5978-1	1989	1992	$48	**$90**	6%

Particulars: Four stories with ground floor art gallery, double wood doors lead to apartments, blue canopy over entry. Earlier pieces had gilded trim at top of building, later production has dull gold colored paint. This does not affect secondary market value.

'91	'92	'93	'94	'95	'96	'97
$48	50	78	82	80	80	85

RED BRICK FIRE STATION

ITEM #	INTRO	RETIRED	OSRP	GBTRU	↑
5536-0	1990	1995	$55	**$85**	6%

Particulars: Brick Station House for Hook & Ladder Company. Large wood doors lead to equipment with separate door for upper level. Stone block detailing on turret and above upper floor windows. Formal pediment at front gate.

'91	'92	'93	'94	'95	'96	'97
$55	55	55	55	55	75	80

WONG'S IN CHINATOWN

ITEM #	INTRO	RETIRED	OSRP	GBTRU	NO
5537-9	1990	1994	$55	**$80**	CHANGE

Particulars: Chinese restaurant and a laundry in brick building. Canopy over entry and at roof feature pagoda shape. Fire escape for second- and third-story tenants. Chinese writing: Above the door –"Good Luck," on right side of the building– "Cantonese Cuisine," on left side of building–"Laundry," and on the Wong's sign–"Restaurant." In the first version the top window is red. In the second version the top window is gold.

'91	'92	'93	'94	'95	'96	'97
$55	55	55	55	70	70	80

HOLLYDALE'S DEPARTMENT STORE

ITEM #	INTRO	RETIRED	OSRP	GBTRU	↑
5534-4	1991	1997	$75	**$90**	6%

Particulars: First shipments are from Taiwan and have holly on the first floor canopies only. The second version is from China and has holly on all canopies. The third version is from the Philippines. Building has corner curved front with awnings on windows, domed cupola, skylights on roof, and carved balustrade design on second story windows highlight store.

'91	'92	'93	'94	'95	'96	'97
$75	75	85	85	85	85	85

"LITTLE ITALY" RISTORANTE

ITEM #	INTRO	RETIRED	OSRP	GBTRU	NO
5538-7	1991	1995	$50	**$85**	CHANGE

Particulars: Three-story tall, narrow, stucco finish upper level above brick street level entry. Outdoor cafe serving pizza is on side.

'91	'92	'93	'94	'95	'96	'97
$50	50	52	52	52	75	85

WEST VILLAGE SHOPS

Item #	Intro	Retired	OSRP	GBTru	
5880-7	1993	1996	$90	**$120**	NO CHANGE

Particulars: Set of 2 includes *Potter's Tea Seller*, #58808 and *Spring St. Coffee House*, #58809.

see below

'93	'94	'95	'96	'97
$90	90	90	90	120

POTTER'S TEA SELLER

Item #	Intro	Retired	OSRP	GBTru	↑
58808	1993	1996	$45	**$65**	8%

Particulars: 1 of the 2-piece set—WEST VILLAGE SHOPS. Stone 3-story shop serves tea by the cup or pot. Stone arches decorate windows. Green awing covers upper window above entry. Sign hangs in front of door to alert shoppers.

'93	'94	'95	'96	'97
$45	45	45	45	60

SPRING ST. COFFEE HOUSE

Item #	Intro	Retired	OSRP	GBTru	
58809	1993	1996	$45	**$65**	NO CHANGE

Particulars: 1 of the 2-piece set—WEST VILLAGE SHOPS. Four-story narrow building. Steps lead to entry door covered by small pillared portico. Buy beans ground to order & blended for taste, or have a cup at the shop. Lower level is brick, upper stories are stucco.

'93	'94	'95	'96	'97
$45	45	45	45	65

BROKERAGE HOUSE

Item #	Intro	Retired	OSRP	GBTru	↑
5881-5	1994	1997	$48	**$60**	25%

Particulars: Stone building gives impression of invincibility. Four pillars support large entry pediment which has name of Exchange carved into stone. Feeling of wealth is reinforced by gold embellishments. "18" is symbolic of initial Department 56, Inc. stock offering at $18.00. "Price & Price" is in honor of Mr. & Mrs. Price. Judith Price is Department 56, Inc.'s Ms. Lit Town.

'94	'95	'96	'97
$48	48	48	48

First Metropolitan Bank

Item #	Intro	Retired	OSRP	GBTru	↑
5882-3	1994	1997	$60	$75	25%

Particulars: Domed, three-story building presents solid edifice. Four columns reach to third story and create covered entry and area for name inscription. Bank has gilt trim on dome, windows and door.

'94	'95	'96	'97
$60	60	60	60

Heritage Museum Of Art

Item #	Intro	Retired	OSRP	GBTru	NO
5883-1	1994	Current	$96	$96	CHANGE

Particulars: A stately, symmetrical structure with large windows. Names of famous artists are displayed around the top of the building and Thomas Nast's rendition of Santa Claus is on display above the entrance.

'94	'95	'96	'97
$96	96	96	96

Ivy Terrace Apartments

Item #	Intro	Retired	OSRP	GBTru	↑
5887-4	1995	1997	$60	$70	17%

Particulars: Midyear release. 3-story brick building with two canopy covered entries. 3rd-floor apartment has terrace with wrought iron enclosure.

'95	'96	'97
$60	60	60

Holy Name Church

Item #	Intro	Retired	OSRP	GBTru	NO
58875	1995	Current	$96	$96	CHANGE

Particulars: Brick church with entry and steeple with ornate pediment and molding topped by golden dome and cross. Stained glass fills rose window and lancet windows. Niche for statuary in steeple. Ribbed roof with carved design in ridge edging. Design adaptation— Cathedral of the Immaculate Conception, Kansas City, MO.

'95	'96	'97
$96	96	96

CHRISTMAS IN THE CITY®

HI-DE-HO NIGHTCLUB

Item #	Intro	Retired	OSRP	GBTru	NO
58884	1997	Current	$52	**$52**	CHANGE

Particulars: Midyear release. Posters on three-story red brick nightclub highlight present and future club acts. Marquee over double door entry. Club name highlights a Cab Calloway jazz riff.

'97
$52

JOHNSON'S GROCERY & DELI

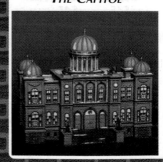

Item #	Intro	Retired	OSRP	GBTru
58886	1997	Current	$60	**$60**

Particulars: Corner store typical of NY's Soho district for groceries, produce, baked goods and prepared ready-to-eat take-out. Combination of three shops create a one-stop shop. Brick construction with awnings over windows and produce bins. Some second story windows have ornamental ironwork.

THE CAPITOL

Item #	Intro	Retired	OSRP	GBTru
58887	1997	Current	$110	**$110**

Particulars: Fortress like formal edifice is softened by the domes on the four corners and the central gold trimmed rotunda. Golden lions guard the rotunda. Broad steps lead up to the main entrance.

RIVERSIDE ROW SHOPS

Item #	Intro	Retired	OSRP	GBTru
58888	1997	Current	$52	**$52**

Particulars: Clustered together tightly along the riverside, these three shops include the North Branch of the National Bank, the Riverside Barber Shop and the Crosby & Smith Stationers. Made of red brick, each shop has its own facade design. Pillars flank the Bank entry and night deposit box and a barber pole hangs outside the barber shop.

THE GRAND MOVIE THEATER

ITEM #	INTRO	RETIRED	OSRP	GBTRU
58870	1998	CURRENT	$50	**$50**

Particulars: Midyear release. Colorful design of movie theater is fashioned after early movie houses in the cities. Ticket stall is designed as an attachment and painted with 18 karat gold. Double entry doors flank ticket booth.

SCOTTIE'S TOY SHOP EXCLUSIVE GIFT SET

ITEM #	INTRO	RETIRED	OSRP	GBTRU
58871	1998	1998 ANNUAL	$65	**$65**

Particulars: Set of 10. Gift Set is midyear release featured at Department 56, Inc.'s National Home For The Holidays Open House Event 11/5/98 - 11/9/98. Established in 1904, this 3 story toy emporium has a large bay window to display toys. Doors flank large window. Holiday wreaths decorate windows and doors. Accessory Set of 3, 5¢ Pony Rides features children and a pony on a spring and metal base. Also included are 4 sisal trees, Cobblestone Road and 1.5 oz. Bag Of Fresh Fallen Snow.

Q & A

Q. I've heard that the electro-mechanical items produced by Department 56, Inc. have a warranty. Is this true?

A. Yes, they do. All the village-related electro-mechanical items sold by Department 56, Inc. carry a one year warranty.

the **Village Chronicle.**

Q & A

Q. Why does Department 56, Inc. classify some pieces as "village accessories"?

A. The items that are placed in this category are those that can be used in either The Original Snow Village® and/or any of The Heritage Village Collections®. These may include such items as lights, trees, bridges, etc.

the **Village Chronicle.**

North Pole Series™

How could Department 56, Inc. have introduced a more appropriate Christmas series than the North Pole Series™? The sixth porcelain series features the make believe world of Santa's village complete with his workshop, toy shops, candy makers, elves and reindeer.

North Pole Series™ received its first limited piece in 1997 when *Elsie's Gingerbread* was introduced.

North Pole Series™ was an instant hit when it debuted in 1990. Collectors of other villages added it to their collections and non-collectors became collectors. This Series, with its universal appeal, may someday be the most popular village offered by Department 56, Inc.

THE BOTTOM LINE:

Cost of all pieces introduced to North Pole Series™ through the 1998 midyear introductions, including variations: **$1,758**

GREENBOOK TruMarket Value of all pieces through the 1998 midyear introductions, including variations: **$2,417**

The North Pole Series™ Since We Last Met...

... NEW FOR SALE LISTINGS

Mrs. Claus' Greenhouse - 1997

Now we know that Mrs. Claus does more than just bake cookies and keep Santa on schedule. You can look through the greenhouse windows and see the plants growing inside.

Glass Ornament Works - 1997

Fragile is a word that can't be taken too lightly in a shop that makes glass ornaments. Some ornaments adorn the building.

Santa's Light Shop - 1997

Here's another of Santa's ventures. The lights around the sign are lit by the bulb inside the building. What else would you expect for a light shop?

Elsie's Gingerbread - 1997

North Pole Series™ has its first limited building. Limited to the year of production 1998, this building is also the Village's first smoking building.

... NO LONGER ON THE MARKET

5633-2	Elfin Snow Cone Works
5634-0	Beard Barber Shop
5635 9	North Pole Dolls & Santa's Bear Works
5638-3	Tin Soldier Shop
56388	Popcorn & Cranberry House

RETIRED BUILDINGS

5600-6	1993	Santa's Workshop
56016	1996	Elf Bunkhouse*
5620-0	1995	NeeNee's Dolls And Toys
5621-9	1995	NORTH POLE SHOPS
5621-9	1995	Orly's Bell & Harness Supply
5621-9	1995	Rimpy's Bakery
5622-7	1995	Tassy's Mitten & Hassel's Woolies
5624-3	1996	Obbie's Books & Letrinka's Candy
5625-1	1996	Elfie's Sleds & Skates
5628-6	1996	Santa's Woodworks
5633-2	1997	Elfin Snow Cone Works
5634-0	1997	Beard Barber Shop
5635-9	1997	North Pole Dolls & Santa's Bear Works
5638-3	1997	Tin Soldier Shop
56388	1997	Popcorn & Cranberry House
56390	1996	North Pole Start A Tradition Set
56390	1996	Candy Cane & Peppermint Shop
56390	1996	Gift Wrap & Ribbons

*Note: Only 1 of the 2 buildings in NORTH POLE, Set of 2, was retired. 56015, Reindeer Barn, has not been retired.

HOMES FOR THE HOLIDAYS

56390	North Pole Start A Tradition Set, 1996

CANDY CANE LANE, Set of 2
- Candy Cane Lane & Peppermint Shop Building
- Gift Wrap & Ribbons Building
- Candy Cane Elves Accessory

GREENBOOK History List

ITEM #	NAME	ISSUED	RETIRED	GBTRU$
5600-6	Santa's Workshop	1990	1993	395.00
5601-4	NORTH POLE, Set/2	1990	*	*
56015	Reindeer Barn	1990	Current	40.00
56016	Elf Bunkhouse	1990	1996	60.00
5620-0	NeeNee's Dolls And Toys	1991	1995	60.00
5621-9	NORTH POLE SHOPS, Set/2	1991	1995	135.00
5621-9	Orly's Bell & Harness Supply	1991	1995	70.00
5621-9	Rimpy's Bakery	1991	1995	75.00
5622-7	Tassy's Mitten & Hassel's Woolies	1991	1995	80.00
5623-5	Post Office	1992	Current	50.00
5624-3	Obbie's Books & Letrinka's Candy	1992	1996	85.00
5625-1	Elfie's Sleds & Skates	1992	1996	60.00
5626-0	North Pole Chapel	1993	Current	45.00
5627-8	North Pole Express Depot	1993	Current	48.00
5628-6	Santa's Woodworks	1993	1996	65.00
5629-4	Santa's Lookout Tower	1993	Current	48.00
5633-2	Elfin Snow Cone Works	1994	1997	55.00
5634-0	Beard Barber Shop	1994	1997	40.00
5635-9	North Pole Dolls &			
	Santa's Bear Works	1994	1997	115.00
5638-3	Tin Soldier Shop	1995	1997	60.00
56384	Elfin Forge & Assembly Shop	1995	Current	65.00
56385	Weather & Time Observatory	1995	Current	50.00
56386	Santa's Rooming House	1995	Current	50.00
56387	Elves' Trade School	1995	Current	50.00
56388	Popcorn & Cranberry House	1996	1997	80.00
56389	Santa's Bell Repair	1996	Current	45.00
56390	North Pole Start A Tradition Set	1996	1996	110.00
56391	Route 1, North Pole,			
	Home Of Mr. & Mrs. Claus	1996	Current	110.00
56392	Hall Of Records	1996	Current	50.00
56393	Christmas Bread Bakers	1996	Current	55.00
56394	The Glacier Gazette	1997	Current	48.00
56395	Mrs. Claus' Greenhouse	1997	Current	68.00
56396	Glass Ornament Works	1997	Current	60.00
56397	Santa's Light Shop	1997	Current	52.00
56398	Elsie's Gingerbread	1997	1998 Annual	65.00

Santa's Workshop

Item #	Intro	Retired	OSRP	GBTru	↓
5600-6	1990	1993	$72	**$395**	6%

Particulars: Multi-chimnied, many gabled home and workshop. Stone foundation with stucco and timber upper stories. Balconies extend off windows and hold garlands. Mailbox by front door.

'91	'92	'93	'94	'95	'96	'97
$72	75	75	150	375	485	420

NORTH POLE

Item #	Intro	Retired	OSRP	GBTru	NO
5601-4	1990	*	$70	*	CHANGE

Particulars: Set of 2 includes *Reindeer Barn*, #56015 and *Elf Bunkhouse*, #56016. *Set is split between Current and Retired—the *Elf Bunkhouse* was retired in 1996.

see below

'91	'92	'93	'94	'95	'96	'97
$70	75	80	80	80	80	*

Reindeer Barn

Item #	Intro	Retired	OSRP	GBTru	NO
56015	1990	Current	$35	**$40**	CHANGE

Particulars: 1 of the 2-piece set—NORTH POLE. Stone and stucco has stalls for all reindeer. Steeply pitched roof has cupola on ridge and step design on front of dormers. Roof vents and Dutch stall doors provide ventilation. A common variation is a name duplicated, another omitted on reindeer stalls.

'91	'92	'93	'94	'95	'96	'97
$35	37.50	40	40	40	40	40

Elf Bunkhouse

Item #	Intro	Retired	OSRP	GBTru	NO
56016	1990	1996	$35	**$60**	CHANGE

Particulars: 1 of the 2-piece set—NORTH POLE. Home for Santa's helpers, 3 stories with steeply pitched roof and protected chimney. Made of wood, stone, and stucco featuring bay windows, dormers, and a balcony. The box and bottomstamp both read "Elf Bunkhouse," while the sign on the front of the building reads "Elves Bunkhouse."

'91	'92	'93	'94	'95	'96	'97
$35	37.50	40	40	40	40	60

North Pole Series™

NeeNee's Dolls And Toys

Item #	Intro	Retired	OSRP	GBTru	NO
5620-0	1991	1995	$36	**$60**	CHANGE

Particulars: Rough finish stucco and stone house. Steeply pitched rear roof, red shuttered lattice-paned front second-story windows. Early release to Showcase Dealers and Gift Creations Concepts (GCC). "N" monogram within wreath begins spelling out of N-O-R-T-H P-O-L-E.

'91	'92	'93	'94	'95	'96	'97
$36	37.50	37.50	37.50	37.50	55	60

NORTH POLE SHOPS

Item #	Intro	Retired	OSRP	GBTru	↑
5621-9	1991	1995	$75	**$135**	4%

Particulars: Set of 2 includes *Orly's Bell & Harness Supply* and *Rimpy's Bakery*.

see below

'91	'92	'93	'94	'95	'96	'97
$75	75	75	75	75	105	130

Orly's Bell & Harness Supply

Item #	Intro	Retired	OSRP	GBTru	↑
5621-9	1991	1995	$37.50	**$70**	8%

Particulars: 1 of the 2-piece set—NORTH POLE SHOPS. Stone steps lead to bell shop doorway with brick work design to frame it. Sleigh strap with bells above sign. Harness area has large wood doors that open to allow horse drawn carriage or wagon to enter. Window with balcony above, on 2nd story. "O" monogram within wreath, part of spelling out of N-O-R-T-H P-O-L-E.

'91	'92	'93	'94	'95	'96	'97
$37.50	37.50	37.50	37.50	37.50	55	65

Rimpy's Bakery

Item #	Intro	Retired	OSRP	GBTru	↑
5621-9	1991	1995	$37.50	**$75**	7%

Particulars: 1 of the 2-piece set—NORTH POLE SHOPS. Three storied, half wood timbered narrow building. Hipped-roof with gable on facade. Large eight paned front window with wood crib in front and on side. "R" monogram within wreath, part of spelling out of N-O-R-T-H P-O-L-E.

'91	'92	'93	'94	'95	'96	'97
$37.50	37.50	37.50	37.50	37.50	55	70

North Pole Series™

Tassy's Mitten & Hassel's Woolies

Item #	Intro	Retired	OSRP	GBTru	
5622-7	1991	1995	$50	**$80**	NO CHANGE

Particulars: Two shops in connected buildings. Hassel's has corner turret window and oriel turret upper window. Tassy's has angled front window at ground and three arched windows on overhang second story. Gable has carved bough and berry design—roof angles steeply pitched. "T" and "H" monograms within wreaths, part of spelling out of N-O-R-T-H P-O-L-E.

'91	'92	'93	'94	'95	'96	'97
$50	50	50	50	50	75	80

Post Office

Item #	Intro	Retired	OSRP	GBTru	
5623-5	1992	Current	$45	**$50**	NO CHANGE

Particulars: Basis for building is turret with what appears to be a half-house on one side of main tower. Second floor features multi-paned windows, small curved turret between second and third floor could hold staircase and take up little wall space. Third floor has low balcony outside windows. Early release to Showcase Dealers. "P" monogram within wreath, part of spelling out of N-O-R-T-H P-O-L-E.

'92	'93	'94	'95	'96	'97
$45	50	50	50	50	50

Obbie's Books & Letrinka's Candy

Item #	Intro	Retired	OSRP	GBTru	↓
5624-3	1992	1996	$70	**$85**	6%

Particulars: The tall narrow book and toy shop contrasts sharply with the shorter, wider, candy shop. Both shops have steep pitched roofs. A bay window on Obbie's side wall plus a number of dormer windows reinforce the angular look of the shop. Onion dome shaped chimney and cupola on roof ridge are unique to Letrinka's which also has a vertical timbered ground level design. "O" and "L" monograms within wreaths, part of spelling out of N-O-R-T-H P-O-L-E.

'92	'93	'94	'95	'96	'97
$70	70	70	70	70	90

Elfie's Sleds & Skates

Item #	Intro	Retired	OSRP	GBTru	
5625-1	1992	1996	$48	**$60**	NO CHANGE

Particulars: Distinctive roof design with chimneys that are only visible outside from the second story. Roof hood projects out from walls to protect windows on house sides as well as sweeping down to help form large front window. "E" monogram within wreath, part of spelling out of N-O R-T-H P-O-L-E.

'92	'93	'94	'95	'96	'97
$48	48	48	48	48	60

North Pole Series™

NORTH POLE CHAPEL

ITEM #	INTRO	RETIRED	OSRP	GBTRU	
5626-0	1993	CURRENT	$45	**$45**	NO CHANGE

Particulars: Spire, containing brass bell, rises at rear of Chapel. Fieldstone topped by timbered upper story. Double door front entry flanked by evergreens. Side chimney rises through roof with flue pipe capped by onion cap. Large wreath encircled clock above entry. Early release to Showcase Dealers and select buying groups.

'93	'94	'95	'96	'97
$45	45	45	45	45

NORTH POLE EXPRESS DEPOT

ITEM #	INTRO	RETIRED	OSRP	GBTRU	
5627-8	1993	CURRENT	$48	**$48**	NO CHANGE

Particulars: Receiving area for people and deliveries in and out of North Pole not going by Santa's sled. Roof line at lowest point is pagoda-like with an A-frame gable transversing a ridge. Stone chimney rises at rear of roof. Separate doors for passengers and freight.

'93	'94	'95	'96	'97
$48	48	48	48	48

SANTA'S WOODWORKS

ITEM #	INTRO	RETIRED	OSRP	GBTRU	
5628-6	1993	1996	$42	**$65**	↑ 8%

Particulars: Lower level contains heavy equipment for sawing, debarking and trimming wood. Main level reached by wood stairs at side of open porch. Structure is a log house.

'93	'94	'95	'96	'97
$42	42	45	45	60

SANTA'S LOOKOUT TOWER

ITEM #	INTRO	RETIRED	OSRP	GBTRU	
5629-4	1993	CURRENT	$45	**$48**	NO CHANGE

Particulars: Pennants fly above door and top of tower which rises above trees to give Santa a clear picture of flight conditions. Balcony around highest story lets Santa check wind velocity.

'93	'94	'95	'96	'97
$45	45	48	48	48

NORTH POLE SERIES™

ELFIN SNOW CONE WORKS

ITEM # 5633-2	INTRO 1994	RETIRED 1997	OSRP $40	GBTRU **$55**	↑ 38%

Particulars: Snow cones on shutters and sign of steep roofed shop. Roof molding trim resembles icing. Oriole window extends from 3rd floor to rooftop.

'94	'95	'96	'97
$40	40	40	40

BEARD BARBER SHOP

ITEM # 5634-0	INTRO 1994	RETIRED 1997	OSRP $27.50	GBTRU **$40**	↑ 45%

Particulars: Small shop with 3 tall front windows allowing light to enter. Barber pole at entry and banner of shears establish function of shop.

'94	'95	'96	'97
$27.50	27.50	27.50	27.50

NORTH POLE DOLLS & SANTA'S BEAR WORKS

ITEM # 5635-9	INTRO 1994	RETIRED 1997	OSRP $96	GBTRU **$115**	↑ 20%

Particulars: Set of 3 consists of *North Pole Dolls*, *Santa's Bear Works* and *Entrance*. Entrance is non-lit. Two 3-story mirror image buildings with 2-story center connecting entrance way. Shops have signs by doors. A "NP" pennant flies from the cupola in the center.

'94	'95	'96	'97
$96	96	96	96

TIN SOLDIER SHOP

ITEM # 5638-3	INTRO 1995	RETIRED 1997	OSRP $42	GBTRU **$60**	↑ 43%

Particulars: Midyear release. Tall, narrow shop with garland draped balcony. Toy soldiers decorate base of 2-story turret at side of entry.

'95	'96	'97
$42	42	42

NORTH POLE SERIES™

ELFIN FORGE & ASSEMBLY SHOP

ITEM #	INTRO	RETIRED	OSRP	GBTRU	NO
56384	1995	CURRENT	$65	**$65**	CHANGE

Particulars: North Pole folks make all the necessary iron works at the forge. Steps lead up to entry that connects two building wings. The forge furnaces are housed in the 3-story building with the tall furnace pipes. Design and assembly takes place in attached turret, with finished product exiting through large double doors.

'95	'96	'97
$65	65	65

WEATHER & TIME OBSERVATORY

ITEM #	INTRO	RETIRED	OSRP	GBTRU	NO
56385	1995	CURRENT	$50	**$50**	CHANGE

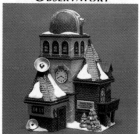

Particulars: Santa has to know all time zones and prevailing climate to plan his big sleigh trip as well as conditions for visiting folk, elves and animals. Telescope located in rooftop observatory, clocks are set for all time zones. Satellite dish brings in news on weather. Fortress-like turret for astronomy and smaller attached areas for offices.

'95	'96	'97
$50	50	50

SANTA'S ROOMING HOUSE

ITEM #	INTRO	RETIRED	OSRP	GBTRU	NO
56386	1995	CURRENT	$50	**$50**	CHANGE

Particulars: Visitors to the North Pole stay at this red clapboard inn. Stairs lead up to entry door for bedrooms. Lower level houses kitchen, dining and sitting rooms, as well as the cloak room.

'95	'96	'97
$50	50	50

ELVES' TRADE SCHOOL

ITEM #	INTRO	RETIRED	OSRP	GBTRU	NO
56387	1995	CURRENT	$50	**$50**	CHANGE

Particulars: All Toy Workshop, Forge & Assembly, Astronomy and Charting skills are taught at the school for elves. Stone pillars form part of sturdy base to support wood structure. Hammer holds school sign above red door.

'95	'96	'97
$50	50	50

POPCORN & CRANBERRY HOUSE

Item #	Intro	Retired	OSRP	GBTru	↑
56388	1996	1997	$45	**$80**	78%

Particulars: Midyear release. Tall chimney separates front part of house from rear work area. Elves work on the berries and corn preparing them for stringing into garlands and creation of holiday trim. Berries trim front sign accented by red roof, door and windows.

'96	'97
$45	45

SANTA'S BELL REPAIR

Item #	Intro	Retired	OSRP	GBTru	NO
56389	1996	Current	$45	**$45**	CHANGE

Particulars: Midyear release. Bells that no longer ring, chime or jingle are sent to the repair shop to be fixed and shined. Brass bells over entry, tall fieldstone chimney, and combination bell tower dormer set this design apart.

'96	'97
$45	45

NORTH POLE START A TRADITION SET

Item #	Intro	Retired	OSRP	GBTru	↑
56390	1996	1996	$85	**$110**	5%

Particulars: Set of 12 includes CANDY CANE LANE, Set of 2—*Candy Cane & Peppermint Shop* and *Gift Wrap & Ribbons.* Accessories: Set of 2—*Candy Cane Elves,* 6 Trees, Brick Road and a Bag of Snow. Starter Set was midyear release featured at Department 56, Inc. National Homes For The Holidays Open House Event, November 7–11, 1996. Special packaging for promotion. Starter Set was priced at $65.00 during the Event.

'96	'97
$85	105

ROUTE 1, NORTH POLE, HOME OF MR. & MRS. CLAUS

Item #	Intro	Retired	OSRP	GBTru	NO
56391	1996	Current	$110	**$110**	CHANGE

Particulars: Steep red rooftop, double turrets flank entry door. Rear turret flies a North Pole banner. Mailbox on front stone wall. The first shipments came with the green gates separate in the box. A short time later, the pieces arrived with the gates already inserted into the fence.

'97
$110

HALL OF RECORDS

ITEM #	INTRO	RETIRED	OSRP	GBTRU	
56392	1996	CURRENT	$50	**$50**	NO CHANGE

Particulars: Central fortress-like tower with clock provides record-keeping on naughty and nice files for Santa and elves. Side wings of building have bright red rooftops with green struts and saw-toothed trim. Staff out for hot chocolate break.

'97
$50

CHRISTMAS BREAD BAKERS

ITEM #	INTRO	RETIRED	OSRP	GBTRU	
56393	1996	CURRENT	$55	**$55**	NO CHANGE

Particulars: Bright blue curved roof with wheat grain symbols on red trim. Domed awnings cover front windows and door. Special treats listed on facade above bay window.

'97
$55

THE GLACIER GAZETTE

ITEM #	INTRO	RETIRED	OSRP	GBTRU	
56394	1997	CURRENT	$48	**$48**	NO CHANGE

Particulars: Midyear release. North Pole newspaper and telegraph office.

'97
$48

MRS. CLAUS' GREENHOUSE

ITEM #	INTRO	RETIRED	OSRP	GBTRU
56395	1997	CURRENT	$68	**$68**

Particulars: Poinsettias, holly and evergreens are available at the greenhouse. The flowering plants are visible through the "glass" of the growing area.

NORTH POLE SERIES™

GLASS ORNAMENT WORKS

ITEM #	INTRO	RETIRED	OSRP	GBTRU
56396	1997	CURRENT	$60	**$60**

Particulars: Glass blown, silvered and painted ornaments are made In this special shop. They also decorate the front of the building creating a festive design. The bright red and green painted trim of the shop is enhanced by the garlands and evergreen boughs.

SANTA'S LIGHT SHOP

ITEM #	INTRO	RETIRED	OSRP	GBTRU
56397	1997	CURRENT	$52	**$52**

Particulars: Shop produces strings of brightly colored lights for holiday trim. Lights surround Santa's building sign and decorate the make-believe trees out front.

ELSIE'S GINGERBREAD

ITEM #	INTRO	RETIRED	OSRP	GBTRU
56398	1997	1998 ANNUAL	$65	**$65**

Particulars: Contains smoking element to produce smoke. Magic smoke used smells like cinnamon. Bake shop specializes in Mrs. Claus' secret gingerbread recipe. Steep tiled roof, large gingerbread baking oven on side of building, main entrance plus a special on-sale location in side section of shop.

NOTES: _____

_____

_____

_____

_____

_____

NORTH POLE SERIES™

DISNEY PARKS VILLAGE™

To non-Department 56, Inc. collectors, the most significant aspect of the company's seventh porcelain village is its association with the Disney theme parks. To Department 56, Inc. collectors, the most significant aspect is the fact that Disney Parks Village™ is the only village to be retired in its entirety.

Introduced in 1994, it was retired in 1996 after only six buildings and four accessories were produced. This is the village for collectors who want to have an entire village on display all year long.

THE BOTTOM LINE:

Cost of all pieces introduced to Disney Parks Village™: **$439**

GREENBOOK TruMarket Value of all pieces without "Holiday Collection" bottomstamp: **$795**

With "Holiday Collection" bottomstamp: **$1,230**

RETIRED BUILDINGS

5350-3	1996	Mickey's Christmas Carol
5351-1	1996	OLDE WORLD ANTIQUES SHOPS
5351-1	1996	Olde World Antiques I
5351-1	1996	Olde World Antiques II
5352-0	1996	Disneyland Fire Department #105
53521	1996	Silversmith
53522	1996	Tinker Bell's Treasures

GREENBOOK HISTORY LIST

ITEM #	NAME	ISSUED	RETIRED	GBTRU$
5350-3	Mickey's Christmas Carol–10 Points	1994	1996	175.00
742-0	(Disney Theme Parks–10 Points)			345.00
5350-3	Mickey's Christmas Carol–6 Points	1994	1996	145.00
742-0	(Disney Theme Parks–6 Points)			265.00
5351-1	OLDE WORLD ANTIQUES SHOPS, S/2	1994	1996	90.00
743-9	(Disney Theme Parks)			145.00
5351-1	Olde World Antiques I	1994	1996	45.00
743-9	(Disney Theme Parks)			75.00
5351-1	Olde World Antiques II	1994	1996	45.00
743-9	(Disney Theme Parks)			75.00
5352-0	Disneyland Fire Department #105	1994	1996	45.00
744-7	(Disney Theme Parks)			85.00
53521	Silversmith	1995	1996	265.00
7448	(Disney Theme Parks)			325.00
53522	Tinker Bell's Treasures	1995	1996	265.00
7449	(Disney Theme Parks)			325.00

RETIRED ACCESSORIES

5353-8	1996	Mickey & Minnie
53539	1996	Balloon Seller
5354-6	1996	Disney Parks Family
5355-4	1996	Olde World Antiques Gate
5516-6	1992	Boulevard
5517-4	1990	Mailbox & Fire Hydrant
5532-8	1995	Don't Drop The Presents!
5533-6	1995	Welcome Home
5535-2	1992	Busy Sidewalks
5539-5	1994	'Tis The Season
5545-0	1993	All Around The Town
5546-8	1995	The Fire Brigade
5547-6	1995	"City Fire Dept." Fire Truck
5551-4	1992	David Copperfield Characters
5554-9	1993	Oliver Twist Characters
5556-5	1996	Playing In The Snow
5559-0	1995	Poultry Market
5560-3	1994	Come Into The Inn
5564-6	1997	Street Musicians
5570-0	1993	Carolers On The Doorstep
5572-7	1994	Village Sign With Snowman
5578-6	1992	Royal Coach
5579-4	1991	Constables
5580-8	1992	Violet Vendor/Carolers/ Chestnut Vendor
5602-2	1995	Toymaker Elves
5603-0	1995	Baker Elves
5604-9	1994	Letters For Santa
5608-1	1993	Trimming The North Pole
5610-3	1993	Santa's Little Helpers
5619-7	1995	Buying Bakers Bread
5630-8	1995	Woodsmen Elves
56364	1997	Charting Santa's Course
5637-5	1997	Snow Cone Elves
5641-3	1993	Market Day
5645-6	1995	Harvest Seed Cart
5646-4	1995	Town Tinker
5649-9	1996	Knife Grinder
5650-2	1997	Blue Star Ice Harvesters
5656-1	1997	Two Rivers Bridge
5802-5	1995	The Old Puppeteer
5803-3	1995	The Bird Seller
5804-1	1994	Village Street Peddlers
5806-8	1997	Churchyard Gate & Fence
5807-6	1997	Churchyard Fence Extensions
5813-0	1997	Chelsea Market Fruit Monger & Cart
5814-9	1997	Chelsea Market Fish Monger & Cart
5817-3	1996	Vision Of A Christmas Past
5818-1	1996	C. Bradford, Wheelwright & Son
5829-7	1997	Thatchers
5831-9	1997	Christmas Carol Revisited Holiday Trimming Set
58394	1997	Cobbler & Clock Peddler
58397	1997	Yeomen Of The Guard
5864-5	1997	Lionhead Bridge
5865-3	1996	Village Express Van
5886-6	1997	Hot Dog Vendor
5901-3	1989	Farm People & Animals
5903-0	1991	Childe Pond And Skaters
5928-5	1990	Fezziwig And Friends
5929-3	1991	Nicholas Nickleby Characters
5934-0	1990	Blacksmith
5938-2	1994	Snow Children
5941-2	1991	Village Harvest People
5945-5	1991	Farm Animals
5948-0	1992	Amish Family—"W/ Mustache"
5948-0	1992	Amish Family—"No Mustache"
5949-8	1992	Amish Buggy
5950-1	1989	Silo & Hay Shed
5951-0	1989	Ox Sled—"Tan Pants"
5951-0	1989	Ox Sled—"Blue Pants"
5951-0	1989	Ox Sled—"Blue Pants/ Mold Change"
5956-0	1992	Sleepy Hollow Characters
5957-9	1991	Organ Grinder
5958-7	1992	Popcorn Vendor
5959-5	1991	River Street Ice House Cart
5960-9	1993	Christmas In The City Sign
5964-1	1996	Automobiles
5965-0	1990	City People

5966-8	1988	Shopkeepers
5967-6	1988	City Workers
5971-4	1991	City Newsstand
5981-1	1990	Village Train Trestle
5982-0	1993	One Horse Open Sleigh
5983-8	1991	City Bus & Milk Truck
5985-4	1991	Salvation Army Band
5986-2	1990	Woodcutter And Son
5987-0	1994	Red Covered Bridge
6501-3	1990	Christmas Carol Figures
6510-2	1989	Lighted Tree W/Children & Ladder
6511-0	1990	Sleighride
6526-9	1990	Carolers—"White Post"
6526-9	1990	Carolers—"Black Post"
6527-7	1986	Village Train
6531-5	1990	Covered Wooden Bridge
6532-3	1990	New England Winter Set
6537-4	1992	Porcelain Trees
6542-0	1992	Alpine Villagers
6545-5	1990	Skating Pond
6546-3	1990	Stone Bridge
6547-1	1989	Village Well & Holy Cross
6569-2	1993	Dickens' Village Sign
6570-6	1993	New England Village Sign
6571-4	1993	Alpine Village Sign
6589-7	1989	Maple Sugaring Shed
6590-0	1990	Dover Coach—"First Version"
6590-0	1990	Dover Coach—"Second Version"
6590-0	1990	Dover Coach—"Third Version"
9953-8	1990	Heritage Village Promotional Sign

QUIKREFERENCE

The Heritage Village Collection® Accessories Quikreference

CAROLERS— "WHITE POST"

ITEM #	INTRO	RETIRED	OSRP	GBTRU	NO
6526-9	1984	1990	$10	**$110**	CHANGE

Particulars: Set of 3. Dickens' Village Series® accessory. 3 versions of set exist. Version 1—White Post, Viola is very light with dark brown trim, little detail in figures, made in Taiwan. This version is the more difficult version to find. Group of village people sing or listen to carols.

'91	'92	'93	'94	'95	'96	'97
$135	120	152	120	120	120	110

CAROLERS—"BLACK POST"

ITEM #	INTRO	RETIRED	OSRP	GBTRU	↑
6526-9	1984	1990	$10	**$40**	8%

Particulars: Version 2—Black post, viola is one color, more detail in figures, made in Taiwan. Version 3—Black post, viola has dark trim, largest set, made in Philippines.

'91	'92	'93	'94	'95	'96	'97
$25	28	45	36	38	40	37

VILLAGE TRAIN

ITEM #	INTRO	RETIRED	OSRP	GBTRU	↓
6527-7	1985	1986	$12	**$395**	4%

Particulars: Set of 3. Dickens' Village Series® accessory. Known as the "Brighton Train" because of the name on the side of the middle car. Three-car porcelain train, with engine, passenger car and caboose mail/freight car.

'91	'92	'93	'94	'95	'96	'97
$450	475	455	455	475	395	410

CHRISTMAS CAROL FIGURES

ITEM #	INTRO	RETIRED	OSRP	GBTRU	↓
6501-3	1986	1990	$12.50	**$80**	6%

Particulars: Set of 3. Dickens' Village Series® accessory. Ebenezer Scrooge, Bob Cratchit carrying Tiny Tim and young boy with poulterer/goose. The box shows Tiny Tim carrying a crutch, but there isn't one in the figurine.

'91	'92	'93	'94	'95	'96	'97
$20	28	42	65	80	85	85

LIGHTED TREE W/ CHILDREN & LADDER

ITEM #	INTRO	RETIRED	OSRP	GBT<small>RU</small>	↓
6510-2	1986	1989	$35	**$245**	20%

Particulars: Set of 3. Lighted. Christmas In The City® accessory. Children climb ladder to decorate tree. The tree is battery operated. Many have been sold on the secondary market as defective, but it's usually just a matter of crossed wires. Once they are switched, the unit works nicely. Check the boy on the ladder carefully as he often falls off the ladder and gets damaged. The sleeve of the first shipments read "Christmas In The City" though that Village didn't make its debut for another year.

'91	'92	'93	'94	'95	'96	'97
$225	285	290	350	350	320	305

SLEIGHRIDE

ITEM #	INTRO	RETIRED	OSRP	GBT<small>RU</small>	↑
6511-0	1986	1990	$19.50	**$55**	10%

Particulars: Dickens' Village Series® and New England Village® accessory. Couple enjoys ride in old fashioned sleigh drawn by two horses. Inspired by a Nathaniel Currier print. The Sleighride has 2 versions. Version 1 —Original sleeve reads, "Dickens Sleighride"—man has narrow white scarf with red polka dots. Version 2—Man's scarf and lapels are white with red polka dots. Gray horse is more spotted.

'91	'92	'93	'94	'95	'96	'97
$35	38	50	58	50	50	50

COVERED WOODEN BRIDGE

ITEM #	INTRO	RETIRED	OSRP	GBT<small>RU</small>	↑
6531-5	1986	1990	$10	**$42**	5%

Particulars: New England Village® accessory. Simple wooden bridge with shingle roof, protects travelers from weather while crossing river. Variations in color from light to dark. Variations do not affect secondary market value.

'91	'92	'93	'94	'95	'96	'97
$25	28	32	32	35	38	40

We'll Cross that Bridge...

"You can't get there from here." In many areas, this tongue-in-cheek saying is true—especially in mountainous areas where the roads generally run along either side of the ranges, but seldom across them. Another area where this held true is anywhere in The Original Snow Village® where there may be a river separating two land areas.

Have you ever noticed that there simply aren't any bridges in the oldest village? It occurred to me only recently. Why is that, and when will it be remedied? Who knows! Until it is, however, cars in the village won't be able to cross rivers, and people won't be able to traverse streams or grassy areas.

continued page 242

We'll Cross that Bridge...

continued from 241

But...in The Heritage Village Collection®, there have been bridges. The first bridge, *Covered Wooden Bridge* (1986-1990), was introduced just three years into the Collection. It's interesting to note that *Sleighride* was introduced in the same year. Perhaps the designer(s) envisioned a vignette—a couple gliding along in their sleigh on a tranquil wintry night—the light of a full moon reflecting off the virgin snow that fell earlier in the day. You can practically hear the sound of the horse's hooves "clip-cloping" across the bridge's wooden deck.

Bridge-lovers had to wait only one more year to get their next one. The *Stone Bridge* (1987-1990) appears to be more suited to cross a stream in a park or a town center than to span a river along a well-traveled route. Like the *Covered Wooden Bridge,* it had a "sister" accessory introduced in the same year—in this case, 1987. Take a look at the variegated stonework on the *Stone Bridge.* Compare it to a *Skating Pond.* They're very similar.

In 1988, Department 56, Inc. introduced two bridges, and each had the distinction of being the first for something. Ironically, it is a bridge that was introduced many years later that often gets credited with both of these.

Not only was the *Village Train Trestle* (1988-1990) the first bridge for a train, but it was also the first bridge to have a center support allowing or creating two separate flows of water. If you own this bridge, you'll notice that the sleeve reads "Stone Train Trestle."

The other bridge introduced that year was the *Red Covered Bridge* (1988-1994). It was the first bridge to name what it crossed. On one of its gables are the words "Maple Creek."

Have you noticed that for two years all four bridges were current and that two of them were covered bridges? Have you also noticed that three of the four retired in 1990?

No bridge was introduced for four years. It was then that the *Lionhead Bridge* (1992-1997) came on the scene. This was the most ornate bridge yet. At one end are two lions—one on either side—each with a paw on a sphere. Like the *Stone Bridge*, this seems to be a "walking" or foot bridge.

It seemed when the *Red Covered Bridge* retired in 1994 that the collection would be without a covered bridge for the first time since the original bridge was introduced. But that wasn't to be the case; the introduction of the *Two Rivers Bridge* (1994-1997) saw to that.

It's the *Two Rivers Bridge* that is often credited with being the first to have a center support allowing two rivers to pass under, and the first to name the waterway(s) it crosses. But as you have already read, it wasn't the first to have either. It is the first, however, to be manufactured with both porcelain and resin. The others are all porcelain.

In one manner of speaking, The Original Snow Village® finally got bridges with the addition of *Village Mill Creek Bridge* (1996) *and Village Mill Creek Wooden Bridge* (1997). Along with the *Village Stone Foot Bridge* and *Village Stone Trestle Bridge* (both introduced in 1997), they are considered by Department 56, Inc. to be a "village accessory" (to be used with either The Heritage Village Collection® or The Original Snow Village®), so The Original Snow Village® technically is still lacking a bridge among its accessories. In any case, these latest bridges offer villagers another means of "getting there from here."

the **Village Chronicle**.

NEW ENGLAND WINTER SET

ITEM #	INTRO	RETIRED	OSRP	GBTRU	↓
6532-3	1986	1990	$18	**$48**	4%

Particulars: Set of 5. Stone well, man pushes sleigh as woman rides, snow covered trees, man pulls cut tree.

'91	'92	'93	'94	'95	'96	'97
$35	35	50	46	45	47	50

PORCELAIN TREES

ITEM #	INTRO	RETIRED	OSRP	GBTRU	↑
6537-4	1986	1992	$14	**$40**	14%

Particulars: Set of 2. Two different size snow covered evergreens.

'91	'92	'93	'94	'95	'96	'97
$16	17	25	36	35	35	35

ALPINE VILLAGERS

ITEM #	INTRO	RETIRED	OSRP	GBTRU	↓
6542-0	1986	1992	$13	**$35**	8%

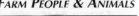

Particulars: Set of 3. Seated man, walking woman carrying book, dog pulling wagon with milk cans. Figurines got thinner in later years of production. This does not affect secondary market value.

'91	'92	'93	'94	'95	'96	'97
$15	15	36	36	35	38	38

FARM PEOPLE & ANIMALS

ITEM #	INTRO	RETIRED	OSRP	GBTRU	↓
5901-3	1987	1989	$24	**$95**	5%

Particulars: Set of 5. Dickens' Village Series® accessory. Man hauling logs. Woman and girl feeding geese. Goat pulls wagon and deer eat winter hay.

'91	'92	'93	'94	'95	'96	'97
$55	60	72	80	90	94	100

The Heritage Village Collection® Accessories

SHOPKEEPERS

ITEM #	INTRO	RETIRED	OSRP	GBT_{RU}	↓
5966-8	1987	1988	$15	**$36**	10%

Particulars: Set of 4. Dickens' Village Series® accessory. *Shopkeepers* and *City Workers* are the only figures to have "snow" sprinkled on them. Vendors of fruits, vegetables, breads, cakes.

'91	'92	'93	'94	'95	'96	'97
$35	30	35	35	38	38	40

CITY WORKERS

ITEM #	INTRO	RETIRED	OSRP	GBT_{RU}	↑
5967-6	1987	1988	$15	**$48**	7%

Particulars: Set of 4. Dickens' Village Series® accessory. *Shopkeepers* and *City Workers* are the only figures to have "snow" sprinkled on them. Some boxes read "City People." Police constable, nurse, driver, tradesman with packages.

'91	'92	'93	'94	'95	'96	'97
$35	35	38	38	40	35	45

SKATING POND

ITEM #	INTRO	RETIRED	OSRP	GBT_{RU}	↓
6545-5	1987	1990	$24	**$68**	9%

Particulars: Dickens' Village Series®, New England Village® & Christmas In The City® accessory. There are two color variations. Version 1 is made in Taiwan, the ice has generally very light blue streaks. Version 2 is made in the Philippines, blue covers most of ice surface. Variations do not affect secondary market value. Low stone wall circles pond. One child watches other child skating. Two snowy trees.

'91	'92	'93	'94	'95	'96	'97
$65	60	60	75	75	75	75

STONE BRIDGE

ITEM #	INTRO	RETIRED	OSRP	GBT_{RU}	NO
6546-3	1987	1990	$12	**$75**	CHANGE

Particulars: Variegated fieldstone arches over river. Corner post has lamp. Variations in color from light to dark do not affect secondary market value.

'91	'92	'93	'94	'95	'96	'97
$40	60	70	80	80	80	75

VILLAGE WELL & HOLY CROSS

ITEM #	INTRO	RETIRED	OSRP	GBTRU	NO
6547-1	1987	1989	$13	**$150**	CHANGE

Particulars. Set of 2. Dickens' Village Series® accessory. There are two variations in color. The first version has blue water and dark birds. The second version has colorless water and the birds are light in color. Variations do not affect secondary market value. Old fashioned hand pump for water housed in small gazebo. Cross upon pedestal on stone step base.

'91	'92	'93	'94	'95	'96	'97
$70	98	145	130	160	165	150

DICKENS' VILLAGE SIGN

ITEM #	INTRO	RETIRED	OSRP	GBTRU	NO
6569-2	1987	1993	$6	**$18**	CHANGE

Particulars: The village signs are the only pieces to identify the actual manufacturer of the piece. The bottomstamp reads "Handcrafted by Jiean Fung Porcelains, Taiwan." The early signs have a dark background. This does not affect secondary market value.

'91	'92	'93	'94	'95	'96	'97
$6.50	6.50	6.50	18	20	18	18

NEW ENGLAND VILLAGE SIGN

ITEM #	INTRO	RETIRED	OSRP	GBTRU	↑
6570-6	1987	1993	$6	**$18**	6%

Particulars: The village signs are the only pieces to identify the actual manufacturer of the piece. The bottomstamp reads "Handcrafted by Jiean Fung Porcelains, Taiwan." The early signs are more detailed and have richer colors. This does not affect secondary market value.

'91	'92	'93	'94	'95	'96	'97
$6.50	6.50	6.50	14	15	16	17

ALPINE VILLAGE SIGN

ITEM #	INTRO	RETIRED	OSRP	GBTRU	NO
6571-4	1987	1993	$6	**$18**	CHANGE

Particulars: The village signs are the only pieces to identify the actual manufacturer of the piece. The bottomstamp reads "Handcrafted by Jiean Fung Porcelains, Taiwan." The early signs are more detailed and have richer colors. This does not affect secondary market value.

'91	'92	'93	'94	'95	'96	'97
$6.50	6.50	6.50	28	20	17	18

VILLAGE HARVEST PEOPLE

ITEM #	INTRO	RETIRED	OSRP	GBTRU	NO
5941-2	1988	1991	$27.50	**$50**	CHANGE

Particulars: Set of 4. New England Village® accessory. Sleeve reads "Harvest Time." Woman with butter churn, man loads pumpkins on cart, corn shocks, and pumpkins.

'91	'92	'93	'94	'95	'96	'97
$28	50	55	45	45	45	50

CITY NEWSSTAND

ITEM #	INTRO	RETIRED	OSRP	GBTRU	↑
5971-4	1988	1991	$25	**$65**	8%

Particulars: Set of 4. Christmas In The City® accessory. News vendor, magazine and newspaper wooden stand, woman reading paper, newsboy showing headlines.

'91	'92	'93	'94	'95	'96	'97
$25	48	48	42	48	52	60

VILLAGE TRAIN TRESTLE

ITEM #	INTRO	RETIRED	OSRP	GBTRU	↓
5981-1	1988	1990	$17	**$67**	4%

Particulars: Double arch trestle spans river. Single track on stone train overpass. Sleeve reads "Stone Train Trestle."

'91	'92	'93	'94	'95	'96	'97
$35	42	60	60	60	70	70

ONE HORSE OPEN SLEIGH

ITEM #	INTRO	RETIRED	OSRP	GBTRU	↑
5982-0	1988	1993	$20	**$38**	9%

Particulars: Couple out for a ride in sleigh with canopy. Lap robes protect against cold.

'91	'92	'93	'94	'95	'96	'97
$21	24	25	30	35	38	35

CITY BUS & MILK TRUCK

ITEM #	INTRO	RETIRED	OSRP	GBTRU	↑
5983-8	1988	1991	$15	**$38**	9%

Particulars: Set of 2. Christmas In The City® accessory. Box reads "Transport." Open back milk truck carries large milk cans. Old fashioned city bus.

'91	'92	'93	'94	'95	'96	'97
$16	25	36	36	32	32	35

SALVATION ARMY BAND

ITEM #	INTRO	RETIRED	OSRP	GBTRU	↓
5985-4	1988	1991	$24	**$88**	2%

Particulars: Set of 6. Christmas In The City® accessory. Five uniformed musicians and conductor represent charitable organization.

'91	'92	'93	'94	'95	'96	'97
$24	40	42	50	65	75	90

WOODCUTTER AND SON

ITEM #	INTRO	RETIRED	OSRP	GBTRU	↑
5986-2	1988	1990	$10	**$48**	7%

Particulars: Set of 2. New England Village® accessory. Father splits logs as son carries firewood.

'91	'92	'93	'94	'95	'96	'97
$25	25	32	50	40	42	45

RED COVERED BRIDGE

ITEM #	INTRO	RETIRED	OSRP	GBTRU	↑
5987-0	1988	1994	$15	**$28**	12%

Particulars: New England Village® accessory. Wooden bridge spans Maple Creek supported by stone bases.

'91	'92	'93	'94	'95	'96	'97
$16	16	17	17	22	24	25

VIOLET VENDOR/CAROL-ERS/CHESTNUT VENDOR

ITEM #	INTRO	RETIRED	OSRP	GBTRU	NO
5580-8	1989	1992	$23	**$45**	CHANGE

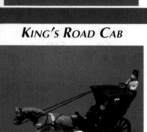

Particulars: Set of 3. Dickens' Village Series® accessory. Elderly woman sells bunches of violets from basket, man sells fresh roasted nuts, and two women singing carols.

'91	'92	'93	'94	'95	'96	'97
$23	24	52	45	40	40	45

KING'S ROAD CAB

ITEM #	INTRO	RETIRED	OSRP	GBTRU	NO
5581-6	1989	CURRENT	$30	**$30**	CHANGE

Particulars: Dickens' Village Series® accessory. Two-wheeled horse drawn carriage. Driver sits high and behind cab. Passengers protected from weather.

'91	'92	'93	'94	'95	'96	'97
$30	30	30	30	30	30	30

CHRISTMAS CAROL CHRISTMAS MORNING FIGURES

ITEM #	INTRO	RETIRED	OSRP	GBTRU	NO
5588-3	1989	CURRENT	$18	**$18**	CHANGE

Particulars: Set of 3. Dickens' Village Series® accessory. Scrooge transformed—smiling, small boy by fence and lamppost—waving, couple carrying presents. Early release to National Association Of Limited Edition Dealers (NALED). Addition to *Christmas Carol* grouping.

'91	'92	'93	'94	'95	'96	'97
$18	18	18	18	18	18	18

CHRISTMAS CAROL CHRISTMAS SPIRITS FIGURES

ITEM #	INTRO	RETIRED	OSRP	GBTRU	NO
5589-1	1989	CURRENT	$27.50	**$27.50**	CHANGE

Particulars: Set of 4. Dickens' Village Series® accessory. Scrooge with Ghost of...1) Christmas Past, 2) Christmas Present, and 3) Future...&...Marley. Addition to *Christmas Carol* grouping.

'91	'92	'93	'94	'95	'96	'97
$27.50	27.50	27.50	27.50	27.50	27.50	27.50

FARM ANIMALS

ITEM #	INTRO	RETIRED	OSRP	GBTRU	↓
5945-5	1989	1991	$15	**$42**	7%

Particulars: Set of 4. New England Village® accessory. Chickens, geese, sheep, ewe and lamb.

'91	'92	'93	'94	'95	'96	'97
$15	25	33	36	40	40	45

ORGAN GRINDER

ITEM #	INTRO	RETIRED	OSRP	GBTRU	NO
5957-9	1989	1991	$21	**$36**	CHANGE

Particulars: Set of 3. Christmas In The City® accessory. Man turns handle to produce music for little monkey to dance. Woman and children watch monkey. (Woman and girl missing from photo).

'91	'92	'93	'94	'95	'96	'97
$21	38	40	40	35	36	36

POPCORN VENDOR

ITEM #	INTRO	RETIRED	OSRP	GBTRU	↓
5958-7	1989	1992	$22	**$36**	5%

Particulars: Set of 3. Christmas In The City® accessory. Truck with red and white striped top. Vendor fills red and white bag. Little girl has a full bag of popcorn.

'91	'92	'93	'94	'95	'96	'97
$22	22	40	35	40	32	38

RIVER STREET ICE HOUSE CART

ITEM #	INTRO	RETIRED	OSRP	GBTRU	NO
5959-5	1989	1991	$20	**$55**	CHANGE

Particulars: Christmas In The City® accessory. Horse pulls a blue and gray ice wagon for ice man.

'91	'92	'93	'94	'95	'96	'97
$20	40	45	45	50	50	55

The Heritage Village Collection® Accessories

CENTRAL PARK CARRIAGE

ITEM #	INTRO	RETIRED	OSRP	GBTRU	NO
5979-0	1989	CURRENT	$30	**$30**	CHANGE

Particulars: Christmas In The City® accessory. Gray horse pulls red and black carriage. Driver has mother and child as passengers.

'91	'92	'93	'94	'95	'96	'97
$30	30	30	30	30	30	30

HERITAGE VILLAGE PROMOTIONAL SIGN

ITEM #	INTRO	RETIRED	OSRP	GBTRU	↓
9953-8	1989	1990	$5	**$24**	14%

Particulars: Vertical sign with arched top and brick base. Gold lettering on white facade. Variation exists of green lettering on green facade. This does not affect secondary market value. Earthenware.

'91	'92	'93	'94	'95	'96	'97
$-	-	-	18	20	25	28

MAILBOX & FIRE HYDRANT

ITEM #	INTRO	RETIRED	OSRP	GBTRU	NO
5214-0	1990	CURRENT	$5	**$5**	CHANGE

Particulars: Set of 2. Christmas In The City® accessory. Red & green H.V. mailbox & red fire hydrant. Replaced 1989, #5517-4. Metal.

'91	'92	'93	'94	'95	'96	'97
$5	5	5	5	5	5	5

BUSY SIDEWALKS

ITEM #	INTRO	RETIRED	OSRP	GBTRU	↑
5535-2	1990	1992	$28	**$50**	11%

Particulars: Set of 4. Christmas In The City® accessory. Delivery boy, doorman, two elderly ladies, mother with toddler and baby in carriage.

'91	'92	'93	'94	'95	'96	'97
$28	28	42	42	45	45	45

5018-0	1990	Snowman With Broom
5038-5	1985	Scottie With Tree
5040-7	1988	Monks-A-Caroling
5053-9	1987	Singing Nuns
5056-3	1987	Snow Kids Sled, Skis
5057-1	1988	Family Mom/Kids, Goose/Girl
5059-8	1988	Santa/Mailbox
5064-1	1986	Carolers
5069-0	1986	Ceramic Car
5079-2	1986	Ceramic Sleigh
5094-6	1990	Kids Around The Tree
5095-4	1987	Girl/Snowman, Boy
5096-2	1988	Shopping Girls With Packages
5102-0	1988	3 Nuns With Songbooks
5103-9	1988	Praying Monks
5104-7	1989	Children In Band
5105-5	1990	Caroling Family
5107-1	1990	Christmas Children
5108-0	1989	For Sale Sign
5113-6	1990	Snow Kids
5116-0	1992	Man On Ladder Hanging Garland
5117-9	1990	Hayride
5118-7	1990	School Children
5129-2	1990	Apple Girl/ Newspaper Boy
5130-6	1991	Woodsman And Boy
5131-4	1992	Doghouse/Cat In Garbage Can
5133-0	1991	Water Tower
5134-9	1993	Kids Decorating The Village Sign
5136-5	1990	Woody Station Wagon
5137-3	1991	School Bus, Snow Plow
5146-2	1995	Village Gazebo
5147-0	1992	Choir Kids
5148-9	1990	Special Delivery
5158-6	1993	Down The Chimney He Goes
5159-4	1993	Sno-Jet Snowmobile
5160-8	1992	Sleighride
5161-6	1992	Here We Come A Caroling
5162-4	1992	Home Delivery
5163-2	1993	Fresh Frozen Fish
5164-0	1995	A Tree For Me
5165-9	1996	A Home For The Holidays
5168-3	1991	Kids Tree House
5169-1	1992	Bringing Home The Tree
5170-5	1991	Skate Faster Mom
5171-3	1996	Crack The Whip
5172-1	1991	Through The Woods
5173-0	1991	Statue Of Mark Twain
5174-8	1991	Calling All Cars
5179-9	1990	Mailbox
5180-2	1994	Village Birds
5197-7	1992	Special Delivery
5408-9	1994	Wreaths For Sale
5409-7	1993	Winter Fountain
5410-0	1994	Cold Weather Sports
5411-9	1992	Come Join The Parade
5412-7	1992	Village Marching Band
5413-5	1994	Christmas Cadillac
5414-3	1993	Snowball Fort
5415-1	1993	Country Harvest
5418-6	1994	Village Greetings
5428-3	1997	Village Used Car Lot
5430-5	1994	Nanny And The Preschoolers
5431-3	1995	Early Morning Delivery
5432-1	1996	Christmas Puppies
5433-0	1995	Round & Round We Go!
5435-6	1994	We're Going To A Christmas Pageant
5436-4	1995	Winter Playground
5440-2	1996	Spirit Of Snow Village Airplane
5449-6	1997	Safety Patrol
5450-0	1996	Christmas At The Farm
5451-8	1995	Check It Out Bookmobile
5452-6	1997	Tour The Village
5453-4	1996	Pint-Size Pony Rides
5455-0	1997	A Herd Of Holiday Heifers
5458-5	1996	Spirit Of Snow Village Airplane
5459-3	1996	Village News Delivery
5462-3	1996	Sunday School Seranade
5473-9	1997	Feeding The Birds
5474-7	1997	Mush!
5481-0	1997	Coca-Cola® brand Billboard
54860	1997	Frosty Playtime
54867	1997	Grand Ole Opry Carolers
54875	1997	A Ride On The Reindeer Lines
6459-9	1984	Monks-A-Caroling
8183-3	1991	Sisal Tree Lot

The Original Snow Village® Accessories—Retired

CAROLERS

ITEM #	INTRO	RETIRED	OSRP	GBTru	NO
5064-1	1979	1986	$12	**$125**	CHANGE

Particulars: Set of 4. Couple, girl, garlanded lamppost, snowman. First people in the Village and first non-lit accessory.

'91	'92	'93	'94	'95	'96	'97
$95	105	110	125	125	125	125

CERAMIC CAR

ITEM #	INTRO	RETIRED	OSRP	GBTru	NO
5069-0	1980	1986	$5	**$60**	CHANGE

Particulars: First vehicle, no other cars were available until 1985. Did not come in a box. Open roadster holds lap rugs, Christmas tree and wrapped presents.

'91	'92	'93	'94	'95	'96	'97
$20	42	48	52	50	55	60

CERAMIC SLEIGH

ITEM #	INTRO	RETIRED	OSRP	GBTru	↓
5079-2	1981	1986	$5	**$60**	8%

Particulars: Patterned after old-fashioned wood sleigh, holds Christmas tree and wrapped presents. Did not come in a box.

'91	'92	'93	'94	'95	'96	'97
$20	52	55	55	55	55	65

SNOWMAN WITH BROOM

ITEM #	INTRO	RETIRED	OSRP	GBTru	↑
5018-0	1982	1990	$3	**$15**	25%

Particulars: Snowman with top hat and red nose holds straw broom.

'91	'92	'93	'94	'95	'96	'97
$10	15	15	15	10	12	12

MONKS-A-CAROLING

ITEM #	INTRO	RETIRED	OSRP	GBTRU	⬆
6460-2	1982	N/A	$6	**$205**	3%

Particulars: These original four friars singing carols were giftware adopted as a Original Snow Village™ piece by collectors. The piece is unglazed, the Monks carry paper song books and have real cord for sashes.

	'97
	$200

MONKS-A-CAROLING

ITEM #	INTRO	RETIRED	OSRP	GBTRU	NO
6459-9	1983	1984	$6	**$65**	CHANGE

Particulars: This is the 2nd *Monks-A-Caroling*. It was retired after one year due to the maker's inability to supply. This version is slightly smaller than the giftware piece, glazed, and the Monks carry ceramic songbooks and have painted-on ropes. The diffused rosy blush in the Monks' cheeks differentiate this piece from the 3rd version Monks (1984, Item #5040-7, from another supplier).

'91	'92	'93	'94	'95	'96	'97
$70	70	75	75	70	65	65

SCOTTIE WITH TREE

ITEM #	INTRO	RETIRED	OSRP	GBTRU	⬆
5038-5	1984	1985	$3	**$175**	6%

Particulars: A black dog waits by a snow covered tree. Some pieces have a white star on top of the tree.

'91	'92	'93	'94	'95	'96	'97
$95	115	132	140	150	165	165

MONKS-A-CAROLING

ITEM #	INTRO	RETIRED	OSRP	GBTRU	⬆
5040-7	1984	1988	$6	**$65**	30%

Particulars: Replaced the 1983 *Monks-A Caroling*, Item #6459-9. On this piece the Monks have a distinct pink circle to give the cheeks blush.

'91	'92	'93	'94	'95	'96	'97
$25	25	30	38	40	38	50

SINGING NUNS

ITEM #	INTRO	RETIRED	OSRP	GBTRU	↓
5053-9	1985	1987	$6	**$130**	4%

Particulars: Four nuns in habits, sing carols.

'91	'92	'93	'94	'95	'96	'97
$65	75	85	105	125	130	135

AUTO WITH TREE— "SQUASHED"

ITEM #	INTRO	RETIRED	OSRP	GBTRU	↑
5055-5	1985	VARIATION	$5	**$90**	20%

Particulars: First version of red VW Beetle with sisal tree strapped to roof looks as if the tree's weight crushed the car. Approximately 3 3/8" long. Did not come in a box.

'97
$75

AUTO WITH TREE

ITEM #	INTRO	RETIRED	OSRP	GBTRU	NO
5055-5	1985	CURRENT	$5	**$6.50**	CHANGE

Particulars: Second version of red VW Beetle with sisal tree strapped to roof. Approximately 3" long. Did not come in a box.

'91	'92	'93	'94	'95	'96	'97
$6.50	6.50	6.50	6.50	6.50	6.50	6.50

SNOW KIDS SLED, SKIS

ITEM #	INTRO	RETIRED	OSRP	GBTRU	↓
5056-3	1985	1987	$11	**$50**	9%

Particulars: Set of 2. Three children on a toboggan and one child on skis. See *Snow Kids,* 1987, #5113-6, for these kids as part of a set of 4 in a scaled down size.

'91	'92	'93	'94	'95	'96	'97
$20	48	48	50	50	50	55

The Original Snow Village® Accessories

FAMILY MOM/KIDS, GOOSE/GIRL–"LARGE"

ITEM #	INTRO	RETIRED	OSRP	GBTRU	↑
5057-1	1985	1988	$11	$50	19%

Particulars: Set of 2. Mother holds hands of two children, one girl feeds corn to geese. First version. This is the original larger size. By 1987 the piece was downscaled.

'91	'92	'93	'94	'95	'96	'97
$30	35	35	45	45	48	42

FAMILY MOM/KIDS, GOOSE/GIRL–"SMALL"

ITEM #	INTRO	RETIRED	OSRP	GBTRU	↑
5057-1	1985	1988	$11	$45	7%

Particulars: Set of 2. Second version. This is the downscaled version. In addition to being smaller, there is more detail in the pieces.

'91	'92	'93	'94	'95	'96	'97
$30	35	35	45	45	48	42

SANTA/MAILBOX–"LARGE"

ITEM #	INTRO	RETIRED	OSRP	GBTRU	↓
5059-8	1985	1988	$11	$55	8%

Particulars: Set of 2. Santa with toy bag and girl mails letter to Santa as dog watches. First version. This is the original larger size. Girl has brown hair. By 1987 the piece was downscaled. 1997 was the first year we tracked secondary market performance separately.

'91	'92	'93	'94	'95	'96	'97
$25	40	46	48	50	53	60

SANTA/MAILBOX–"SMALL"

ITEM #	INTRO	RETIRED	OSRP	GBTRU	↓
5059-8	1985	1988	$11	$50	12%

Particulars: Set of 2. Second version. This is the downscaled version. In addition to being shorter, Santa and the girl are also trimmer. In this version the girl has blonde hair. 1997 was the first year we tracked secondary market performance separately.

'91	'92	'93	'94	'95	'96	'97
$25	40	46	48	50	53	57

The Original Snow Village® Accessories

KIDS AROUND THE TREE– "LARGE"

ITEM #	INTRO	RETIRED	OSRP	GBTRU	↑
5094-6	1986	1990	$15	**$60**	9%

Particulars: First version of *Kids Around The Tree*. This is the original larger size, 5 ³/₄" in height. By 1987 the piece was dramatically downscaled. Children join hands to make a ring around the snow covered tree with a gold star.

'91	'92	'93	'94	'95	'96	'97
$60	60	60	70	60	60	55

KIDS AROUND THE TREE– "SMALL"

ITEM #	INTRO	RETIRED	OSRP	GBTRU	↑
5094-6	1986	1990	$15	**$46**	15%

Particulars: Second version of *Kids Around The Tree*. This is the downscaled version, 4 ¹/₂" in height.

'91	'92	'93	'94	'95	'96	'97
$30	32	32	40	35	38	40

GIRL/SNOWMAN, BOY

ITEM #	INTRO	RETIRED	OSRP	GBTRU	↑
5095-4	1986	1987	$11	**$72**	11%

Particulars: Set of 2. Girl puts finishing touches on snowman as boy reaches to place decorated hat atop head. See *Snow Kids,* 1987, #5113-6, for these kids as part of a set of 4 in a scaled down size.

'91	'92	'93	'94	'95	'96	'97
$35	50	55	70	70	62	65

SHOPPING GIRLS WITH PACKAGES–"LARGE"

ITEM #	INTRO	RETIRED	OSRP	GBTRU	NO
5096-2	1986	1988	$11	**$50**	CHANGE

Particulars: Set of 2. Girls dressed toasty for shopping with hats, mittens, coats, boots, stand by some of their wrapped packages. First version. This is the original larger size–3" in height. By 1987 the piece was downscaled. 1997 was the first year we tracked secondary market performance separately.

'91	'92	'93	'94	'95	'96	'97
$25	35	38	44	45	48	50

SHOPPING GIRLS WITH PACKAGES—"SMALL"

ITEM #	INTRO	RETIRED	OSRP	GBTRU	↓
5096-2	1986	1988	$11	**$45**	4%

Particulars: Set of 2. Second version. This is the downscaled version—2 ¾" in height. 1997 was the first year we tracked secondary market performance separately.

'91	'92	'93	'94	'95	'96	'97
$25	35	38	44	45	48	47

SNOW VILLAGE HOUSE FOR SALE SIGN

ITEM #	INTRO	RETIRED	OSRP	GBTRU
NONE	1987	N/A	GIFT	NE

Particulars: This sign was given to dealers who attended trade shows and showrooms around the country. It was never intended for resale and is one of the rarest Original Snow Village® accessories. It came packed in a blister pack.

3 NUNS WITH SONGBOOKS

ITEM #	INTRO	RETIRED	OSRP	GBTRU	↑
5102-0	1987	1988	$6	**$140**	4%

Particulars: Three nuns in habits standing side-by-side carry songbooks to sing carols. Available for only one year.

'91	'92	'93	'94	'95	'96	'97
$50	75	95	115	125	128	135

PRAYING MONKS

ITEM #	INTRO	RETIRED	OSRP	GBTRU	↓
5103-9	1987	1988	$6	**$48**	4%

Particulars: Three monks, standing side-by-side, praying. Available for only one year.

'91	'92	'93	'94	'95	'96	'97
$30	32	42	42	40	44	50

The Original Snow Village® Accessories

CHILDREN IN BAND

ITEM #	INTRO	RETIRED	OSRP	GBTRU	↑
5104-7	1987	1989	$15	**$35**	17%

Particulars: One child conducts three band players: horn, drum and tuba.

'91	'92	'93	'94	'95	'96	'97
$25	35	28	24	25	32	30

CAROLING FAMILY

ITEM #	INTRO	RETIRED	OSRP	GBTRU	NO
5105-5	1987	1990	$20	**$35**	CHANGE

Particulars: Set of 3. Father holds baby, mother and son, and girl with pup.

'91	'92	'93	'94	'95	'96	'97
$25	35	30	32	30	28	35

TAXI CAB

ITEM #	INTRO	RETIRED	OSRP	GBTRU	NO
5106-3	1987	CURRENT	$6	**$6.50**	CHANGE

Particulars: Yellow Checker cab. Size is 3 1/2" x 2".

'91	'92	'93	'94	'95	'96	'97
$6.50	6.50	6.50	6.50	6.50	6.50	6.50

CHRISTMAS CHILDREN

ITEM #	INTRO	RETIRED	OSRP	GBTRU	NO
5107-1	1987	1990	$20	**$35**	CHANGE

Particulars: Set of 4. Children at outdoor activities: girl and pup on sled, boy, girl holding wreath and girl feeding carrot to bunny.

'91	'92	'93	'94	'95	'96	'97
$25	35	35	30	30	35	35

FOR SALE SIGN

Item #	Intro	Retired	OSRP	GBTru	NO
5108-0	1987	1989	$3.50	**$10**	CHANGE

Particulars: First "For Sale Sign." This ceramic sign is trimmed with holly. See also *For Sale Sign,* 1989, #5166-7.

'91	'92	'93	'94	'95	'96	'97
$8	12	12	10	10	10	10

FOR SALE SIGN— "GCC BLANK"

Item #	Intro	Retired	OSRP	GBTru	↓
581-9	1987	Promo	*	**$22**	12%

Particulars: Gift Creations Concepts (GCC) 1989 Christmas Catalog Exclusive, *free with any $100 Department 56 purchase. Holly trims blank sign for personalization.

'97
$25

SNOW KIDS

Item #	Intro	Retired	OSRP	GBTru	↑
5113-6	1987	1990	$20	**$56**	2%

Particulars: Set of 4 incorporates *Snow Kids Sled, Skis,* 1985, Item #5056-3, and *Girl/Snowman, Boy,* 1986, Item #5095-4, re-scaled to the smaller size. Three kids on toboggan, child on skis, boy and girl putting finishing touches on snowman.

'91	'92	'93	'94	'95	'96	'97
$30	52	52	48	45	50	55

MAN ON LADDER HANGING GARLAND

Item #	Intro	Retired	OSRP	GBTru	↑
5116-0	1988	1992	$7.50	**$19**	19%

Particulars: Man carries garland up ladder to decorate eaves of house. Man is ceramic, ladder is wooden, garland is sisal.

'91	'92	'93	'94	'95	'96	'97
$8	8	18	16	18	16	16

The Original Snow Village® Accessories

HAYRIDE

ITEM #	INTRO	RETIRED	OSRP	GBTRU	↑
5117-9	1988	1990	$30	**$68**	13%

Particulars: Farmer guides horse-drawn hay-filled sleigh with children as riders.

'91	'92	'93	'94	'95	'96	'97
$45	65	70	65	60	60	60

SCHOOL CHILDREN

ITEM #	INTRO	RETIRED	OSRP	GBTRU	↑
5118-7	1988	1990	$15	**$32**	7%

Particulars: Set of 3. Three children carrying school books.

'91	'92	'93	'94	'95	'96	'97
$20	30	25	28	25	25	30

APPLE GIRL/ NEWSPAPER BOY

ITEM #	INTRO	RETIRED	OSRP	GBTRU	↑
5129-2	1988	1990	$11	**$25**	14%

Particulars: Set of 2. Girl holds wood tray carrier selling apples for 5¢, newsboy sells the Village News.

'91	'92	'93	'94	'95	'96	'97
$20	25	20	22	20	22	22

WOODSMAN AND BOY

ITEM #	INTRO	RETIRED	OSRP	GBTRU	↑
5130-6	1988	1991	$13	**$36**	20%

Particulars: Set of 2. Man chops and splits logs and boy prepares to carry supply to fireplace.

'91	'92	'93	'94	'95	'96	'97
$13	26	22	25	30	30	30

DOGHOUSE/CAT IN GARBAGE CAN

ITEM #	INTRO	RETIRED	OSRP	GBTru	↑
5131-4	1988	1992	$15	**$30**	11%

Particulars: Set of 2. Dog sits outside doghouse decorated with wreath; cat looks at empty boxes and wrappings in garbage can.

'91	'92	'93	'94	'95	'96	'97
$15	15	30	30	25	27	27

FIRE HYDRANT & MAILBOX

ITEM #	INTRO	RETIRED	OSRP	GBTru	NO
5132-2	1988	CURRENT	$6	**$6**	CHANGE

Particulars: Set of 2. Red fire hydrant and rural curbside mailbox on post. Sizes are 1 1/2" & 2 3/4", respectively.

'91	'92	'93	'94	'95	'96	'97
$6	6	6	6	6	6	6

WATER TOWER

ITEM #	INTRO	RETIRED	OSRP	GBTru	↑
5133-0	1988	1991	$20	**$90**	20%

Particulars: 2 pieces. Metal scaffold base holds red ceramic Original Snow Village® water container with green top, ladder leads to top.

'91	'92	'93	'94	'95	'96	'97
$22	48	48	52	65	70	75

WATER TOWER– "JOHN DEERE"

ITEM #	INTRO	RETIRED	OSRP	GBTru	↓
2510-4	1988	PROMO	$24	**$625**	10%

Particulars: Special piece, *John Deere Water Tower* is exactly the same as the *Original Snow Village® Water Tower* with the exception of it reads, "Moline Home of John Deere." It was offered for sale through the John Deere catalog.

'91	'92	'93	'94	'95	'96	'97
$125	125	150	395	650	675	695

The Original Snow Village® Accessories

NATIVITY

ITEM #	INTRO	RETIRED	OSRP	GBTRU	NO
5135-7	1988	CURRENT	$7.50	**$7.50**	CHANGE

Particulars: Holy Family, lamb, in crèche scene.
Size is 2 ¼".

'91	'92	'93	'94	'95	'96	'97
$7.50	7.50	7.50	7.50	7.50	7.50	7.50

WOODY STATION WAGON

ITEM #	INTRO	RETIRED	OSRP	GBTRU	↑
5136-5	1988	1990	$6.50	**$35**	17%

Particulars: "Wood" paneled sides on station wagon.

'91	'92	'93	'94	'95	'96	'97
$12	20	22	30	25	25	30

SCHOOL BUS, SNOW PLOW

ITEM #	INTRO	RETIRED	OSRP	GBTRU	↑
5137-3	1988	1991	$16	**$67**	22%

Particulars: Set of 2. Yellow school bus and red sand gravel truck with snow plow.

'91	'92	'93	'94	'95	'96	'97
$16	25	25	55	50	57	55

TREE LOT

ITEM #	INTRO	RETIRED	OSRP	GBTRU	NO
5138-1	1988	CURRENT	$33.50	**$37.50**	CHANGE

Particulars: Christmas lights on tree lot's fence plus decorated shack and trees for sale. The shack is ceramic, the fence is wood and the trees are sisal.
Size is 9 ½" x 5" x 4 ½".

'91	'92	'93	'94	'95	'96	'97
$37.50	37.50	37.50	37.50	37.50	37.50	37.50

SISAL TREE LOT

ITEM #	INTRO	RETIRED	OSRP	GBTRU	↓
8183-3	1988	1991	$45	**$90**	5%

Particulars: A variety of cut trees for sale at a street lot. Signs identify the trees in each row.

'91	'92	'93	'94	'95	'96	'97
$45	80	85	85	75	85	95

VILLAGE GAZEBO

ITEM #	INTRO	RETIRED	OSRP	GBTRU	↑
5146-2	1989	1995	$27	**$42**	5%

Particulars: Small, open, red roofed garden structure that will protect folks from rain and snow, or be a private place to sit.

'91	'92	'93	'94	'95	'96	'97
$27.50	28	30	30	30	42	40

CHOIR KIDS

ITEM #	INTRO	RETIRED	OSRP	GBTRU	↑
5147-0	1989	1992	$15	**$30**	7%

Particulars: Four kids in white and red robes with green songbooks caroling.

'91	'92	'93	'94	'95	'96	'97
$15	15	20	28	25	25	28

SPECIAL DELIVERY

ITEM #	INTRO	RETIRED	OSRP	GBTRU	↑
5148-9	1989	1990	$16	**$57**	14%

Particulars: Set of 2. Mailman and mailbag with his mail truck in USPO colors of red, white and blue with the eagle logo. Discontinued due to licensing problems with the U.S. Postal Service. Replaced with 1990, *Special Delivery*, Item #5197-7.

'91	'92	'93	'94	'95	'96	'97
$45	42	42	42	45	40	50

The Original Snow Village® Accessories

FOR SALE SIGN

ITEM #	INTRO	RETIRED	OSRP	GBTRU	NO
5166-7	1989	CURRENT	$4.50	**$4.50**	CHANGE

Particulars: Enameled metal sign can advertise "For Sale" or "SOLD" depending which side is displayed. Birds decorate and add color. Size is 3".

'91	'92	'93	'94	'95	'96	'97
$4.50	4.50	4.50	4.50	4.50	4.50	4.50

FOR SALE SIGN— "BACHMAN'S®"

ITEM #	INTRO	RETIRED	OSRP	GBTRU	NO
539-8	1989	PROMO	$4.50	**$25**	CHANGE

Particulars: Bachman's Exclusive for their Village Gathering in 1990. Enameled metal sign reads "Bachman's Village Gathering 1990". Birds decorate and add color. Size is 3".

'96	'97
$25	25

STREET SIGN

ITEM #	INTRO	RETIRED	OSRP	GBTRU	↑
5167-5	1989	1992	$7.50	**$12**	20%

Particulars: 6 pieces per package. Green metal street signs. Use the street names provided (Lake St., Maple Dr., Park Ave., River Rd., Elm St., Ivy Lane ...) or personalize to give each village street a unique name. Size: 4 $1/4$" tall.

'91	'92	'93	'94	'95	'96	'97
$7.50	7.50	NE	8	8	12	10

KIDS TREE HOUSE

ITEM #	INTRO	RETIRED	OSRP	GBTRU	↑
5168-3	1989	1991	$25	**$65**	8%

Particulars: Decorated club house built on an old dead tree. Steps lead up to the hideaway. Material is resin.

'91	'92	'93	'94	'95	'96	'97
$25	48	45	45	50	55	60

BRINGING HOME THE TREE

ITEM #	INTRO	RETIRED	OSRP	GBTRU	↑
5169-1	1989	1992	$15	**$28**	12%

Particulars: A man pulls a sled holding the tree as the girl watches to make sure it doesn't fall off. Tree is sisal.

'91	'92	'93	'94	'95	'96	'97
$15	15	20	22	25	27	25

SKATE FASTER MOM

ITEM #	INTRO	RETIRED	OSRP	GBTRU	↓
5170-5	1989	1991	$13	**$28**	7%

Particulars: Two children sit in the sleigh as their skating Mom pushes them across the ice

'91	'92	'93	'94	'95	'96	'97
$13	30	28	24	20	28	30

CRACK THE WHIP

ITEM #	INTRO	RETIRED	OSRP	GBTRU	↓
5171-3	1989	1996	$25	**$30**	6%

Particulars: Set of 3. A fast moving line of skaters hold tightly to the person in front of them. The first person does slow patterns but as the line snakes out, the last people are racing to keep up and they whip out.

'91	'92	'93	'94	'95	'96	'97
$25	25	25	25	25	25	32

THROUGH THE WOODS

ITEM #	INTRO	RETIRED	OSRP	GBTRU	↑
5172-1	1989	1991	$18	**$30**	7%

Particulars: Set of 2. Children bring a tree and a basket of goodies to Grandma.

'91	'92	'93	'94	'95	'96	'97
$18	30	30	22	25	23	28

The Original Snow Village® Accessories

STATUE OF MARK TWAIN

ITEM #	INTRO	RETIRED	OSRP	GBTRU	↑
5173-0	1989	1991	$15	**$45**	13%

Particulars: A tribute to the author who wrote about lives of American folk.

'91	'92	'93	'94	'95	'96	'97
$15	28	28	30	30	35	40

CALLING ALL CARS

ITEM #	INTRO	RETIRED	OSRP	GBTRU	↑
5174-8	1989	1991	$15	**$70**	8%

Particulars: Set of 2. Police car and patrolman directing traffic.

'91	'92	'93	'94	'95	'96	'97
$15	32	30	30	35	35	65

MAILBOX

ITEM #	INTRO	RETIRED	OSRP	GBTRU	NO
5179-9	1989	1990	$3.50	**$20**	CHANGE

Particulars: Freestanding public mailbox in U.S.P.O. colors red, white and blue with logo. Discontinued due to licensing problems with the U.S. Postal Service. Replaced with *Mailbox*, 1990, Item #5198-5, page 99.

'91	'92	'93	'94	'95	'96	'97
$20	20	15	20	20	20	20

SNOW VILLAGE PROMOTIONAL SIGN

ITEM #	INTRO	RETIRED	OSRP	GBTRU	↑
9948-1	1989	Disc. '90	PROMO	**$25**	14%

Particulars: Earthenware sign intended to be used by Department 56, Inc. retailers as a promotional item. Sign displays the Original Snow Village® logo. Brickwork at the base supports the sign.

'95	'96	'97
$15	20	22

BRINGING FLEECES TO THE MILL

ITEM #	INTRO	RETIRED	OSRP	GBTRU	NO
5819-0	1993	CURRENT	$35	**$35**	CHANGE

Particulars: Set of 2. Dickens' Village Series® accessory. Shepherd takes wagon load of fleeces to market. Child stands with sheep.

'93	'94	'95	'96	'97
$35	35	35	35	35

DASHING THROUGH THE SNOW

ITEM #	INTRO	RETIRED	OSRP	GBTRU	NO
5820-3	1993	CURRENT	$32.50	**$32.50**	CHANGE

Particulars: Dickens' Village Series® accessory. Horse drawn sleigh takes couple for ride across snowy roads.

'93	'94	'95	'96	'97
$32.50	32.50	32.50	32.50	32.50

CHRISTMAS AT THE PARK

ITEM #	INTRO	RETIRED	OSRP	GBTRU	NO
5866-1	1993	CURRENT	$27.50	**$27.50**	CHANGE

Particulars: Set of 3. Christmas In The City® accessory. Seated father, mother and child. Seated boy and girl with dog.

'93	'94	'95	'96	'97
$27.50	27.50	27.50	27.50	27.50

VILLAGE EXPRESS VAN— GOLD

ITEM #	INTRO	RETIRED	OSRP	GBTRU	↑
9977-5	1993	PROMO	$25	**$845**	2%

Particulars: Gold "Road Show" Edition of the Village Express Van. Packed in a special gold box. Presented to potential investors before initial public offering.

'95	'96	'97
$1200	945	825

VILLAGE EXPRESS VAN FOR GATHERINGS

ITEM #	INTRO	RETIRED	OSRP	GBTRU
VARIOUS	1994	PROMO	$25	SEE BELOW

Particulars: Black van for store delivery service. Right side is Department 56, Inc. logo and left side features specific Department 56, Inc. dealer name logo. 14 Vans were produced—13 for dealer Department 56, Inc. sponsored Village Gatherings where the Van was sold. The Lemon Tree received the other Van to be sold to members of the store's Collector's Club:

Bachman's	#729-3	$70
Bronner's Christmas Wonderland	#737-4	$50
European Imports	#739-0	$50
Fortunoff	#735-8	$100
Lemon Tree	#721-8	$45
Lock, Stock & Barrel	#731-5	$100
North Pole City	#736-6	$50
Robert's Christmas Wonderland	#734-0	$50
Stats	#741-2	$50
The Christmas Dove	#730-7	$50
The Incredible Christmas Place	#732-3	$50
The Limited Edition	#733-1	$95
The Windsor Shoppe	#740-4	$50
William Glen	#738-2	$50

MICKEY & MINNIE

ITEM #	INTRO	RETIRED	OSRP	GBTRU	
5353-8	1994	1996	$22.50	**$35**	NO CHANGE

Particulars: Set of 2. Disney Parks Village™ accessory. Mickey and Minnie characters welcome guests to the Disney Theme Parks.

'94	'95	'96	'97
$22.50	22.50	22.50	35

DISNEY PARKS FAMILY

ITEM #	INTRO	RETIRED	OSRP	GBTRU	
5354-6	1994	1996	$32.50	**$38**	↑ 9%

Particulars: Set of 3. Disney Parks Village™ accessory. Family of seven enjoys a day at a Disney Park. Mom photographs kids in Mouse ears, as two others eat ice cream cones, and one tot is seated on Dad's shoulders for best view.

'94	'95	'96	'97
$32.50	32.50	32.50	35

The Heritage Village Collection® Accessories

OLDE WORLD ANTIQUES GATE

ITEM #	INTRO	RETIRED	OSRP	GBTʀᴜ	↑
5355-4	1994	1996	$15	**$20**	11%

Particulars: Disney Parks Village™ accessory. Entry gate with wooden door. Brick frames door and is base for wrought iron fencing.

'94	'95	'96	'97
$15	15	15	18

POLKA FEST

ITEM #	INTRO	RETIRED	OSRP	GBTʀᴜ	NO
5607-3	1994	CURRENT	$30	**$30**	CHANGE

Particulars: Set of 3. Alpine Village Series™ accessory. Musicians play polka as a couple dances. Boy sings and yodels to the music.

'94	'95	'96	'97
$30	30	30	30

LAST MINUTE DELIVERY

ITEM #	INTRO	RETIRED	OSRP	GBTʀᴜ	NO
5636-7	1994	CURRENT	$35	**$35**	CHANGE

Particulars: North Pole Series™ accessory. Elves hand-power a rail car pulling doll car and teddy car as another elf hangs onto rear bumper. Shipping was delayed until 1996 due to production problems.

'94	'95	'96	'97
$35	35	35	35

SNOW CONE ELVES

ITEM #	INTRO	RETIRED	OSRP	GBTʀᴜ	↑
5637-5	1994	1997	$30	**$36**	20%

Particulars: Set of 4. North Pole Series™ accessory. Elves taste test new batch of snow cones. Cart holds more flavors. Icicles form on snow cone sign.

'94	'95	'96	'97
$30	30	30	30

OVER THE RIVER AND THROUGH THE WOODS

ITEM #	INTRO	RETIRED	OSRP	GBTʀᴜ	NO
5654-5	1994	CURRENT	$35	**$35**	CHANGE

Particulars: New England Village® accessory. After cutting tree for home, father and kids use horse-drawn sleigh to bring it in. Their dog runs along side.

'94	'95	'96	'97
$35	35	35	35

THE OLD MAN AND THE SEA

ITEM #	INTRO	RETIRED	OSRP	GBTʀᴜ	NO
5655-3	1994	CURRENT	$25	**$25**	CHANGE

Particulars: Set of 3. New England Village® accessory. Two children listen closely as the man tells stories of the sea. Boy holds telescope.

'94	'95	'96	'97
$25	25	25	25

TWO RIVERS BRIDGE

ITEM #	INTRO	RETIRED	OSRP	GBTʀᴜ	↑
5656-1	1994	1997	$35	**$40**	14%

Particulars: New England Village® accessory. Wooden bridge on 3 sets of pilings spans 2 rivers. Horses, carriages and carts use center. Walkers use side passages. Porcelain and Resin. Size: 8 1/2" x 4 1/2" x 4".

'94	'95	'96	'97
$35	35	35	35

WINTER SLEIGHRIDE

ITEM #	INTRO	RETIRED	OSRP	GBTʀᴜ	NO
5825-4	1994	CURRENT	$18	**$18**	CHANGE

Particulars: Dickens' Village Series® accessory. Ice-skating boys give a sleigh ride to a friend. In the proofs, the handle attached to the sleigh with wires that were curled at the ends.

'94	'95	'96	'97
$18	18	18	18

CHELSEA MARKET MISTLETOE MONGER & CART

ITEM #	INTRO	RETIRED	OSRP	GBTRU	NO
5826-2	1994	CURRENT	$25	**$25**	CHANGE

Particulars: Set of 2. Dickens' Village Series® accessory. Vendor sells greens from basket as wife sells from cart.

'94	'95	'96	'97
$25	25	25	25

CHELSEA MARKET CURIOSITIES MONGER & CART

ITEM #	INTRO	RETIRED	OSRP	GBTRU	NO
5827-0	1994	CURRENT	$27.50	**$27.50**	CHANGE

Particulars: Set of 2. Dickens' Village Series® accessory. Vendor stands next to cart playing concertina. He sells everything from toys to clocks to quilts.

'94	'95	'96	'97
$27.50	27.50	27.50	27.50

PORTOBELLO ROAD PEDDLERS

ITEM #	INTRO	RETIRED	OSRP	GBTRU	NO
5828-9	1994	CURRENT	$27.50	**$27.50**	CHANGE

Particulars: Set of 3. Dickens' Village Series® accessory. Peddlers sell toys and carol song sheets to passing villagers.

'94	'95	'96	'97
$27.50	27.50	27.50	27.50

THATCHERS

ITEM #	INTRO	RETIRED	OSRP	GBTRU	↑
5829-7	1994	1997	$35	**$38**	9%

Particulars: Set of 3. Dickens' Village Series® accessory. Workers gather up and place thatch bundles on cart.

'94	'95	'96	'97
$35	35	35	35

The Heritage Village Collection® Accessories

A Peaceful Glow On Christmas Eve

Item #	Intro	Retired	OSRP	GBTru	
5830-0	1994	Current	$30	**$30**	NO CHANGE

Particulars: Set of 3. Dickens' Village Series® accessory. Clergyman watches children sell candles for church service.

'94	'95	'96	'97
$30	30	30	30

Christmas Carol Holiday Trimming Set

Item #	Intro	Retired	OSRP	GBTru	↑
5831-9	1994	1997	$65	**$72**	11%

Particulars: Set of 21. Dickens' Village Series® accessory. Holiday trimming set with gate, fence, lamppost, trees, garlands, wreaths, and 3 figurine groupings.

'94	'95	'96	'97
$65	65	65	65

Chamber Orchestra

Item #	Intro	Retired	OSRP	GBTru	
5884-0	1994	Current	$37.50	**$37.50**	NO CHANGE

Particulars: Set of 4. Christmas In The City® accessory. Conductor and four musicians play outdoor holiday music concert.

'94	'95	'96	'97
$37.50	37.50	37.50	37.50

Holiday Field Trip

Item #	Intro	Retired	OSRP	GBTru	
5885-8	1994	Current	$27.50	**$27.50**	NO CHANGE

Particulars: Set of 3. Christmas In The City® accessory. Five students walk with their teacher as they visit the City sights.

'94	'95	'96	'97
$27.50	27.50	27.50	27.50

HOT DOG VENDOR

ITEM #	INTRO	RETIRED	OSRP	GBTRU	↑
5886-6	1994	1997	$27.50	**$33**	20%

Particulars: Set of 3. Christmas In The City® accessory. Mother buys hot dog for son from a street vendor.

'94	'95	'96	'97
$27.50	27.50	27.50	27.50

POSTERN

ITEM #	INTRO	RETIRED	OSRP	GBTRU	NO
9871-0	1994	1994	$17.50	**$27**	CHANGE

Particulars: Dickens' Village Series® Ten Year Anniversary Piece. Cornerstone with dates. Special commemorative imprint on bottom. Arched, timbered entry connected to gatehouse. Flag flies at top of arch; village sign hangs below it. Posterns were entrances to important places or village gathering areas.

'94	'95	'96	'97
$17.50	25	25	27

PROMOTIONAL VILLAGE EXPRESS VANS

ITEM #	INTRO	RETIRED	OSRP	GBTRU
VARIOUS	1995	PROMO	SEE BELOW	**SEE BELOW**

Particulars: The Black Village Express Promotional Van design introduced in 1994 was continued in 1995 adding the following special pieces:

1) *St. Nick's Van*, #7560, was produced for St. Nick's in Littleton, CO. This van does not say Department 56, Inc. on the passenger door. Both doors read "1995."
GBTru: $60

2) *Parkwest Van*, #7522, was produced for the NALED affiliated Parkwest Catalog Group to commemorate their 10th Anniversary. The group has 350 dealers. The panel of the van featured the symbol of a running deer, "Parkwest, 10th Anniversary" was printed below.
GBTru: $575

3) *Canadian Van*, #21637, was produced for Canadian dealers and distributed by Millard Lister Sales Ltd. The 10 Canadian Provinces were listed on the van's top rail. One side panel says "On-Time Delivery Since 1976: The Village Express." The other panel has a Red Maple Leaf, Canadian Event 1995. Doors have 1995. SRP was $40.00. **GBTru: $45**

The Heritage Village Collection® Accessories

SQUASH CART

Item #	Intro	Retired	OSRP	GBTru	↑
0753-6	1995	Promo	$50	**$100**	5%

Particulars: New England Village® accessory. Commemorates 110th Anniversary of Bachman's. Special bottomstamp. Introduced at the Bachman's Village Gathering, 1995. Green squash are taken to market in horse drawn burgundy wagon by Bachman's workers. See 1995, *Harvest Pumpkin Wagon*, Item #56591, for the Heritage Village Collection® dealers piece with the orange pumpkins in place of green squash.

'95	'96	'97
$50	95	95

BALLOON SELLER

Item #	Intro	Retired	OSRP	GBTru	↑
53539	1995	1996	$25	**$58**	5%

Particulars: Set of 2. Disney Parks Village™ accessory. Girl buys her brother a helium balloon from park vendor.

'95	'96	'97
$25	25	55

"SILENT NIGHT" MUSIC BOX

Item #	Intro	Retired	OSRP	GBTru	NO
56180	1995	Current	$32.50	**$32.50**	CHANGE

Particulars: Music Box which commemorates Christmas song "Silent Night," debuted at Bronner's Christmas Wonderland, Frankenmuth, MI, a Gold Key Dealer. It is based on Silent Night Memorial Chapel in Oberndorf, Austria. A replica of the Chapel is at Bronner's. Music box was available to all Heritage Village Collection® dealers as of 6/1/96.

'95	'96	'97
$32.50	32.50	32.50

"ALPENHORN PLAYER" ALPINE VILLAGE SIGN

Item #	Intro	Retired	OSRP	GBTru	NO
56182	1995	Current	$20	**$20**	CHANGE

Particulars: Alpen horn player in Tyrollean outfit plays long mountain horn.

'95	'96	'97
$20	20	20

The Heritage Village Collection® Accessories

CHARTING SANTA'S COURSE

ITEM #	INTRO	RETIRED	OSRP	GBTRU	↑
56364	1995	1997	$25	**$30**	20%

Particulars. Set of 2. North Pole Series™ accessory. Elves plan Santa's sleigh ride. One checks skies with telescope as other checks constellation maps with globe of earth.

'95	'96	'97
$25	25	25

I'LL NEED MORE TOYS

ITEM #	INTRO	RETIRED	OSRP	GBTRU	NO
56365	1995	CURRENT	$25	**$25**	CHANGE

Particulars: Set of 2. North Pole Series™ accessory. Santa tells elf that more toys are needed from the workshop.

'95	'96	'97
$25	25	25

"A BUSY ELF" NORTH POLE SIGN

ITEM #	INTRO	RETIRED	OSRP	GBTRU	NO
56366	1995	CURRENT	$20	**$20**	CHANGE

Particulars: Red bird watches carver elf create village sign. Porcelain and Acrylic.

'95	'96	'97
$20	20	20

FARM ANIMALS

ITEM #	INTRO	RETIRED	OSRP	GBTRU	NO
56588	1995	CURRENT	$32.50	**$32.50**	CHANGE

Particulars: Set of 8 with 8 hay bales. New England Village® accessory. Cows, horses, sheep, pig, goat, hen and rooster.

'95	'96	'97
$32.50	32.50	32.50

LOBSTER TRAPPERS

ITEM #	INTRO	RETIRED	OSRP	GBTRU	
56589	1995	CURRENT	$35	**$35**	NO CHANGE

Particulars: Set of 4. New England Village® accessory. Boat at dock with lobster filled traps. Boy checks traps and lobsterman holds up a three pounder.

'95	'96	'97
$35	35	35

LUMBERJACKS

ITEM #	INTRO	RETIRED	OSRP	GBTRU	
56590	1995	CURRENT	$30	**$30**	NO CHANGE

Particulars: Set of 2. New England Village® accessory. One man chops tree with ax as second worker saws trunk into logs. Porcelain and Wood.

'95	'96	'97
$30	30	30

HARVEST PUMPKIN WAGON

ITEM #	INTRO	RETIRED	OSRP	GBTRU	
56591	1995	CURRENT	$45	**$45**	NO CHANGE

Particulars: New England Village® accessory. Farm workers gather pumpkins which are loaded onto green wagon. Driver and helper with horse drawn wagon. Though there are slight color modifications, this piece is based on the Bachman's 110th Anniversary Squash Cart sold at the Bachman's Village Gathering in 1995, #753-6.

'95	'96	'97
$45	45	45

"FRESH PAINT" NEW ENGLAND VILLAGE SIGN

ITEM #	INTRO	RETIRED	OSRP	GBTRU	
56592	1995	CURRENT	$20	**$20**	NO CHANGE

Particulars: Sign maker completes lettering of village sign.

'95	'96	'97
$20	20	20

A PARTRIDGE IN A PEAR TREE—#1	ITEM #	INTRO	RETIRED	OSRP	GBTRU	NO
	5835-1	1995	CURRENT	$35	$35	CHANGE

Particulars: Dickens' Village Series® accessory. The 12 Days Of Dickens' Village. Three children dance around tree as a partridge sits on top.

'95	'96	'97
$35	35	35

Twelve Days of Dickens' Village Series

Since the *Twelve Days of Dickens' Village Series* was introduced at the Stationery Show in May 1995, it has lived a misunderstood existence. Many collectors have not ventured past the Series' name. Confined to that series or simply a series of its own, the versatility of these accessories, each with gold-plated adornments, has escaped the imagination of many collectors.

It could be that you can discover something for all twelve pieces. On the other hand, maybe only two or three are for you. In any case, a second look is certainly warranted. Let's take a look at some of the ideas that we have.

A Partridge In A Pear Tree This accessory fits in many village scenes, especially near a school or church. To me, it's a natural near the 1996 special event piece, *Christmas Bells*.

Two Turtle Doves How can you have the *Bird Seller* and not have this nearby?

Three French Hens The woman feeding the hens and the one collecting eggs look great in just about any farm scene—Dickens' Village Series®, Alpine Village Series™, or New England Village® (though they are a little colorful for an Amish farm). The well goes with the same farms, and can also be placed virtually anywhere in a village scene.

Four Calling Birds The clock is as well suited for any village as it is Dickens' Village Series®. The men playing the instruments are a great way to expand the ensemble that makes up the *Chamber Orchestra* in Christmas In The City®. Speaking of the City, they could even go with the *Street Musicians*. Have you ever noticed how similar the instruments that appear in all three accessories are? Trivia: Did you know that the song originally had Four **Colly** Birds?

Five Golden Rings Along with Dickens' Village Series®, since the juggler is in costume, this set appears at home in just about any village. We have even used the juggler in a parade in Christmas In The City®.

Six Geese A-Laying They fit in any village's farm or rural scene. If you have a display featuring the farm animals, the geese are sure to follow.

Seven Swans A-Swimming The swans bring a sense of beauty and gentleness to any scene with an unfrozen lake or pond.

Eight Maids A-Milking This is a great addition for any farm. See *Hens* and *Geese* above.

Nine Ladies Dancing Place these ladies anywhere people are having fun. See *A Partridge in a Pear Tree*.

continued page 284

Twelve Days of Dickens' Village Series

continued from 283

Ten Pipers Piping The pipers can join the juggler from *Five Golden Rings* in a parade in any village. You may think about putting them in front of the *Ramsford* or *Kensington Palace*, too.

Eleven Lords-A-Leaping Looks like a fox hunter in costume to me. It's a perfect companion for the Dickens' Village Series® accessory, *Tallyho!*

Twelve Drummers Drumming The twelve drummers provide the cadence for the parade that also features the pipers and the juggler from *Five Golden Rings.* They can also join the pipers at the *Palace,* adding even more color and fanfare.

the **Village Chronicle**.

TWO TURTLE DOVES—#II

ITEM #	INTRO	RETIRED	OSRP	GBTRU	NO
5836-0	1995	CURRENT	$32.50	**$32.50**	CHANGE

Particulars: Set of 4. Dickens' Village Series® accessory. The 12 Days Of Dickens' Village. Woman carries two turtle doves and boy carries cage. Another woman and daughter watch.

'95	'96	'97
$32.50	32.50	32.50

THREE FRENCH HENS—#III

ITEM #	INTRO	RETIRED	OSRP	GBTRU	NO
58378	1995	CURRENT	$32.50	**$32.50**	CHANGE

Particulars: Set of 3. Dickens' Village Series® accessory. The 12 Days Of Dickens' Village. Farmyard with water pump, farm worker collecting eggs, farm worker scattering grain feed for hen and rooster.

'95	'96	'97
$32.50	32.50	32.50

FOUR CALLING BIRDS—#IV

ITEM #	INTRO	RETIRED	OSRP	GBTRU	NO
58379	1995	CURRENT	$32.50	**$32.50**	CHANGE

Particulars: Set of 2. Dickens' Village Series® accessory. The 12 Days Of Dickens' Village. Street musicians play violin and bass as birds atop clock respond with song.

'95	'96	'97
$32.50	32.50	32.50

FIVE GOLDEN RINGS—#V

ITEM #	INTRO	RETIRED	OSRP	GBTRU	NO
58381	1995	CURRENT	$27.50	**$27.50**	CHANGE

Particulars: Set of 2. Dickens' Village Series® accessory. The 12 Days Of Dickens' Village. Townsfolk watch as juggler balances five rings.

'95	'96	'97
$27.50	27.50	27.50

SIX GEESE A-LAYING—#VI

ITEM #	INTRO	RETIRED	OSRP	GBTRU	NO
58382	1995	CURRENT	$30	**$30**	CHANGE

Particulars: Set of 2. Dickens' Village Series® accessory. The 12 Days Of Dickens' Village. Six geese follow boy and girl.

'95	'96	'97
$30	30	30

BRIXTON ROAD WATCHMAN

ITEM #	INTRO	RETIRED	OSRP	GBTRU	NO
58390	1995	CURRENT	$25	**$25**	CHANGE

Particulars: Set of 2. Dickens' Village Series® accessory. Early method of protection and enforcement of village rules and regulations. Watchman gave warnings, assistance and monitored activities. Guard house used for rest and foul weather.

'95	'96	'97
$25	25	25

"TALLYHO!"

ITEM #	INTRO	RETIRED	OSRP	GBTRU	NO
58391	1995	CURRENT	$50	**$50**	CHANGE

Particulars: Set of 5. Dickens' Village Series® accessory. Country aristocracy ride Hunters for the sport of following scent hounds as they pick up the trail of a fox. Jumping fences and hedges, they ride the countryside, guided by the Whipper-in who sounds the tallyho.

'95	'96	'97
$50	50	50

The Heritage Village Collection® Accessories

CHELSEA MARKET HAT MONGER & CART

ITEM #	INTRO	RETIRED	OSRP	GBTRU	NO
58392	1995	CURRENT	$27.50	**$27.50**	CHANGE

Particulars: Set of 2. Dickens' Village Series® accessory. Hat maker seated on trunk holds up hats for sale for every occasion. Apprentice sits on hand cart with cat on lap.

'95	'96	'97
$27.50	27.50	27.50

"YE OLDE LAMPLIGHTER" DICKENS' VILLAGE SIGN

ITEM #	INTRO	RETIRED	OSRP	GBTRU	NO
58393	1995	CURRENT	$20	**$20**	CHANGE

Particulars: Lamplighter reaches up to light lamp wick in lantern on village sign.

'95	'96	'97
$20	20	20

COBBLER & CLOCK PEDDLER

ITEM #	INTRO	RETIRED	OSRP	GBTRU	↑
58394	1995	1997	$25	**$28**	12%

Particulars: Set of 2. Dickens' Village Series® accessory. Clock peddler sells and repairs clocks and timepieces while cobbler makes and repairs shoes.

'95	'96	'97
$25	25	25

"YES, VIRGINIA..."

ITEM #	INTRO	RETIRED	OSRP	GBTRU	NO
58890	1995	CURRENT	$12.50	**$12.50**	CHANGE

Particulars: Set of 2. Christmas In The City® accessory. Young girl speaks to gentleman with close resemblance to Santa Claus. Famous letter to the editor once written by Virginia is remembered every holiday.

'95	'96	'97
$12.50	12.50	12.50

ONE-MAN BAND & THE DANCING DOG

Item #	Intro	Retired	OSRP	GBTru	NO
58891	1995	Current	$17.50	**$17.50**	CHANGE

Particulars: Set of 2. Christmas In The City® accessory. Man wears contraption to allow playing of 5 instruments as costumed dog dances to the music.

'95	'96	'97
$17.50	17.50	17.50

CHOIR BOYS ALL-IN-A-ROW

Item #	Intro	Retired	OSRP	GBTru	NO
58892	1995	Current	$20	**$20**	CHANGE

Particulars: Christmas In The City® accessory. Choir boys in red, white and gold robes sing Christmas service.

'95	'96	'97
$20	20	20

"A KEY TO THE CITY" CHRISTMAS IN THE CITY SIGN

Item #	Intro	Retired	OSRP	GBTru	NO
58893	1995	Current	$20	**$20**	CHANGE

Particulars: Mayor stands at city gate to welcome dignitary and give the key to the city. Porcelain and Metal.

'95	'96	'97
$20	20	20

ELVES ON ICE

Item #	Intro	Retired	OSRP	GBTru	NO
52298	1996	Current	$7.50	**$7.50**	CHANGE

Particulars: Set of 4. North Pole Series™ accessory. Midyear release. Four skating elves can be used on *Village Animated Skating Pond.* One skates as he rings bells. One pushes another on skates. One speeds on ice with stocking hat blown by wind. One hatless elf glides along ice. Resln.

'96	'97
$7.50	7.50

The Heritage Village Collection® Accessories

287

NUTCRACKER VENDOR & CART	ITEM # 56183	INTRO 1996	RETIRED CURRENT	OSRP $20	GBTRU **$25**	↑ 25%

Particulars: Alpine Village Series™ accessory. Track Compatible. Movable metal wheels allow vendor to sell his nutcrackers throughout the village. A metal arch above cart advertises the finely crafted pieces.

'97
$20

NORTH POLE EXPRESS	ITEM # 56368	INTRO 1996	RETIRED CURRENT	OSRP $37.50	GBTRU **$37.50**	NO CHANGE

Particulars: Set of 3. North Pole Series™ accessory. Train brings vacationing elves and polar bear home to North Pole. Wood fire box engine, open freight car and passenger car topped with a gift carrier arrive at depot.

'97
$37.50

EARLY RISING ELVES	ITEM # 56369	INTRO 1996	RETIRED CURRENT	OSRP $32.50	GBTRU **$32.50**	NO CHANGE

Particulars: Set of 5. North Pole Series™ accessory. Elves dressed in traditional costumes make early bakery deliveries.

'97
$32.50

END OF THE LINE	ITEM # 56370	INTRO 1996	RETIRED CURRENT	OSRP $28	GBTRU **$28**	NO CHANGE

Particulars: Set of 2. North Pole Series™ accessory. Elf in ticket booth welcomes home vacationers from Miami. Crate of oranges will fill many stockings with treats.

'97
$28

BUSINESS REPLY MAIL

FIRST-CLASS MAIL PERMIT 9640 PACIFIC GROVE, CALIFORNIA

POSTAGE WILL BE PAID BY ADDRESSEE

GREENBOOK

Collectors' Information Services
P.O. Box 645
Pacific Grove CA 93950-9989

Thank You for purchasing this GREENBOOK Guide. We'd like to let you know when updates are published and to learn a little bit more about you and how we can help you. Please return this postage-paid card to us and we'll also enter your name in our Quarterly GREENBOOK Guide and Collectible Thank You Giveaway Drawing. We'll be giving away a Guide and a current piece from the Collection covered four times a year...at the end of March, June, September and December. All responses received that quarter will go into the drawing. *Please visit our website at: www.greenbooks.com*

Name: _____

Complete Street Address: _____

Town & Zip: _____

Telephone: _____   Email Address: _____

❑ I own a computer w/CD drive & would like information on GREENBOOK Contemporary Collectible CD Roms.

I purchased/received the GREENBOOK Guide to: *(Check All That Apply)* ❑ Beanie Babies ❑ Boyds Collectibles ❑ Charming Tails ❑ Cherished Teddies by Enesco ❑ Department 56® Villages ❑ Department 56® Snowbabies™ ❑ Hallmark Keepsake Ornaments ❑ Hallmark Kiddie Cars ❑ Harbour Lights ❑ Precious Moments Company Dolls ❑ Precious Moments Figurines by Enesco ❑ Walt Disney Classics Collections

I collect: *(Check All That Apply)* ❑ Annalee Dolls ❑ Armani Figurines ❑ Barbie ❑ Beanie Babies ❑ Thomas Blackshear Sculptures ❑ Boyds Collectibles ❑ Cat's Meow ❑ Charming Tails ❑ Cherished Teddies by Enesco ❑ Christopher Radko Ornaments ❑ Coca Cola Collectibles ❑Department 56® Villages ❑Department 56® Snowbabies™ ❑ Dreamsicles ❑ Fenton Glass ❑ Greenwich Workshop ❑ Hallmark Keepsake Ornaments ❑ Hallmark Kiddie Cars ❑ Harbour Lights ❑ Harmony Kingdom Collectibles ❑ Hummel Figurines by Goebel ❑ Berta Hummel Collectibles ❑ Emmet Kelly, Jr. ❑ Thomas Kinkaide ❑ Sandra Kuck Figurines ❑ Lefton Carousel Collection ❑ LLadro ❑ Precious Moments Company Dolls ❑ Precious Moments Figurines by Enesco ❑ Sarah's Attic ❑ Seraphim Angels by Roman ❑ Sheila's Collectibles ❑ Steiff ❑ Swarovski Silver Crystal ❑ Walt Disney Classics Collection ❑ Other _____

HOLIDAY DELIVERIES

ITEM #	INTRO	RETIRED	OSRP	GBTRU	NO
56371	1996	CURRENT	$16.50	$16.50	CHANGE

Particulars: North Pole Series™ accessory. Track Compatible. Elf pedals three-wheeled velocipede with rear basket filled with gifts to deliver.

'97
$16.50

A NEW POTBELLIED STOVE FOR CHRISTMAS

ITEM #	INTRO	RETIRED	OSRP	GBTRU	NO
56593	1996	CURRENT	$35	$35	CHANGE

Particulars: Set of 2. New England Village® accessory. Track Compatible.

'97
$35

CHRISTMAS BAZAAR: HANDMADE QUILTS

ITEM #	INTRO	RETIRED	OSRP	GBTRU	NO
56594	1996	CURRENT	$25	$25	CHANGE

Particulars: Set of 2. New England Village® accessory. Woman holds up a quilt while child admires assortment piled on display table and shelves.

'97
$25

CHRISTMAS BAZAAR: WOOLENS & PRESERVES

ITEM #	INTRO	RETIRED	OSRP	GBTRU	NO
56595	1996	CURRENT	$25	$25	CHANGE

Particulars: Set of 2. New England Village® accessory. Young boy at street stall sells preserves and pies while a woman and child sell knitted woolen items. Early shipments read "Jams & Jellies" on the sign.

'97
$25

The Heritage Village Collection® Accessories

SEVEN SWANS-A-SWIMMING—#VII	ITEM # 58383	INTRO 1996	RETIRED CURRENT	OSRP $27.50	GBTRU $27.50	NO CHANGE

Particulars: Set of 4. Dickens' Village Series® accessory. The 12 Days Of Dickens' Village. Dickensian couple watch swimming swans.

'97
$27.50

EIGHT MAIDS-A-MILKING—#VIII	ITEM # 58384	INTRO 1996	RETIRED CURRENT	OSRP $25	GBTRU $25.00	NO CHANGE

Particulars: Set of 2. Dickens' Village Series® accessory. The 12 Days Of Dickens' Village. Maid carries milk pails on shoulder yoke after milking the cow.

'97
$25

TENDING THE NEW CALVES	ITEM # 58395	INTRO 1996	RETIRED CURRENT	OSRP $30	GBTRU $30	NO CHANGE

Particulars: Set of 3. Dickens' Village Series® accessory. Midyear release. Boy leads calf. Girl churns butter from fresh milk. Small building to house young calves.

'96   '97
$30   30

CAROLING WITH THE CRATCHIT FAMILY (REVISITED)	ITEM # 58396	INTRO 1996	RETIRED CURRENT	OSRP $37.50	GBTRU $37.50	NO CHANGE

Particulars: Set of 3. Dickens' Village Series® accessory. Midyear release. An addition to the *Christmas Carol Revisited Series.* Bob Cratchit pushes sleigh of family carolers as two sons lead the way, one with lantern and the other with songbook.

'96   '97
$37.50 37.50

YEOMEN OF THE GUARD

Item #	Intro	Retired	OSRP	GBTru	↑
58397	1996	1997	$30	**$68**	127%

Particulars: Set of 5. Dickens' Village Series® accessory. Midyear release. Head Warder and Guards that protect royal buildings and residences. Can be used with *The Tower of London* .

'96	'97
$30	30

THE FEZZIWIG DELIVERY WAGON (REVISITED)

Item #	Intro	Retired	OSRP	GBTru	NO
58400	1996	Current	$32.50	**$32.50**	CHANGE

Particulars: Dickens' Village Series® accessory. Track Compatible. An addition to the *Christmas Carol Revisited Series*. Piece comes with a miniature storybook created and written by designers which sets scene for piece. Metal wheels turn on horse-drawn delivery wagon driven by Mr. Fezziwig.

'97
$32.50

RED CHRISTMAS SULKY

Item #	Intro	Retired	OSRP	GBTru	NO
58401	1996	Current	$30	**$30**	CHANGE

Particulars: Dickens' Village Series® accessory. Track Compatible. Horse-drawn two metal wheels movable carriage carries driver and one passenger.

'97
$30

GINGERBREAD VENDOR

Item #	Intro	Retired	OSRP	GBTru	NO
58402	1996	Current	$22.50	**$22.50**	CHANGE

Particulars: Set of 2. Dickens' Village Series® accessory. Track Compatible. Vendor sells large baked gingerbread cakes from a sleigh. Boy and girl hold their purchase as they nibble pieces.

'97
$22.50

	ITEM #	INTRO	RETIRED	OSRP	GBTRU	NO
"A CHRISTMAS CAROL" READING BY CHARLES DICKENS	58403	1996	CURRENT	$45	**$45**	CHANGE

Particulars: Set of 4. Dickens' Village Series® accessory. This fewer piece set (than #58404) is non-limited and non-numbered. Color palette changes for all pieces except Dickens. Department 56, Inc. logo on bottomstamp. Dickens reads his *A Christmas Carol* story to spectators in park setting. This is an addition to the *Christmas Carol Revisited Series*.

'97
$45

	ITEM #	INTRO	RETIRED	OSRP	GBTRU	↑
"A CHRISTMAS CAROL" READING BY CHARLES DICKENS	58404	1996	LTD ED 42,500	$75	**$145**	93%

Particulars: Set of 7. Dickens' Village Series® accessory. This limited edition set is based on the 4 piece set by the same name. Additional characters and ornaments make up the difference. The edition number is on the base of platform piece with Crest and Lion Badge of the Charles Dickens Heritage Ltd. Foundation. 6 pieces will have Lion decal. This is an addition to the *Christmas Carol Revisited Series*.

'97
$75

	ITEM #	INTRO	RETIRED	OSRP	GBTRU	NO
CITY TAXI	58894	1996	CURRENT	$12.50	**$12.50**	CHANGE

Particulars: Christmas In The City® accessory. Track Compatible. Green fender trim on brown cabs with metal wheels. Roof rack holds packages and holiday tree.

'97
$12.50

	ITEM #	INTRO	RETIRED	OSRP	GBTRU	NO
THE FAMILY TREE	58895	1996	CURRENT	$18	**$18**	CHANGE

Particulars: Christmas In The City® accessory. Track Compatible. Father pulls sled with evergreen tree as son, daughter and family pet help bring it home to trim.

'97
$18

GOING HOME FOR THE HOLIDAYS

ITEM #	INTRO	RETIRED	OSRP	GBTRU	NO
58896	1996	CURRENT	$27.50	**$27.50**	CHANGE

Particulars: Set of 3. Christmas In The City® accessory, Mother, father and two children carry gifts, family pet, and luggage. Train porter with other luggage whistles for taxi.

'97
$27.50

CHRISTMAS BELLS

ITEM #	INTRO	RETIRED	OSRP	GBTRU	NO
98711	1996	1996 ANNUAL	$35	**$50**	CHANGE

Particulars: This is the Homes For The Holidays, November 1996 Event Piece. Gazebo with boy ringing town bell as one child holds ears and another watches.

'96	'97
$35	50

BACHMAN'S® WILCOX TRUCK

ITEM #	INTRO	RETIRED	OSRP	GBTRU	↑
8803	1997	1997 ANNUAL	$29.95	**$75**	150%

Particulars: 2nd Issue in Bachman's Exclusive Accessories. Replica of a Wilcox truck modeled after a 1919 Wilcox restored by the Bachman family.

'97
$29.95

THE HOLLY & THE IVY

ITEM #	INTRO	RETIRED	OSRP	GBTRU	↑
56100	1997	1997 ANNUAL	$17.50	**$25**	43%

Particulars: Set of 2. This was the Homes For The Holiday, November 1997 Event piece.

'97
$17.50

A NEW BATCH OF CHRISTMAS FRIENDS

ITEM #	INTRO	RETIRED	OSRP	GBTRU	NO
56175	1997	CURRENT	$27.50	**$27.50**	CHANGE

Particulars: Set of 3. Midyear release. Alpine Village Series™ accessory. St. Bernard pup plays with little girl. Lederhosen dressed boy pulls pups on a sled.

'97
$27.50

HEIDI & HER GOATS

ITEM #	INTRO	RETIRED	OSRP	GBTRU
56201	1997	CURRENT	$30	**$30**

Particulars: Set of 4. Alpine Village Series™ accessory. Grandpa and Peter join Heidi and her goats. Characters, in traditional alpine dress, based on a favorite children's book.

DON'T BREAK THE ORNAMENTS

ITEM #	INTRO	RETIRED	OSRP	GBTRU
56372	1997	CURRENT	$27.50	**$27.50**

Particulars: Set of 2. North Pole Series™ accessory. Elves carefully hang ornaments on display boughs.

DELIVERING THE CHRISTMAS GREENS

ITEM #	INTRO	RETIRED	OSRP	GBTRU
56373	1997	CURRENT	$27.50	**$27.50**

Particulars: Set of 2. North Pole Series™ accessory. Mrs. Santa sets plants on delivery tray so elves can deliver for the holidays.

UNTANGLE THE CHRISTMAS LIGHTS

ITEM #	INTRO	RETIRED	OSRP	GBTRU
56374	1997	CURRENT	$35	$35

Particulars: North Pole Series™ accessory, Elves check string of lights to make sure they are tangle-free.

CHRISTMAS BAZAAR ... FLAPJACKS & HOT CIDER

ITEM #	INTRO	RETIRED	OSRP	GBTRU
56596	1997	CURRENT	$27.50	$27.50

Particulars: Set of 2. New England Village® accessory. Just the treat for a cold wintry day, flapjacks plus a hot drink. Uniquely American, the griddlecake, johnnycake, hotcake, pancake or flapjack, is a popular food item that is fast and easy to make.

CHRISTMAS BAZAAR... TOY VENDOR & CART

ITEM #	INTRO	RETIRED	OSRP	GBTRU
56597	1997	CURRENT	$27.50	$27.50

Particulars: Set of 2. New England Village® accessory. Children check out and choose toys and games sold by vendor from his wheeled cart.

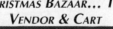

CHRISTMAS BAZAAR... SIGN

ITEM #	INTRO	RETIRED	OSRP	GBTRU
56598	1997	CURRENT	$16	$16

Particulars: Set of 2. New England Village® accessory. Handcrafted sign announces the street market is present and open for business.

The Heritage Village Collection® Accessories

TAPPING THE MAPLES

Item #	Intro	Retired	OSRP	GBTru
56599	1997	Current	$75	**$75**

Particulars: Set of 7. New England Village® accessory. Taught by the Native Americans, early colonists learned to tap maple trees for the precious sweet syrupy treat. This set shows all phases of tapping and collecting the sap.

DELIVERING COAL FOR THE HEARTH

Item #	Intro	Retired	OSRP	GBTru	
58326	1997	Current	$32.50	**$32.50**	NO CHANGE

Particulars: Set of 2. Midyear release. Dickens' Village Series® accessory. Horse-drawn coal cart comes with a small package of coal. Hanging from the rear is a coal scuttle. Coal merchant with broom and another scuttle completes set. First shipments had maroon wheels and the coal buckets were attached permanently with silver hoops. The carts in subsequent shipments have red wheels and the buckets are hung on hooks.

'97
$32.50

NINE LADIES DANCING–#IX

Item #	Intro	Retired	OSRP	GBTru
58385	1997	Current	$30	**$30**

Particulars: Set of 2. Dickens' Village Series® accessory. The 12 Days Of Dickens' Village. Girls dance as a young boy plays a tune.

TEN PIPERS PIPING–#X

Item #	Intro	Retired	OSRP	GBTru
58386	1997	Current	$30	**$30**

Particulars: Set of 3. Dickens' Village Series® accessory. The 12 Days Of Dickens' Village. Men playing the bagpipes led by a drum major.

ASHLEY POND SKATING PARTY

ITEM #	INTRO	RETIRED	OSRP	GBTRU
58405	1997	CURRENT	$70	**$70**

Particulars: Set of 6. Dickens' Village Series® accessory. Ladies, gentlemen, family groups and children skate on the local frozen pond using old-fashioned long blade skates. Small warming house.

THE FIRE BRIGADE OF LONDON TOWN

ITEM #	INTRO	RETIRED	OSRP	GBTRU
58406	1997	CURRENT	$70	**$70**

Particulars: Set of 5. Dickens' Village Series® accessory. Horses pull wheeled water tank pumper. Men pull hose cart and carry buckets and axes. One man sounds horn to clear the roadway.

FATHER CHRISTMAS'S JOURNEY

ITEM #	INTRO	RETIRED	OSRP	GBTRU
58407	1997	CURRENT	$30	**$30**

Particulars: Set of 2. Dickens' Village Series® accessory. Track Compatible. First Santa representation for the Dickens' Village Series®. Santa pulls a colorful old-fashioned sleigh with toys, trinkets and ornaments.

CHRISTMAS PUDDING COSTERMONGER

ITEM #	INTRO	RETIRED	OSRP	GBTRU
58408	1997	CURRENT	$32.50	**$32.50**

Particulars: Set of 3. Dickens' Village Series® accessory. Festive seasonal booth sells holiday dinner treats. Family chooses a Plum Pudding for Christmas dinner.

STEPPIN' OUT ON THE TOWN

ITEM #	INTRO	RETIRED	OSRP	GBTRU	NO
58885	1997	CURRENT	$35	**$35**	CHANGE

Particulars: Set of 5. Midyear release. Christmas In The City® accessory. Track Compatible limo. Doorman stands by limo that transports a couple in evening clothes ready for an evening on the town. Musicians hurry to the nightclub to take their places on the bandstand.

'97
$35

JOHNSON'S GROCERY ... HOLIDAY DELIVERIES

ITEM #	INTRO	RETIRED	OSRP	GBTRU
58897	1997	CURRENT	$18	**$18**

Particulars: Christmas In The City® accessory. Track Compatible. Delivery man pedals a three-wheeled cart bringing holiday treats to shoppers' homes.

SPIRIT OF THE SEASON

ITEM #	INTRO	RETIRED	OSRP	GBTRU
58898	1997	CURRENT	$20	**$20**

Particulars: Christmas In The City® accessory. Winged Angel statue captures the spirit of the holiday. Pigeons rest on the base.

LET'S GO SHOPPING IN THE CITY

ITEM #	INTRO	RETIRED	OSRP	GBTRU
58899	1997	CURRENT	$35	**$35**

Particulars: Set of 3. Christmas In The City® accessory. Women shopping, Grandmother and grandson, and two girls with baby carriage.

BIG SMILE FOR THE CAMERA

ITEM #	INTRO	RETIRED	OSRP	GBTRU
58900	1997	CURRENT	$27.50	**$27.50**

Particulars: Set of 2. Christmas In The City® accessory. Photographer gets ready to take picture of celebrity signing girl's autograph book.

POINSETTIA DELIVERY TRUCK

ITEM #	INTRO	RETIRED	OSRP	GBTRU
59000	1997	CURRENT	$32.50	**$32.50**

Particulars: Old-fashioned wood paneled truck with roll-up canvas top delivers holiday flowers.

TENDING THE COLD FRAME

ITEM #	INTRO	RETIRED	OSRP	GBTRU
2208	1998	1998 ANNUAL	$35	**$35**

Particulars: Created for Bachman's Village Gathering. Henry and Hattie Bachman are seen with several of their children. The children care for young plants in a cold frame–a makeshift greenhouse made from window frames. Tiny plants can be seen. Frames have tiny window hinges.

VILLAGE CAMDEN PARK FOUNTAIN

ITEM #	INTRO	RETIRED	OSRP	GBTRU
52705	1998	CURRENT	$84	**$84**

Particulars: Set of 3. Midyear release. Dickens' Village Series® accessory. Compatible w/Camden Park Square pieces. Complete with a water pump. Working fountain. Water comes out of lion's mouths as well as up from the central sculpture.

The Heritage Village Collection® Accessories

PEPPERMINT SKATING PARTY

ITEM #	INTRO	RETIRED	OSRP	GBTRU
56363	1998	CURRENT	$64	**$64**

Particulars: Set of 6. North Pole Series™ accessory. Skating party consists of Mr. and Mrs. Claus, elves and a fallen-down reindeer. Warming hut helps take out the chill of winter. The weathervane always points to the North.

SEA CAPTAIN & HIS MATES

ITEM #	INTRO	RETIRED	OSRP	GBTRU
56587	1998	CURRENT	$32.50	**$32.50**

Particulars: Set of 4. New England Village® accessory. Captain and crew from the Emily Louise sailing ship. Girl holds ship in bottle and boy sails play boat tied to a tiny rope.

NOTES: _____

_____

_____

_____

_____

_____

_____

_____

_____

_____

_____

_____

_____

_____

_____

This short-lived series was produced for Bachman's Inc. of Minneapolis, MN, the original parent company of Department 56, Inc. Three buildings were manufactured and distributed, but a planned fourth building, a bookstore, never made it past the drawing board.

HOMETOWN BOARDING HOUSE

ITEM #	INTRO	RETIRED	OSRP	GBTRU	↑
670-0	1987	1988	$34	**$345**	15%

Particulars: Inspired by the Sprague House in Red Wing, MN. Three story brick building with rented rooms above the main floor parlor and dining room.

'92	'93	'94	'95	'96	'97
$275	330	330	325	300	300

HOMETOWN CHURCH

ITEM #	INTRO	RETIRED	OSRP	GBTRU	↑
671-8	1987	1988	$40	**$365**	20%

Particulars: Designed after a St. Paul, MN church. Building has cross-shaped floor plan with a spire rising from one side of the transept. A simple entry door at the base of the spire is in contrast to the large arched windows that fill the end walls.

'92	'93	'94	'95	'96	'97
$300	300	300	325	305	305

HOMETOWN DRUGSTORE

ITEM #	INTRO	RETIRED	OSRP	GBTRU	↑
672-6	1988	1989	$40	**$600**	1%

Particulars: Same mold as the Christmas In The City® *Variety Store*, #5972-2. Inspired by a store in Stillwater, MN. Drugstore is corner store in a two attached buildings structure. Taller three story building houses barber shop on main level and eye glass shop above. Garlands decorate the awnings over display windows.

'92	'93	'94	'95	'96	'97
$675	675	675	625	565	595

THE HEINZ HOUSE

ITEM #	INTRO	RETIRED	OSRP	GBTRU	↑
7826	1996	N/A	$28	**$80**	7%

Particulars: This building was manufactured by Department 56, Inc. for the H.J. Heinz Company for them to use in promotions. Heinz gave it as a gift to its vendors and suppliers in late 1996 and sold it to their stockholders by a direct mail campaign in early 1997. It is packed in a white, flap-top box with red lettering.

'97
$75

STATE FARM—MAIN STREET MEMORIES

ITEM #	INTRO	RETIRED	OSRP	GBTRU
56000	1997	N/A	$35.50	**$95**

Particulars: The Main Street Memories building was made available by State Farm Insurance to its agents, employees and their families. The building depicts building highlighted in Randy Souders painting that is also called Main Street Memories. A State Farm agent is located on the right side of the building, a barber shop is on the left side and a drug store in the corner shop.

NOTES:

Profiles™

Trees

1988–1991
#5112-8
SV GARLAND TRIM

3 pieces per package.
Each piece is
24" long.

LSRP: $4.50/pkg

?–1997
#5205-1
EVERGREEN TREES

Set of 3.
Sizes: 3 1/4", 4 1/4"
& 6 1/2".
Cold cast porcelain.

LSRP: $12.95/set

1988–1989
#5115-2
FROSTED TOPIARY VILLAGE GARDEN

photo not
available

Set of 8.
4 cones & 4 ovals.

LSRP: $16/set

?–1996
#6582-0
FROSTED EVERGREEN TREES

Set of 3.
Sizes: 8 1/2", 6 1/2"
& 4 1/2".

LSRP: $16/set

1989–1990
#5184-5
WINTER OAK TREE WITH 2 RED BIRDS

LSRP: $16/ea

1988–1991
#5111-0
CHRISTMAS WREATHS

8 pieces per package.
Sizes: 1" & 3/4".

LSRP: $5/pkg

1989–1994
#5192-6
VILLAGE POTTED TOPIARY PAIR

Sisal trees in white
resin planters.
2 pieces per package.
Size: 4 3/4".

LSRP: $5/pkg

1990–1990
#5183-7
SISAL TREE SET

Set of 7.
4 cones & 3 ovals.

LSRP: $16/set

photo not available

1991–Current
#5202-7
VILLAGE FROSTED TOPIARY, LARGE

Set of 8.
Sizes: 4 cones & 4 oblong, 4" each.

SRP: $12.50/set

1991–Current
#5175-6
VILLAGE FROSTED NORWAY PINES

Set of 3.
Sizes: 7", 9" & 11".

SRP: $12.95/set

1991–Current
#5203-5
VILLAGE FROSTED TOPIARY, SMALL

Set of 8.
Sizes:
4 @ 2" round,
4 @ 3" high.

SRP: $7.50/set

1991–Current
#5200-0
VILLAGE FROSTED TOPIARY, LARGE

2 pieces per package.
Size: 11 1/2".

SRP: $12.50/pkg.

1991–Current
#5419-4
SISAL WREATHS

6 pieces per package.
Size: 1" diameter.

SRP: $4/pkg

1991–Current
#5201-9
VILLAGE FROSTED TOPIARY, MEDIUM

Set of 4.
Sizes:
2 @ 7 1/2"
& 2 @ 6".

SRP: $10/set

1991–Current
#5527-1
VILLAGE POLE PINE FOREST

Set of 5.
4 trees in a snow base.
Size: 10" x 5" x 12".

SRP: $48/set

Trees

1991–Current
#5528-0
***VILLAGE POLE PINE
TREE, SMALL***
Size: 8".
SRP: $10/ea

1992–1997
#5219-1
***VILLAGE PORCELAIN
PINE TREE, SMALL***
Size is 7".
LSRP: $10

1991–Current
#5529-8
***VILLAGE POLE PINE
TREE, LARGE***
Size: 10 1/2".
SRP: $12.50/ea

1993–1993
#5181-0
***VILLAGE WINTER OAK,
SMALL***
Size: 4 1/4".
LSRP: $4.50/ea

photo not
available

1992–1992
#5185-3
***TOPIARY GARDEN
SISAL***
36 pieces assorted.
Sizes:
2 1/2", 4", 6", 8" &
12".
LSRP: $50/set

1993–1993
#5182-9
***VILLAGE WINTER OAK,
LARGE***
Size: 7 3/4".
LSRP: $8/ea

1992–1997
#5218-3
***VILLAGE PORCELAIN
PINE, LARGE***
Size is 8 1/2".
LSRP: $12.50

1993–1996
#5216-7
***VILLAGE WINTER
BIRCH TREE***
Size: 11 1/2".
LSRP: $12.50/ea

Trees

1993–1995
#5221-3

VILLAGE PINE CONE TREES

Set of 2.
Sizes: 8 ³/₄" & 7 ¹/₄".
Resin.

LSRP: $15/set

1994–1996
#5231-0

VILLAGE FROSTED SPRUCE TREE

Size: 15".

LSRP: $12.50/ea

1993–1995
#6595-1

SPRUCE TREE WITH WOODEN BASE, SMALL

Size: 6".

LSRP: $3.50/ea

1994–1996
#5232-9

VILLAGE FROSTED SPRUCE TREE

Size: 22".

LSRP: $27.50/ea

1993–1995
#6597-8

SPRUCE TREE WITH WOODEN BASE, MEDIUM

Size: 9".

LSRP: $5/ea

1994–Current
#5243-4

VILLAGE BARE BRANCH TREE, W/25 LIGHTS

This item is Battery Operated or can be used with Adapter, Item #5225-6.
Size: 9".

SRP: $13.50/ea

1993–1995
#6598-6

SPRUCE TREE WITH WOODEN BASE, LARGE

Size: 12".

LSRP: $7/ea

1994–Current
#5246-9

VILLAGE PENCIL PINES

Set of 3.
Sizes: 12", 8" & 5".

SRP: $15/set

Trees

1994–1997
#5251-5

PORCELAIN PINE TREE

Set of 2.
Sizes: 4 ³/₄" & 3 ³/₄".

LSRP: $15

1995–1996
#5248-5

SPRUCE TREE FOREST

Set of 4.
Size: 16" x 14".

LSRP: $25/set

1994–1997
#5254-0

VILLAGE AUTUMN MAPLE TREE

Size: 11".

LSRP: $15/ea

1995–1996
#5249-3

VILLAGE FROSTED ZIG-ZAG TREE, WHITE

Set of 3.
Sizes: 9", 7" & 4 ¹/₂".

LSRP: $15/set

1995–1996
#5241-8

VILLAGE FROSTED BARE BRANCH TREE, SMALL

Size: 9 ¹/₂".

LSRP: $6.50/ea

1995–1996
#5250-7

VILLAGE FROSTED ZIG-ZAG TREE, GREEN

Set of 3.
Sizes: 9", 7" & 4 ¹/₂".

LSRP: $15/set

1995–1996
#5242-6

VILLAGE FROSTED BARE BRANCH TREE, LARGE

Size: 13".

LSRP: $12.50/ea

1995–1996
#5255-8

SNOWY WHITE PINE TREE, SMALL

Size: 18".

LSRP: $15/ea

Trees

1995–1996
#5256-6
***SNOWY WHITE PINE
TREE, LARGE***
Size: 24".
LSRP: $20/ea

1995–1997
#52603
***LIGHTED SNOWCAPPED
REVOLVING TREE***
Lighted. Battery
Operated or can be
used with Adapter,
Item #5225-6.
Size: 8". Resin.

LSRP: $35/ea

1995–Current
#52590
VILLAGE LANDSCAPE
Set of 14.
SRP: $16.50/set

1995–1997
#52604
***LIGHTED SNOWCAPPED
TREES***
Set of 2.
Lighted.
Sizes: 10" & 8".
Resin.
LSRP: $45/set

1995–Current
#52596
***VILLAGE FLEXIBLE
SISAL HEDGE***
3 pieces per
package.
Each piece is 12"
long.
SRP: $7.50/pkg

1995–Current
#52605
***VILLAGE FROSTED FIR
TREES***
Set of 4.
Sizes:
15", 12", 9" & 6 $^1/4$".
SRP: $15/set

1995–Current
#52600
***VILLAGE HYBRID
LANDSCAPE***
Set of 22.
SRP: $35/set

1995–Current
#52606
***VILLAGE CEDAR PINE
FOREST***
Set of 3.
Sizes: 12", 10" & 8".
SRP: $15/set

Trees

1995–Current
#52607

VILLAGE PONDEROSA PINES

Set of 3.
Sizes: 12", 10" & 9".

SRP: $13/set

1995–Current
#52613

VILLAGE SNOWY EVERGREEN TREES, MEDIUM

Set of 6.
Sizes: 7 1/4", 5 1/2", 5 1/4", 5" & 4 1/4".
Resin.

SRP: $25/set

1995–Current
#52608

VILLAGE ARCTIC PINES

Set of 3.
Sizes: 10", 8" & 6".

SRP: $12/set

1995–Current
#52614

VILLAGE SNOWY EVERGREEN TREES, LARGE

Set of 5.
Sizes:
9 1/4", 9", 7 1/4" & 7".
Resin.

SRP: $32.50/set

1995–Current
#52610

VILLAGE FALLEN LEAVES

Size: 3 oz. bag.
Fabric.

SRP: $5/bag

1995–Current
#52615

VILLAGE SNOWY SCOTCH PINES

Set of 3.
Sizes: 7", 5 1/4" & 5".
Resin.

SRP: $15/set

1995–Current
#52612

VILLAGE SNOWY EVERGREEN TREES, SMALL

Set of 6.
Sizes: 3 1/2", 3", 2 1/4" & 2".
Resin.

SRP: $8.50/set

1995 Current
#52616

VILLAGE AUTUMN TREES

Set of 3.
Sizes:
7 3/4", 6" & 4 3/4".
Resin.

SRP: $13.50/set

Trees

1995–Current
#52617

VILLAGE WAGON WHEEL PINE GROVE

Size:
6 ³/₄" x 6 ¹/₄" x 6 ¹/₂".
Resin.

SRP: $22.50/ea

1996–Current
#52623

VILLAGE BARE BRANCH TREES

Set of 6.

SRP: $22.50/set

1995–Current
#52618

VILLAGE PINE POINT POND

Size:
9 ¹/₄" x 8" x 5 ³/₄".
Resin.

SRP: $37.50/ea

1996–Current
#52630

VILLAGE HOLLY TREE

Size: 7".

SRP: $10/ea

1995–Current
#52619

VILLAGE DOUBLE PINE TREES

Size:
5 ¹/₄" x 5 ¹/₂" x 6".
Resin.

SRP: $13.50/ea

1996–Current
#52631

VILLAGE BIRCH TREE CLUSTER

With 2 mailboxes.

SRP: $20/ea

1996–Current
#52622

VILLAGE JACK PINES

Set of 3.

SRP: $18/set

1996–Current
#52632

VILLAGE TOWERING PINES

Set of 2.
With cardinals.
Sizes: 7" & 9".

SRP: $13.50/set

1996–Current
#52636
VILLAGE WINTER BIRCH
Set of 6.
Sizes:
12", 9 ¹/₂" & 7 ¹/₂".

SRP: $22.50/set

1997–Current
#52655
VILLAGE AUTUMN BIRCH/MAPLE TREE
Set of 4.
Sizes: 12" & 8".

SRP: $27.50/set

1996–Current
#52637
VILLAGE FROSTED SPRUCE
Set of 2.
Sizes: 15 1/2" & 12".

SRP: $25/set

1997–Current
#52660
VILLAGE WINTERGREEN PINES
Set of 3.
Sizes:
3", 4 ¹/₄" & 5 ¹/₄".

SRP: $7.50

1996–Current
#52638
VILLAGE FROSTED HEMLOCK TREES
Set of 2.
Sizes: 15 1/2" & 12".

SRP: $32.50/set

1997–Current
#52661
VILLAGE WINTERGREEN PINES
Set of 2.
Sizes: 7" & 8 ¹/₂".

SRP: $15

1996–Current
#52639
VILLAGE TOWN TREE
With 50 LED Lights.
Size: 14".

SRP: $35/ea

1997–Current
#52662
VILLAGE FLEXIBLE SISAL HEDGE
Set of 3.
Size: 12".

SRP: $10/set

Trees

1997–Current
#52665
VILLAGE LOG PILE

Wood crib holds cut logs.
Size: 4".

SRP: $3/ea

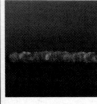

1998–Current
#52703
VILLAGE FLEXIBLE AUTUMN HEDGES

Set of 2. Size: 12" long.

SRP: $10

1997–Current
#52683
VILLAGE LIGHTED SNOWY TREE

45 LED lights/ adapter.
Size: 8.5".

SRP: $27.50/ea

Trims

1997–Current
#52690
VILLAGE LIGHTED CHRISTMAS TREE

With 50 LED lights/ adapter.

SRP: $48/ea

1987–1993
#5109-8
VILLAGE PARK BENCH

Size: 2 ¹/₂".

LSRP: $3.20/ea

1997–Current
#59001
VILLAGE PORCELAIN PINE TREE

Set of 4.

SRP: $17.50/set

1988–Current
#5110-1
VILLAGE TOWN CLOCK

2 assorted–green or black.
Size: 3 ¹/₂" tall.

SRP: $3/ea

1988–Current
#5139-0
UP ON A ROOF TOP
2 pieces.
Size: 4" long.
Pewter.

SRP: $6.50/ea

1989–1994
#5180-2
VILLAGE BIRDS
6 pieces per package.

LSRP: $3.50/pkg

1989–Current
#5176-4
VILLAGE STOP SIGN
2 pieces per
package.
Size: 3" tall.

SRP: $5/pkg

1990–1994
#5206-0
CANDLES BY THE DOORSTEP
4 pieces per package.
2 "AA" Batteries.
Size: 2 1/4".

LSRP: $6.95/pkg

1989–Current
#5177-2
FLAG POLE
Resin base, metal
pole, cloth flag and
thread rope.
Size: 7" high.

SRP: $8.50/ea

1990–Current
#5211-6
VILLAGE ACRYLIC ICICLES
4 pieces per package.
Each piece is 18"
long.

SRP: $4.50/pkg

1989–Current
#5178-0
VILLAGE PARKING METER
4 pieces per
package. Size: 2"
tall.

SRP: $6/pkg

1990–Current
#5511-5
'CHRISTMAS EAVE' TRIM
Non-electric bulb
garland.
Size: 24" long.

SRP: $3.50/ea

Trims

1991–Current
#5208-6

VILLAGE MYLAR SKATING POND

2 sheets per package.
Each sheet is
25 1/4" x 18".

SRP: $6/pkg

1991–Current
#5984-6

VILLAGE COBBLESTONE ROAD

2 strips per package.
Each strip is
4 3/4" x 36".

SRP: $10/pkg

1991–Current
#5210-8

VILLAGE BRICK ROAD

2 strips per package.
Each strip is
4 3/4" x 36".
Vinyl.

SRP: $10/pkg

1992–1992
#948-2

HERITAGE VILLAGE COLLECTION® PROMOTIONAL LOGO BANNER

Giveaway at 1992 events.

LSRP: n/a

1991–1997
#5417-8

"IT'S A GRAND OLD FLAG"

2 pieces per package.
Size: 2 1/4".
Metal.

LSRP: $4/pkg

1992–Current
#5217-5

TACKY WAX

Size: 1" diameter x 1" deep tub.

SRP: $2/tub

1991–1994
#5418-6

VILLAGE GREETINGS

Set of 3.

LSRP: $5/set

1992–1995
#5526-3

HERITAGE BANNERS

Set of 4, 2 each of 2.
Size: 1 1/4".

LSRP: $6/set

Trims

1993–Current
#5230-2

VILLAGE WROUGHT IRON PARK BENCH

Size: 2 ¼".
Metal.

SRP: $5/ea

1993–1994
#5524-7

"VILLAGE SOUNDS" TAPE WITH SPEAKERS

23 minute tape.

LSRP: $25/ea

1993–Current
#5233-7

VILLAGE SLED & SKIS

Set of 2.
Sizes: 2" & 2 ¼".

SRP: $6/set

1993–1994
#5525-5

"VILLAGE SOUNDS" TAPE

23 minutes,
continuous play.

LSRP: $8/ea

1993–Current
#5456-9

WINDMILL

Size: 11 ½" high.
Metal with earthen
base.

SRP: $20/ea

1994–Current
#98841

"THE BUILDING OF A VILLAGE TRADITION" VIDEO, WITH INSTRUCTION BOOKLET

35 Minutes.

SRP: $19.95/ea

1993–Current
#5512-3

UTILITY ACCESSORIES

Set of 8.
2 stop signs,
4 parking meters,
2 traffic lights.
Sizes: 1 ¾", 2" & 3".

SRP: $12.50/set

1995–Current
#52594

VILLAGE LET IT SNOW SNOWMAN SIGN

Size: 6".
Resin.

SRP: $12.50/ea

Trims

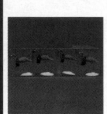

1995–Current
#52595

***VILLAGE PINK
FLAMINGOS***

4 pieces per
package.
Size: 1 ³/₄".

SRP: $7.50/pkg

1996–Current
#52591

***VILLAGE SQUARE
CLOCK TOWER***

Battery-operated
watch.

SRP: $32.50/ea

1995–1997
#52599

***VILLAGE ELECTION
YARD SIGNS***

Set of 6, assorted.
Size: 2 ¹/₄".

LSRP: $10/set

1996–Current
#52620

***VILLAGE MAGIC
SMOKE™***

Pine Scent.
6 oz. bottle.

SRP: $2.50/ea

1995–Current
#52601

***VILLAGE BRICK TOWN
SQUARE***

Size: 23 ¹/₂" square.
Vinyl.

SRP: $15/ea

1996–Current
#52633

***VILLAGE MILL CREEK
(STRAIGHT SECTION)***

Straight section of
creek bed with
evergreens.
Size: 9 ¹/₄" x 4 ¹/₂".

SRP: $12.50/ea

1995–Current
#52602

***VILLAGE COBBLE-
STONE TOWN SQUARE***

Size: 23 ¹/₂" square.
Vinyl.

SRP: $15/ea

1996–Current
#52634

***VILLAGE MILL CREEK
(CURVED SECTION)***

Curved section of
creek bed with
evergreens.
Size: 8 ¹/₂" x 4 ¹/₂".

SRP: $12.50/ea

Trims

1996–Current
#52635

VILLAGE MILL CREEK BRIDGE

Stone bridge over section of creek.
Size: 10 ³/₄" x 5 ³/₄".

SRP: $35/ea

1997–Current
#52649

VILLAGE STONE HOLLY TREE CORNER POSTS

Set of 2.
Size: 4 ¹/₄".

SRP: $8.50/set

1997–Current
#52646

VILLAGE STONE FOOTBRIDGE

Size: 7" x 3 ¹/₂".

SRP: $16/ea

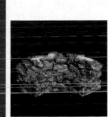

1997–Current
#52650

VILLAGE STONE CURVED WALL/BENCH

Set of 4.

LSRP: $15/set

1997–Current
#52647

VILLAGE STONE TRESTLE BRIDGE

Size: 9" x 4 ³/₄".

SRP: $37.50/ea

1997–Current
#52651

VILLAGE MILL CREEK POND

SRP: $55/ea

1997–Current
#52648

STONE HOLLY CORNER POSTS AND ARCHWAY

Set of 3.
Sizes:
4 ¹/₄", 3 ¹/₂" x 4".

SRP: $20/set

1997–Current
#52652

VILLAGE GAZEBO

SRP: $22.50/ea

Trims

1997–Current
#52653
VILLAGE MILL CREEK WOODEN BRIDGE
Size:
10 3/4" x 5 1/4" x 4 3/4".
SRP: $32.50/ea

1997–Current
#52659
WEATHER VANE
Set of 5 assorted.
SRP: $6.50/set

1997–Current
#52654
VILLAGE MILL CREEK PARK BENCH
Size: 6" x 4 1/2".
SRP: $14/ea

1997–Current
#52666
PEPPERMINT ROAD, STRAIGHT SECTION
SRP: $5/ea

1997–Current
#52656
TELEPHONE POLES
Set of 6. Individual "wires" complete with perched birds can connect poles.
SRP: $15/set

1997–Current
#52667
PEPPERMINT ROAD, CURVED SECTION
SRP: $5/ea

1997–Current
#52658
TELEVISION ANTENNA
Set of 4.
SRP: $5/set

1997–Current
#52668
TWO LANE PAVED ROAD
Set of 2.
SRP: $15/set

1997–Current
#52669
CANDY CANE BENCH

SRP: $5/ea

1997–Current
#52689
***VILLAGE CAMDEN
PARK SQUARE
STONE WALL***

SRP: $2.50/ea

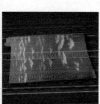

1997–Current
#52685
***VILLAGE BLUE SKIES
BACKDROP***
Size: 39" x 59".
SRP: $7.50/ea

1997–Current
#52691
***VILLAGE CAMDEN
PARK COBBLESTONE
ROAD***
Set of 2.
SRP: $10/set

1997–Current
#52686
***VILLAGE STARRY
NIGHT SKY BACK-
DROP***
Size: 39" x 59".
SRP: $7.50/ea

1998–Current
#52704
***VILLAGE HALLOWEEN
SET***
Set of 22. Includes 1
scarecrow, 3 wheat
shocks, 1 ghost, 2 black
cats, 12 pumpkins, 2
trees & a bag of Village
Fallen Leaves.
SRP: $50/set

1997–Current
#52687
***VILLAGE CAMDEN
PARK SQUARE***
Set of 22.
SRP: $75/set

NOTES: _____
_____
_____
_____
_____
_____
_____

Trims

319

Snow

1991–1992
#4996-4
*"LET IT SNOW"
CRYSTALS, PLASTIC
SNOW*

Size: 8 oz. box.

LSRP: $6.50/box

1977–Current
#4998-1
REAL PLASTIC SNOW

7 oz. bag.

SRP: $3/bag

1995–Current
#49979
*VILLAGE FRESH FALLEN
SNOW*

7 oz. bag.
Compatible with
Let It Snow Machine

SRP: $4/bag

1977–Current
#4999-9
REAL PLASTIC SNOW

2 lb. box.

SRP: $10/box

1995–Current
#49980
*VILLAGE FRESH FALLEN
SNOW*

2 lb. box.
Compatible with
Let It Snow Machine.

SRP: $12/box

1991–Current
#4995-6
*VILLAGE "BLANKET
OF NEW FALLEN
SNOW"*

Size: 2' x 5' 1".

SRP: $7.50/ea

1995–1997
#52592
*VILLAGE LET IT SNOW
MACHINE, WITH 1 LB.
BAG VILLAGE FRESH
FALLEN SNOW*

Size:
38 1/2" x 9" x 5 1/2".
Battery operated.

LSRP: $85/ea

Fences

1989–1991
#5508-5
Lamp Post Fence Extension
Set of 12.
6 posts &
6 fence pieces.

LSRP: $10/set

1987–Current
#5100-4
Village White Picket Fence
One of the first metal accessories.
Size: 6" x 1 ³/₄".
Cast Iron.

SRP: $3/ea

1990–Current
#5212-4
Tree-Lined Court- yard Fence
1 ¹/₂" high x 4" long.
Metal with resin.

SRP: $4/ea

1987–1997
#5101-2
Village White Picket Fence
Set of 4.
Each piece is
6" x 1 ³/₄".
Cast Iron.

LSRP: $12/set

1991–Current
#5204-3
Village Snow Fence, Flexible Wood & Wire
2" high x 36" long.

SRP: $7/ea

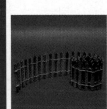

1989–1991
#5506-9
Lamp Post Fence
Set of 10.
2 lamps, 4 posts,
4 fence pieces.

LSRP: $13/set

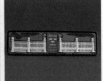

1991–1997
#5207-8
Frosty Tree-Lined Picket Fence
3 posts & 3 attached trees.
Size: 5 ³/₄" x 2 ¹/₂".
Metal with resin.

LSRP: $6.50/ea

1991–Current
#5514-0

Village Wrought Iron Gate And Fence

Set of 9.
Gate & 4 fence pieces with 4 posts.
Size: 9 1/4" x 3".
Metal.

SRP: $15/set

1991–Current
#5999-4

Wrought Iron Fence

4 pieces per package.
White & black.
Size: 4" long.

SRP: $10/pkg

1991–Current
#5515-8

Village Wrought Iron Fence Extensions

Set of 9. 4 fence pieces & 5 posts.
Size: 9 1/4" x 3".
Metal.

SRP: $12.50/set

1992–Current
#5220-5

Courtyard Fence With Steps

1 1/4" high x 4 1/4" long.
Metal with resin.

SRP: $4/ea

1991–Current
#5541-7

City Subway Entrance

Size:
4 1/2" x 2 3/4" x 4 1/2".
Metal.

SRP: $15/ea

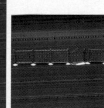

1993–Current
#5234-5

Chain Link Fence With Gate

Set of 3.
Size: 2" high.

SRP: $12/set

1991–Current
#5998-6

Wrought Iron Fence

White & black or white & green.
Each piece is 4" long.

SRP: $2.50/ea

1993–Current
#5235-3

Chain Link Fence Extensions

Set of 4.
Each piece is 4 1/2" long.

SRP: $15/set

Fences

1994–Current
#5252-3

VICTORIAN WROUGHT IRON FENCE WITH GATE

Set of 5.
Size: 5 1/2" x 3".
Metal.

SRP: $15/set

1996–Current
#52624

VILLAGE WHITE PICKET FENCE WITH GATE

Set of 5.
Size: 3" & 3 3/4".

SRP: $10/set

1994–Current
#5253-1

VICTORIAN WROUGHT IRON FENCE EXTENSION

Size: 3".
Metal.

SRP: $2.50/ea

1996–Current
#52625

VILLAGE WHITE PICKET FENCE EXTENSIONS

Set of 6.
Size: 3 3/4"

SRP: $10/set

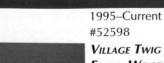

1995–1997
#52597

VILLAGE SPLIT RAIL FENCE, WITH MAILBOX

Set of 4.
Hand-hewn wood.

LSRP: $12.50/set

1996–Current
#52629

VILLAGE STONE WALL

2 assorted.
Size: 5 1/2" x 1 1/2".

SRP: $2.50/ea

1995–Current
#52598

VILLAGE TWIG SNOW FENCE, WOOD

2 3/4" x 4' roll.

SRP: $6/ea

1997–Current
#52657

SNOW FENCE
White.

SRP: $7/ea

Fences

1997–Current
#52664
CANDY CANE FENCE
Size: 24"
SRP: $8.50/ea

1998–Current
#52702
VILLAGE HALLOWEEN FENCE
Set of 2.
Flexible wooden fence with orange pumpkins and a black cat.
SRP: $12.50

OTHER GUIDES FROM GREENBOOK

GREENBOOK Guide to
Ty Beanie Babies

GREENBOOK Guide to
The Enesco Precious Moments Collection

GREENBOOK Guide to
Department 56® Snowbabies™

GREENBOOK Guide to
Hallmark Keepsake Ornaments

GREENBOOK Guide to
Hallmark Kiddie Car Classics

GREENBOOK Guide to
The Walt Disney Classics Collection

GREENBOOK Guide to
Cherished Teddies by Enesco

GREENBOOK Guide to
Precious Moments Company Dolls

GREENBOOK Guide to
Harbour Lights

GREENBOOK Guide to
Boyds Bears

GREENBOOK Guide to
Charming Tails

Fences

Mountains

VILLAGE MOUNTAIN BACKDROP

Set of 2.
Without trees.
Sizes:
27" x 11" & 22" x 9 1/2".
Foam.

SRP: $65/set

1992–Current
#5226-4

VILLAGE MOUNTAIN WITH FROSTED SISAL TREES, SMALL

Set of 5. With 4 trees.
Size:
12" x 10 1/2" x 8".
Foam and sisal.

SRP: $32.50/set

1994–Current
#52582

VILLAGE MOUNTAIN TUNNEL

Size:
19 1/2" x 9 1/2" x 5 1/2".

SRP: $37.50/ea

1992–Current
#5227-2

VILLAGE MOUNTAIN WITH FROSTED SISAL TREES, MEDIUM

Set of 8. With 7 trees
& 1 niche to display
Village piece. Size:
22" x 12" x 10 1/2".

SRP: $65/set

1996–Current
#52643

VILLAGE MOUNTAIN CENTERPIECE

Size:
24" x 15" x 7 1/2".

SRP: $45/ea

1992–Current
#5228-0

VILLAGE MOUNTAINS WITH FROSTED SISAL TREES, LARGE

Set of 14 w/13 trees.
Accommodates 3
lighted pieces. Size:
35" x 13" x 15 1/2".
Foam and sisal.

SRP: $150/set

Lights

1988–1988
#5993-5

STREETLAMP WRAPPED IN GARLAND

2 pieces per package.
Size: 4".

LSRP: $10/pkg

1991–Current
#3636-6

STREET LAMPS

6 pieces per package. Battery Operated (2 "AA" Cells) or can be used with Adapter, Item #5502-6. Cord 60" long, lamps 2 1/4" tall.

SRP: $10/pkg

1989–1991
#5503-4

OLD WORLD STREETLAMP

4 pieces per package.
2 "C" Batteries.
Size: 4".

LSRP: $22/pkg

1991–Current
#5215-9

VILLAGE MINI LIGHTS

14 bulbs. Battery Operated or can be used with Adapter, Item #5502-6.
Size: 27" long cord.

SRP: $12.50/ea

1990–1991
#5505-0

TURN OF THE CENTURY LAMPPOST

6 pieces per package.
2 "C" Batteries.
Size: 4".

LSRP: $22/pkg

1991–Current
#5500-0

TRAFFIC LIGHT

2 lights per package. Battery Operated (2 "C" Cells) or can be used with Adapter, Item #5502-6.
Size: 4 1/4" tall.

SRP: $11/pkg

1990–Current
#5996-0

VILLAGE DOUBLE STREET LAMPS

4 per package. Battery Operated (2 "C" Cells) or can be used w/ Adapter, #5502-6.
3 1/2" tall.

SRP: $13/pkg

1991–Current
#5501-8

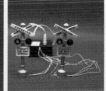

RAILROAD CROSSING SIGN

2 signs per package. Battery Operated or can be used with Adapter, Item #5502-6.
Size: 4 1/4" tall.

SRP: $12.50/pkg

Lights

1991–Current
#5504-2
TURN OF THE CENTURY LAMPPOST

4 pieces per package.
Battery Operated (2 "C" Cells) or can be used with Adapter, Item #5502-6.
Size: 4" tall.
SRP: $16/pkg

1996–Current
#52626
VILLAGE MINI LIGHTS

20-light strand.
SRP: $10/set

1992–1994
#5416-0
YARD LIGHTS (2 SANTAS, 2 SNOWMEN)

Set of 4.
Size: 1 ³/₄".
LSRP: $12.95/set

1996–Current
#52627
VILLAGE BOULEVARD LAMPPOSTS

4 pieces per package.
Size: 3 ³/₄".
SRP: $15/pkg

1996–Current
#52611
VILLAGE SPOTLIGHT

Set of 2. Battery Operated or can be used with Adapter, Item #5225-6.
Size: 1 ³/₄".

SRP: $7/set

1996–1997
#52628
VILLAGE COUNTRY ROAD LAMPPOSTS

2 pieces per package.
LSRP: $12/pkg

1996–Current
#52621
NORTH POLE CANDY CANE LAMPPOSTS

4 pieces per package.
Size: 3".

SRP: $12.50/pkg

1997–Current
#52663
VILLAGE COUNTRY ROAD LAMPPOSTS

Set of 4.
Size: 5".
SRP: $15/set

1997–Current
#52678

VILLAGE 45 LED LIGHT STRAND

With adapter.

SRP: $22.50/ea

1997–Current
#52682

VILLAGE FROSTY LIGHT SPRAYS

Set of 2.

SRP: $12/set

1997–Current
#52679

VILLAGE LIGHTED CHRISTMAS POLE

With 48 LED Lights.
With adapter.
Size: 9".

SRP: $32.50/ea

1997–Current
#52684

VILLAGE STRING OF STARRY LIGHTS

With 20 LED lights.

SRP: $12.50/ea

1997–Current
#52680

ROAD CONSTRUCTION SIGN

Set of 2. Blink on/off to warn of road work.

SRP: $12/set

1998–Current
#52700

VILLAGE STRING OF 12 PUMPKIN LIGHTS

LED lights. Battery operated or Brite Lites™ adapter compatible.

SRP: $13/ea

1997–Current
#52681

VILLAGE WALKWAY LIGHTS

Set of 2.
3-light sections.
Size: 6".

SRP: $12/set

1998–Current
#52701

VILLAGE JACK-O'-LANTERNS

LED lights. Battery operated or AC/DC adapter compatible.

SRP: $10/pair

Lights

1998–Current
#52706

**CARNIVAL CAROUSEL
LED LIGHT SET**

W/adapter.
Special light set to
coordinate with *The
Carnival Carousel.*

SRP: $20/set

1992–Current
#5224-8

**VILLAGE BRITE LITES™
REINDEER, ANIMATED**

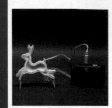

Size: 3 ¼".

SRP: $13.50/ea

Brite Lites™

All Brite Lites are battery
operated or they can be used
with Adapter, Item #5225-6.

1992–Current
#5225-6

**VILLAGE BRITE LITES™
ADAPTER**

For use with 2 "Brites
Lites" only.

SRP: $10/ea

1992–1997
#5222-1

**VILLAGE BRITE LITES™
'I LOVE MY VILLAGE',
ANIMATED**

Size: 6 ½".

LSRP: $15/ea

1993–Current
#5236-1

**VILLAGE BRITE LITES™
FENCE, ANIMATED**

Set of 4.
Size: 11".

SRP: $25/set

1992–Current
#5223-0

**VILLAGE BRITE LITES™
'MERRY CHRISTMAS',
ANIMATED**

Size: 7 ½".

SRP: $15/ea

1993–Current
#5237-0

**VILLAGE BRITE LITES™
SNOWMAN, ANIMATED**

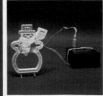

Size: 3 ¾".

SRP: $20/ea

1993–Current
#5238-8
VILLAGE BRITE LITES™ TREE, ANIMATED
Size: 3 ¹/₂".
SRP: $13.50/ea

1994–1997
#5245-0
VILLAGE BRITE LITES™ SET OF 20 RED LIGHTS, FLASHING

LSRP: $9/ea

1993–Current
#5239-6
VILLAGE BRITE LITES™ SANTA, ANIMATED
Size: 3 ¹/₂".
SRP: $20/ea

1994–Current
#5482-8
COCA–COLA® BRAND NEON SIGN
Size: 4 ¹/₂" x 2".
SRP: $16.50/ea

1993–1997
#9846-9
VILLAGE BRITE LITES™ 'DEPARTMENT 56®', ANIMATED
Size: 5".
LSRP: $10/ea

1997–Current
#52670
VILLAGE BRITE LITES™ CANDY CANES
Set of 2.
Size: 3".
SRP: $18/set

1994–1997
#5244-2
VILLAGE BRITE LITES™ WAVING FLAG, ANIMATED
Size: 5".
LSRP: $12.50/ea

1997–Current
#52671
VILLAGE BRITE LITES™ ANGEL
Size: 3 ¹/₄".
SRP: $15/ea

Brite Lites™

1997–Current
#52672
***VILLAGE BRITE LITES*™**
SNOW DRAGON
Size: 9 ¹/₂" x 2".
SRP: $20/ea

Electrical

1997–Current
#52673
***VILLAGE BRITE LITES*™**
SANTA IN CHIMNEY
Size: 3 ¹/₂".
SRP: $15/ea

1990–1990
#9926-0
BATTERY OPERATED
LIGHT
6 watts, 12 volts.
LSRP: $2.50/ea

1997–Current
#52674
***VILLAGE BRITE LITES*™**
CANDLES
Set of 4.
Size: 3".
SRP: $17/set

1991–Current
#5502-6
AC/DC ADAPTER,
FOR BATTERY OPER-
ATED ACCESSORIES
Not for use with
Brites Lites.
SRP: $10/ea

1997–Current
#52675
***VILLAGE BRITE LITES*™**
HOLLY ARCHWAY

SRP: $25/ea

1991–Current
#9902-8
SINGLE CORD SET,
WITH SWITCHED
CORD AND BULB

SRP: $3.50/set

1991–Current
#9924-4

VILLAGE REPLACEMENT LIGHT BULBS

3 pieces per package.
6 Watt, 12 Volt.

SRP: $2/pkg

1996–Current
#99245

VILLAGE REPLACEMENT ROUND LIGHT BULBS

Set of 3.
6 Watts, 120 Volts.

SRP: $2/set

1991–Current
#9927-9

VILLAGE 6 SOCKET LITE SET WITH BULBS, WHITE SWITCHED CORD

Size is 12'.

SRP: $12.50/set

1996–Current
#99247

VILLAGE LED LIGHT BULB

Battery Operated.

SRP: $6.50/ea

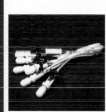

1991–Current
#9933-3

VILLAGE MULTI-OUTLET PLUG STRIP, 6 OUTLETS

UL Approved.
Size:
12" x 2" x 1 1/2".

SRP: $10/ea

1996–Current
#99278

VILLAGE 20 SOCKET LIGHT SET WITH BULBS

SRP: $25/set

1992–1994
#5213-2

VILLAGE "LIGHTS OUT" REMOTE CONTROL

Turns lights on/off in up to 60 houses at once. Electric eye with remote.

LSRP: $25/ea

1997–Current
#99246

VILLAGE SPOTLIGHT REPLACEMENT BULBS

Set of 6.

SRP: $2.50/set

Electrical

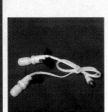

1997–Current
#99280
**VILLAGE DOUBLE
LIGHT SOCKET
ADAPTER**

SRP: $4/ea

1994–Current
#5229-9
**VILLAGE ANIMATED
SKATING POND**

Set of 15.
UL Approved.
Size: 17 $1/2$" x 14".

SRP: $60/ea

Animated

1994–Current
#5240-0
VILLAGE STREETCAR

Set of 10.
With transformer.
Car lights up.

SRP: $65/ea

1987–1988
#5997-8
**VILLAGE EXPRESS
TRAIN—BLACK**

Set of 22. Manufac-
tured by Tyco. Black
locomotive pulls a
coal car, two
passenger cars and a
caboose.

LSRP: $90/set

1994–1996
#5247-7
**VILLAGE ANIMATED
ALL AROUND THE
PARK**

Set of 18. UL
Approved.
Size: 19" x 15" x 16".

LSRP: $95/ea

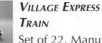

1988–1996
#5980-3
**VILLAGE EXPRESS
TRAIN**

Set of 22. Manufac-
tured by Bachmann
Trains. Red, black
and silver locomo-
tive pulls the cars
around the track.

LSRP: $95

1996–Current
#52593
**VILLAGE UP, UP &
AWAY, ANIMATED
SLEIGH**

UL Approved.
Size: 17" tall.

SRP: $40/ea

Electrical/Animated

1996–Current
#52640

VILLAGE REVOLVING TURNTABLE

SRP: $50/ea

1997–Current
#52645

VILLAGE ANIMATED SLEDDING HILL

SRP: $65/ea

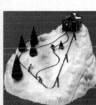
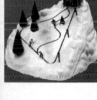

1996–Current
#52641

VILLAGE ANIMATED SKI MOUNTAIN

With 3 skiers.
Size: 20" x 17" x 14".

SRP: $85/ea

1996–Current
#52642

VILLAGE ANIMATED ACCESSORY TRACK

Accepts all Track Compatible pieces by fitting included adapter to base.
Size: 38" x 24".

SRP: $65/ea

1996–Current
#52644

VILLAGE WATERFALL W/ELECTRIC PUMP

Water cascades down hilly terrain to form small lake before entering creek.

SRP: $65/ea

NOTES: _____

_____
_____
_____
_____
_____
_____
_____
_____
_____
_____
_____
_____
_____
_____
_____
_____
_____
_____
_____
_____
_____
_____
_____
_____

Animated

1982–1983

#5099-7

Snow Village Wooden Ornaments

These six wooden ornaments are replicas of six Original Snow Village® buildings from 1982. They include *Carriage House, Centennial House, Countryside Church, Gabled House, Pioneer Church* and *Swiss Chalet*. They have monofilament lines attached to the tops and/or clips attached to the bottoms.

GBTru: $475

1997–1997
#8961

RONALD MCDONALD HOUSE® ORN. (THE HOUSE THAT ♥ BUILT™)

A portion of proceeds will be donated to Ronald McDonald Houses across the country.

GBTru: $15

1997–Current
#98630

NANTUCKET ORNAMENT

Original Snow Village® Classic Ornament Series.

SRP: $15

1997–Current
#98631

STEEPLED CHURCH ORNAMENT

Original Snow Village® Classic Ornament Series.

SRP: $15

1997–Current
#98632

J. YOUNG'S GRANARY ORNAMENT

Original Snow Village® Classic Ornament Series.

SRP: $15

NOTES: _____

_____

_____

_____

_____

_____

_____

_____

_____

_____

_____

_____

_____

_____

_____

_____

_____

_____

_____

_____

_____

_____

_____

_____

_____

_____

_____

_____

_____

1994–1994
#9872-8
DEDLOCK ARMS

Miniature version of Signature Collection lit piece. Special Keepsake box.

GBTru: $17

1996–1996
#98731
THE PIED BULL INN

Miniature version of Signature Collection lit piece. Special Keepsake box.

GBTru: $17

1995–1995
#9870-1
SIR JOHN FALSTAFF INN

Miniature version of Signature Collection lit piece. Special Keepsake box.

GBTru: $18

1997–1997
#98732
GAD'S HILL PLACE

Miniature version of Signature Collection lit piece. Special Keepsake box.

GBTru: $17

1996–1996
#98729
THE GRAPES INN

Miniature version of Signature Collection lit piece. Special Keepsake box.

GBTru: $17

1997–Current
#98733
DICKENS' VILLAGE MILL

The Heritage Village® Classic Ornament Series.

SRP: $15

1996–1996
#98730
CROWN & CRICKET INN

Miniature version of Signature Collection lit piece. Special Keepsake box.

GBTru: $17

1997–Current
#98734
SANTA'S WORKSHOP

The Heritage Village® Classic Ornament Series.

SRP: $16.50

1997–Current
#98737

DICKENS' VILLAGE CHURCH

The Heritage Village® Classic Ornament Series.

SRP: $15

1997–Current
#98740

DOROTHY'S DRESS SHOP

The Heritage Village® Classic Ornament Series.

SRP: $15

1997–Current
#98738

THE OLD CURIOSITY SHOP

The Heritage Village® Classic Ornament Series.

SRP: $15

1997–Current
#98741

CITY HALL

The Heritage Village® Classic Ornament Series.

SRP: $15

1997–Current
#98739

CRAGGY COVE LIGHTHOUSE

The Heritage Village® Classic Ornament Series.

SRP: $15

1997–Current
#98742

SANTA'S LOOKOUT TOWER

The Heritage Village® Classic Ornament Series.

SRP: $15

NOTES:

_____
_____
_____
_____
_____
_____

Number Index

Number Index

Notes:

Number Index

Alphabetical Index

Alphabetical Index

Alphabetical Index

Alphabetical Index

Alphabetical Index